MONKEY HOUSE BLUES

Dominic Stevenson is a writer, musician and videographer. He spent 11 years living and travelling in Asia before settling in the UK, where he works in video. He continues to travel widely.

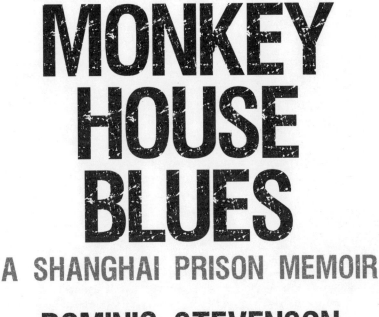

MONKEY HOUSE BLUES

A SHANGHAI PRISON MEMOIR

DOMINIC STEVENSON

MAINSTREAM
PUBLISHING

EDINBURGH AND LONDON

First published in Great Britain in 2010 by
MAINSTREAM PUBLISHING COMPANY
(EDINBURGH) LTD
7 Albany Street
Edinburgh EH1 3UG

ISBN 9781845965662

A catalogue record for this book is available
from the British Library

Typeset in Badhouse and Caslon

Printed in Great Britain by
CPI Mackays of Chatham Ltd, Chatham ME5 8TD

1 3 5 7 9 10 8 6 4 2

Acknowledgements

With thanks to the following for their help in bringing this book to print: Andrea Neville, Robert H. Stevenson, Richard D. Stevenson, Neelia Clabburn, Elspeth Barker, George Szirtes, Stephen Foster, David Holzer, Mark Baber, Sasha Otterburn, Kelvin O'Mard, David Ackles, Bill Campbell and Karyn Millar.

Contents

'The Darkening of the Light'
In this clouded view we forget that all changes are like
streams, which travel a long way underground before they
come to the surface.

A Guide to the I Ching, Carol K. Anthony

Prologue

Not for the first time, Wang sat on the floor, hands cuffed behind his back, staring at the wall. With his shaven head and grey flannel uniform he resembled a wretched Buddha, moving only to reposition his cramped legs from beneath his rigid torso. He'd already had a good kicking from our top prisoner, Mr Zhao, and his crew, but this time the guards were involved, which meant the inmate being handcuffed first. Several prisoners had reported having personal belongings stolen, and a search had revealed a stash of the missing items under Wang's bed. Quite what these missing objects were was a mystery; the Chinese were forbidden any kind of personal effects anyway. The assumption was that Wang had been thieving food from other prisoners, probably some tinned pineapple or dried fish that their families had brought in on visiting days.

I stood on the landing chatting to Larry as the Chinese sat around playing cards and chewing sunflower seeds. Small mountains of sticky husks piled up on the corners of their tables as they slapped cards onto the Formica surfaces as if they were swatting invisible flies. The relative peace of the wing was broken as three guards appeared from round the corner, and the Chinese bolted upright in their seats, hands clasped in front of them. Captain Xu, looking like a man with a job to do for once, led the way, his eyes staring ahead, with Jin and Zhu close behind, glaring dutifully at the back of his head. The Chinese inmates trailed their progress down the block like automated mannequins before they stopped outside Wang's cell. The prisoner glanced sideways, momentarily catching the green uniforms out of the corner of his eye. Xu laid a disconcerting hand on his shoulder and Wang hoisted his contorted frame off the wooden pallet of the cell floor, using his damp forehead for balance as he levered himself into an upright position. The four men walked back down the corridor, Wang's head hanging like a condemned man's, and as they filed past, the Chinese sifted through their pockets for more sunflower seeds and continued their card games.

The guards' office consisted of two cells knocked into one and was situated next to the foreigners' sitting area. The door clicked shut as we sat and looked at each other. Nobody doubted what would happen next. Wang would be gagged with a wet flannel while a second set of handcuffs was put round his ankles and tied to the existing pair round his wrists. A jug of drinking water would be poured over him for added effect and he'd lie on his stomach like the hog-tied pigs I'd seen at the markets in Guangzhou, staring into space, their petrified eyes glazed over like jellied eight-balls as they awaited their fate. But Wang knew what punishment to expect; after all, it had only been a matter of weeks since his last visit to the guards' office.

Someone tried to alleviate the tension by cracking a bad joke. Nobody laughed. A disgruntled card player at the other end of the wing began yelling at his mates, waving a greasy chicken's claw in the air like a bloodthirsty preacher, pointing accusingly at his opponents at the table. Another guy hawked a lump of phlegm into the front of his mouth, swilling the grisly globule around before lobbing the yellow slime into a stainless steel spittoon beneath the cell block window.

A caustic crackle began to radiate from inside the guards' room, the sound punctuated by harsh thuds followed by high-pitched squeals. I looked at Larry, who plunged his head down into a book he was pretending to be interested in. Jürgen appeared from his cell and sat down next to Ludwig, who put his headphones on and began to gnaw on the end of a pencil. Gareth looked over towards me and, shaking his head, turned up his radio, hoping to drown out the hideous din of a convulsing human being eight feet away, but the radio waves picked up the electrical pulse of the cattle prods, amplifying the ghastly hum that ricocheted down the cell block like an epileptic rattlesnake. He looked up, turned off the radio and walked over to the window, where prisoners from 10th Brigade were pouring their night soil into the sewers below.

Moments later, the officers' door sprung open and Wang staggered out, flanked by two guards, their faces flushed by the adrenalin rush of their grisly work. The Chinese sat solemnly as the officers led him back to his cell, hands cuffed behind his back. Wang's face was caked in snot and tears. Pink tracks streamed down his cheeks, which twitched with muscular spasms; his eyelids drooped downwards, zombie-like, and his lashes flickered across his pupils. The three men reached Wang's cell as the Chinese cast their eyes down towards their feet shuffling beneath the tables. The prisoner stepped inside as the steel door clanged shut behind him, and the guards turned on their heels and marched back to their office.

A lone cockroach scuttled across the corridor outside the office in a bid to make it to the other side, before Officer Zhu's boot crushed it into the concrete floor. Within seconds, the officers' flunky Mr Yin appeared with a bucket and mopped up the smear of mucus and carapace. Someone grunted before tossing a nine of spades onto the table, and others followed suit as a packet of dried mango segments was passed around. The stench of slop from 10th Brigade wafted upwards from the courtyard downstairs and filled the air with an oppressive stink.

I twisted a piece of paper between my sweaty fingers, popped the imaginary cigarette into my mouth and took a lungful of make-believe smoke. Someone turned the radio back on and we got on with our work. A week later, Wang was moved to a work farm in Xinjiang. We never saw him again.

[1]

The Poisoned Yangtze

It was dusk as I arrived at the central railway station in Nanjing, the capital city of Jiangsu Province, and like in most Chinese railway stations, a rambling cardboard city of itinerant labourers had sprung up on the forecourt, turning the station into a giant open-air flophouse. They were the flotsam and jetsam of China's rapid transition towards modernity, a vagabond army of involuntary trainspotters huddled under tarpaulin sheets. Their kids rummaged through piles of garbage: a pack of feral munchkins with tiny feet sore and blistered from the cruel work. It was embarrassing for the government to admit there were some 110 million of these people drifting around the country looking for work, and so this official estimate was likely to be conservative. Though the mass exodus of Chinese from the countryside to the vast urban sprawls of the nation's cities had created an endless source of cheap labour for the local factory owners, the limited accommodation had encouraged makeshift shanty towns to spring up, often outside train stations. Having left their poverty-stricken villages with nothing, many were unable to return even if they wanted to. Those unable to find work or accommodation often ended up being arrested for vagrancy and were put into police-owned factories not unlike prisons. Later I would discover that Chinese police officers could put people in these places for three years without even taking them to court.

My hotel room was much fancier than I'd grown accustomed to while travelling in China. I'd generally paid a couple of dollars for a dormitory bed, but since few hotels were allowed to give rooms to tourists, the ones that did tended to be the larger four-star establishments. I was using the room to repackage the hashish I had brought across China from the Hindu Kush and needed complete privacy. I slumped on the bed as the fan blades cut the air above. I was paranoid about my impending mission, and money was low after an epic trek from the mountains of Pakistan to the east coast of China. The last phase of the trip, though comparatively short in distance, had the most obstacles, with the Japanese port of Kobe the final destination. Japanese customs checks were likely to be rigorous, and the best way to avoid detection would be to swallow the hash on the two-day boat ride. First I had the unenviable task of wrapping the dope into individual pellets, a laborious 12-hour job that I was not looking forward to. My room reminded me of a Japanese love hotel, with its large mirrors on the walls and garish furnishings. It was expensive, too, but the receptionist had let me put it on a Visa card, so I could worry about that later.

The next morning, I set to work dismantling my guitar bag. The hash had been rolled into squares, vacuum-packed and slid into the lining of the leather bag. The seams had been sewn together by the wife of an Afghan tribesman above a shop in Peshawar, and I cut through the stitches with a penknife and pulled out the leathery sheets. The hash was perfect for the job, and the summer heat made the bendy sheets easy to roll between my fingers into four-gram pieces.

Five years earlier, I'd sat in a New Delhi hotel room in the middle of a sweltering Indian summer with three hundred grams of *charas* in front of me. Unlike hashish, which is pressed pollen and consequently has a pliable, plasticine quality when warm, *charas* is made by rubbing the heads of marijuana plants until the clammy resin begins to stick to the palms of the hands, after which it is collected and rolled into (usually) ten-gram sticks. It often has a woody, peaty texture that does not like to be reconstituted, and working the stuff into bite-sized pieces was arduous. I'd bought this particular batch from an Indian sadhu (holy man) at short notice, and it was poor quality. The long bus ride from Manikaran, high up above the Kulu Valley in India's northern Himachal Pradesh province, had been uneventful and relatively pleasurable under the circumstances. I'd packed the dope inside a hollowed-out pineapple amongst a bag of fruit in the hold of the bus and felt relaxed with the many police checkpoints on the way down. Wrapping the stuff was more problematic, but I eventually developed a system that involved cutting a tube of cling film into four-inch sections, securing one of the rolls between my knees and stretching the plastic around the hash, while turning the edges inwards. Done properly, the plastic clings tightly to the dope for days inside the body and passes through without any problem.

It was widely believed to be the safest way of transporting smallish quantities of hash before the arrival of X-ray machines. Of course it wasn't foolproof, and if the shit hit the fan there was no way you could deny having it. At least with a suitcase you could plead ignorance and claim to have been duped. As far as I know, no jury has ever acquitted someone with a gutful of hash. What made this method appealing to many people like myself was the low risk factor in the country of departure. You could eat the pellets in your hotel room and forget about them till you arrived at the other end. In the '60s and '70s, very few people got locked up in places like India and Morocco, and if they did, a modest bribe was usually enough to secure a swift release. By the '80s, massive pressures (not to mention 'foreign-aid' enticements) were put on the governments of drug-producing countries to join the West's War on Drugs. International borders became much harder to penetrate, while prison sentences were often longer in the countries where you bought the dope than in the countries where the contraband was headed. At the time of writing, India, for example, is handing out mandatory ten-year sentences for possession of more than ten grams of hashish – an amount that is unlikely to lead to court action in most European countries. Not only were the sentences harsher, but also legal representation was often non-existent, while jail conditions were sometimes medieval and corruption was rife. However, international borders are not as they used to be, as the threat of terrorism has eclipsed even the drugs trade. By the mid-'80s, Asian and South American prisons had begun to see many Westerners being held on various drug charges, and a 'home' bust with access to family, legal representation and decent living conditions was far preferable to being stuck in some dungeon halfway across the world. The discomfort of swallowing and unwrapping hashish became a small price to pay for avoiding that fate.

Although I liked the outlaw factor, I had no great love for the dope business. Some of my mates loved it, but I concentrated on market trading, English teaching, bar work and busking. Living in Japan in the '80s there was plenty of money to be made legitimately, and I enjoyed working for a living, though it could nonetheless be routine and boring. Various foreign friends had been held for long periods of time in solitary confinement for minor hash offences, while Japanese friends had had their lives ruined for years by their intimidating police force. I saw dope smuggling as a way of testing my karma and getting away from the humdrum world of work. It was the last-chance saloon where you stood to lose everything with one roll of the dice, and it made me feel some kind of affinity with the outlaws of my favourite folk songs. I got a buzz from the knowledge that it could all come crashing down at any moment, though with hindsight it was pure foolishness.

The guitar-bag scam had made the endless police checkpoints that litter the journey along the Indus Valley and over the Khunjerab Pass into China relatively hassle-free. I'd lost count of the times officials had looked at the instrument while I grinned and made air guitar gestures before being waved on. Now I was sitting on my bed after several thousand miles, marvelling at the quality of the much sought-after Afghan hash and rolling the sticky strips into torpedoes.

Pakistan is one of the best places in the world to buy hash, and it's pretty hard to find a poor-quality smoke in the entire country. The exported version known as red seal or 'paki black' is another story. The middlemen who shift vast quantities of the stuff around the world mix it with various other materials, creating a cheap, user-friendly product that bears little resemblance to what you can buy on any street corner inside the country. I'd been assured by the Afghan trader I'd bought mine from that it was top-quality produce from the Afghan hash mecca of Mazar I Sharif, the main city of northern Afghanistan. I suspected he told all his customers this, which was exactly what they wanted to hear. The hills around Mazar are said to be one of the oldest hash-growing regions in the world and were a major stopover point for travellers on the hippy trails of the '60s and '70s.

After the Russians invaded Afghanistan in 1979, millions of refugees fled to the border towns of Pakistan's North-West Frontier Province. Peshawar became the main base for the CIA's proxy war with the superpower to Afghanistan's north, and it was here that America first began its unholy alliance with the renegade Saudi warrior Osama bin Laden, arming and training his fighters against the Soviets. By the time I got to Pakistan, in 1993, the invaders had long gone and the country had descended into its now familiar quagmire of feuding warlords and endless civil war. Still, Peshawar had prospered and was now the base for various mujahideen groups vying for control of the country's lucrative opium trade.

I worked on the pellets all day, stretching the cling film tight to keep every piece perfectly sealed, and by six o'clock in the evening had 108 torpedoes to swallow on the boat. Although I didn't consider China's borders to be a serious hurdle, I planned to take the precaution of packing the pieces in foreign food parcels that I'd seen on sale in foreign food or Friendship Stores. These shops were found in all the major Chinese cities and were comparatively expensive. They catered for Westerners and wealthy Chinese and sold things like mini Mars Bars and Milky Ways. I decided that as soon as I got to Shanghai I'd buy a couple of packets of chocolate bars, open the packages individually, remove the chocolate and put two or three pieces of hash in each one before supergluing them up again. It seemed unlikely that any Chinese customs man would know what a Mars Bar was, and it was common practice for passengers to take their own food onto the ferries. The only potential problem was getting the bag of dope to Shanghai. I'd wandered around Nanjing looking for a Friendship Store but had run out of time, and after so many train journeys in China I had no reason to think this one would be any different. I found an obscure inside pocket in my rucksack and decided it would do for the relatively short journey to Shanghai, and with the hash finally wrapped I rolled a large joint with some of the leftovers and drifted into a deep sleep.

Some hours later, the distant sound of firecrackers woke me. It was past midnight and I was hungry, so I wandered into town to find something to eat. All the restaurants in the area had closed, but there were a few mobile street stalls serving noodles and rice with pork and vegetables. I sat and chatted to the vendor in my rather silly combination of pidgin English and sign language that seems to go quite a long way anywhere in the world, and drank a can of Chinese cola. By the time I'd eaten, I'd managed to establish some kind of vague directions to get to the nearest point of the Yangtze River and wandered off into the night to see the Far East's greatest waterway.

Three years earlier, I'd made a similar pilgrimage to the spiritual lifeblood of India, the Ganges. It had been one of the greatest days of my life, a day that had come to represent all that was wonderful about the rambling existence I'd chosen. Walking with my girlfriend, Rosie, by the ghats in Varanasi, I knew that this was as good as it gets; not only was I in one of the most beautiful and fascinating places in the world, but I was in love, too. Sitar and tablas emanated from every doorway, while Hindu pilgrims – intoxicated by the sheer pulsating energy of the place – moved around us in a daze. I'd read about the river's legendary powers and marvelled at the thought of the astonishing faith that billions of people had invested in it for thousands of years. Even the British had bought into the river's magic. There were tales of how the ships of the East India Company had taken the river's sacred drinking water from Calcutta to London without the customary stopover in the Cape since the Ganges' water stayed fresh for the entire voyage.

Once I drank it at a party in Goa – a thimbleful infused with California Sunshine, a particularly potent type of LSD. Within minutes I could see the bones in my hands as the translucent skin fell away. For some time after, every person I saw was a skeleton. It was extraordinary. Everyone at the party was naked. I walked around feeling embarrassed, as if I were fully dressed on a nudist beach. No experience with any drug has ever repeated this unique state of mind, but I'd read of such experiences being attained naturally by Indian yogis after many years of deep meditation, and the Ganges lay at the very centre of these miracles. Now the great river was in front of me, crystal clear and still, as the rains had long since dried up for that year. When I eventually rinsed my hands in the river, I felt a rush of energy through my arms, while my fingers and palms experienced an extraordinary pins-and-needles-type sensation. It reminded me of the electric baths used by elderly arthritic Japanese in their public washhouses, as the currents rippled through my arms and around my torso.

The intervening years had been good to me, the happiest of my life. Now I stood once again in front of a great Eastern river, only this time I was alone. There was very little light as I made my way down a gangway to the water's edge, and it was impossible to see for more than a few metres due to a heavy mist. I thought of Charles Dickens's Pip on the marshlands of *Great Expectations*. Squatting on the riverbank, I sank my hands into the water and felt a shiver down my spine. Unlike the Ganges, the Yangtze had a static, lifeless quality. I quickly withdrew my hands and noticed a pungent, rancid smell. The water was putrid and my hands felt tainted by the texture of the black liquid. Far from feeling energised, I immediately sought out fresh water to wash the slimy sensation off my hands, but had to make do with a piece of grubby old newspaper lying close by. I wandered back to my hotel looking forward to having a shower. My first touch of one of the greatest rivers in the world had been gloomily ominous.

The night train from Beijing stopped in Nanjing at 3 a.m., and I was hoping I'd be able to get a ticket at the station. The Shanghai Express was due to arrive at around six, so I'd have to find somewhere to get breakfast before the hotels opened. My financial problems were compounded by not being able to get any money out on my credit card. My original plan to hang out in Shanghai for a few days began to look unrealistic, and I had no idea how I was going to pay for the ferry to Japan. I took a cab to the station with a sense of foreboding. Three weeks had passed since I'd bought the hash from the Afghan in Peshawar, and I was days away from seeing my friends in Kyoto, but the toughest challenges lay ahead.

As I walked towards Nanjing station with the usual retinue of hustlers and would-be baggage carriers in tow, I noticed a police checkpoint at the entrance to the station. Around a dozen officers were standing around a conveyor belt, loading the luggage into what appeared to be an X-ray machine. I began to feel intensely paranoid and considered making a swift about-turn and returning to the hotel when one of the officers, seeing I was a foreign tourist, signalled to me to walk around the checkpoint. It turned out that there had been a series of explosions on trains in the district caused by passengers carrying fireworks in their luggage. Thankfully, foreign tourists were not deemed a threat and were exempt from these checks. It was unlikely that the contents of my rucksack would be detected by the X-ray, but I became acutely aware of the random nature of the hazards that could appear at any time now that the hash was no longer built into my guitar bag.

I was well aware of the dangers of being caught with hashish in Pakistan or Japan, but China had never seemed the kind of place where the police would want to get involved. I'd had a few brief encounters with the police on trains and once after a dispute over a bar bill in Beijing. A bar owner had tried to charge me ten times the normal price for a bottle of beer on the street, and a passer-by had intervened when it looked like I was about to get a hiding. Later I was embarrassed to discover I'd unwittingly bought an imported beer that was correctly priced. The officers who happened to be walking by at the time went to some lengths to ignore me, partly, no doubt, because they could not speak English, but also because foreigners seemed to be outside of the local laws and customs. Obviously this was an arrogant assumption to make; however, there were good reasons for it. Tourists had their own currency called 'foreign exchange certificates' and were forbidden to stay in the majority of the hotels where Chinese stayed. Since the government went to great lengths to separate foreigners from the general populace, it was more trouble than it was worth to get involved with them, and most Chinese were disinclined to have any contact with tourists. Also, tourists were affectionately called 'guests', and hassling them at checkpoints would be tantamount to inviting friends to dinner and frisking them on the door. Since tourists were considered wealthy it was presumed they would not commit crimes, and even if they did it would be awkward for the average Chinese policeman to intervene.

After the shock of meeting a police checkpoint outside the station, the six-hour train journey from Nanjing to Shanghai passed by uneventfully. The carriage was draughty but humid, and the nicotine-stained windows gave the platform lights an amber glow. An affluent-looking mother and son sat opposite me speaking Mandarin, and I took the opportunity to make small talk to pass the time. They spoke excellent English and came across as the kind of upper-class Chinese I'd had little experience of before. The boy was dressed like an English public schoolboy in a navy-blue blazer and tie, while his mother wore an expensive-looking fur coat. She reminded me of an opera star or the wife of a rich industrialist, while her son was a proper Lord Fauntleroy. They were visiting relatives in

Shanghai and asked me what I liked about their country. It was a question I'd been asked many times before; I had a standard reply in which I praised the delicious food, dramatic scenery and friendly people. It involved a slight bending of the truth. The food was good, but much of the country was now hideously ugly and not always friendly. Communism had ripped the guts out of the place, with its vile architecture and divisive social policies, but I was aware my enthusiasm for the country had begun to wane after I had caught hepatitis A. The debilitating illness had made it difficult to enjoy the most basic pleasures of travelling. Simply leaving my hotel room had become exhausting, so there was no question of sightseeing. I'd had to give up the beer, too, which is one of the pleasures of Chinese travel. It was ridiculously cheap and, when ice-cold, perfectly pleasant. I'd spent many hours on trains enjoying it. Hawkers sold it on railway-station platforms, out of large Perspex iceboxes, and it was fun to share with train-compartment colleagues on long journeys. I'd taken an epic 54-hour train ride from Lanzhou to Guangzhou and had drunk several large bottles on the way. I nodded off and woke up dehydrated, so I headed off down the carriage looking for water. Chinese trains have large boiling-water tanks so everyone can get a free cup of green tea, and I found one soon enough. The tap had a red sign in Chinese hanging over it, but I helped myself anyway. The water was lukewarm, but my thirst couldn't wait. A man saw me drinking it and wagged his finger while pointing at the sign. I carried on. That, I assume, was the night I got hepatitis. Sensible people write off their travels when struck down by such diseases, but I was determined to carry on, stumbling from one escapade to the next, with pallid skin and Lucozade piss, desperately trying to get back to Japan.

As the train neared Shanghai, I managed to cheer myself up at the thought of being back in Kyoto in just a few days. There would be friends to visit, and I'd be able to track down Rosie's whereabouts. I planned a trip to the *sentō*, the hot baths that are found on the street corners of every Japanese residential district. Although I was travelling with a guitar, I missed my musician friends and was getting bored playing alone in hotel rooms. As Japan's cultural centre, Kyoto had an eclectic mixture of different kinds of music, including jazz, blues, house and heavy rock. The Beatles still reigned as the kings of pop and could be heard on every jukebox in every bar across the country. Paul McCartney's early '80s dope bust had been a huge event in the Japanese media and had given even the most squeaky-clean member of the band the kind of outlaw folk-hero status usually reserved for the group's bad boy, John Lennon. I was nervous about arriving in Japan with the hash, well aware of the kind of grilling I could expect if suspected, but I'd run out of money and didn't want to hang out working in Japan any longer than necessary. I'd make some money and buy a plane ticket to wherever Rosie was. All I had to do was get on the boat and relax. There was nothing to it; everything would be fine.

A taxi driver nodded to me outside the station and I threw my guitar and rucksack onto the back seat and slid in next to them. It was my first visit to China's most populated city and I was unsure how long it would take me to get a ticket for the boat to Japan. The journey to the hotel took me through the heart of what was once the centre of Britain's attempt to penetrate the Middle Kingdom. The Bund had few of the charms of its former colonial glory, and the sedan chairs that had carried Europeans around the streets of the city had been replaced by plush taxis that carried the city's well-heeled inhabitants from A to B. Where once an international police force ran a cordoned-off section of the city for the benefit of the expat community, the Chinese were now very much back in command. A Public Security van, siren blazing, belted past the cab as it turned into Nanjing Street, the centre of Shanghai's nightlife. The last of the night's revellers walked down the pavements beneath huge billboards advertising Japanese and American goods, while a tramp in a blue-denim Mao suit rummaged through a rubbish bin outside a Kentucky Fried Chicken outlet. It was the middle of the night, but the street was well lit with gaudy neon signs that splattered down the sides of shop facades, while Western music boomed out of doorways.

The cab pulled up outside the Pujing Hotel, and I passed a 20-yuan note to the driver and waited for the change. A scraggy white cat squealed as the doorman leered at it with a broom from the hotel entrance, and I walked into the huge foyer, where an elderly clerk peered over his glasses.

'No room tonight,' the man said tartly before I had a chance to ask.

'Are there any other hotels in the area? I'm taking a ferry to Japan in the morning and need a place to rest for a few hours.'

'No room.'

He cast his eyes across the room to a large sofa in the corner. I'd been planning to use the room to transfer my newly wrapped dope into the mini-Mars Bar wrappers I intended to buy later in the morning. My scam depended on being able to have my own space for at least an hour or so, but I was too tired to go looking for another hotel so I took a towel out of my bag and lay down. It seemed like I'd barely fallen asleep when an acrid, sulphurous smell wafted up into my nostrils. A janitor was pushing a mop around my makeshift bed, slopping ammonia across the cold stone floor. Glancing up at the clock above the reception desk, I saw it was 6.30, and the clerk I'd met earlier had been replaced by another man, who resembled a Chinese Charles Hawtrey, the actor from the old Carry On films. Unsurprisingly there was still no room, so I asked if I could make use of the shower in the meantime. The receptionist slapped his hand down on the bell on his desk and a small, elderly but sprightly bellhop appeared in a traditional Chinese tunic with a friendly smile.

'How can I be of assistance to you, sir?'

'I'd like a shower and a place to keep my luggage until I can book a room, please.'

'Certainly. I have already taken it upon myself to put your musical instrument into the storage room, thus preventing the possibility of its theft. There is, alas, an escalating incidence of larceny across China's eastern-seaboard towns, sir.'

I was astonished at the bellhop's long-winded use of the English language and was reminded of the occasions on which I'd met educated people on the Indian subcontinent who still spoke in a kind of Raj-era dialect rarely heard in post-'50s Britain. I wanted to stop and have a chat with him, imagining he'd have interesting tales to tell about Shanghai in the colonial period, but the receptionist rudely interrupted us and sent him on his way. I felt sorry for him; he was clearly an educated man forced to accept a menial job, being ordered around by intellectual inferiors who treated him like a worthless flunky. I imagined he'd had a grim time of it during the brain-dead years of Mao's Cultural Revolution, when the educated were endlessly hounded and philistinism was brutally enforced as a state religion. I decided that I'd make an effort to have a chat with him after I'd bought my ticket, and wandered off into the city for breakfast.

In the light of day, the city had lost much of the sparkle of the night before. Without the neon signs the buildings were bland and indifferent, while the crowds had grown into oppressive hordes. There seemed little point in taking a taxi because the traffic did not appear to be moving significantly faster than walking pace, and if the receptionist's directions were accurate I didn't have far to go. Eventually I found a large building that supposedly had a travel agent on the sixth floor, and after a few enquiries I discovered the agency on the eighth. It was good news. A boat was leaving the docks at midday for Kobe, and crucially, I could pay using my credit card, which was not giving me any cash. Since I was down to my last few dollars I had little choice but to buy the ticket, but time was running out and I'd yet to buy the mini Mars Bars that were the key to my safe passage out of China. I headed straight to the nearest Friendship Store on Nanjing Street, a vast emporium of international goods stacked high with everything from Indian spices to Johnnie Walker whisky.

With the benefit of hindsight it's easy to see where we make our mistakes, but I've never managed to work out how I spent a good 45 minutes in the department store and left without what I'd gone in there to buy. I remember the exquisite jade carvings, the high-quality Korean leather jackets, the ginseng elixirs and Dragon Well green teas, but I can't recall even seeing the foreign-food section. I'm sure it was there, and doubtless they had something at least similar to what I was looking for, but I left with nothing.

As well as failing to repack my dope, I didn't have enough money to book a hotel room to make the swap anyway. Had I stopped to think for five minutes, it would have been obvious that my mission was falling apart. The most important part of the Chinese leg of the mission had collapsed, but I was past the point of no return: nothing could stop me now.

It was gone ten when I got back to the hotel and I was frantic to leave. Although the boat left at twelve, passengers were required to board at eleven, and I had no idea how long the journey to the port would take, or if I had enough money for the taxi. My rucksack and guitar were in the hotel's storage room, and I was unable to find anyone to unlock the door for me. The Charles Hawtrey lookalike ignored me, and the bellhop had disappeared. I paced the floor for ten minutes, chain-smoking cheap Chinese cigarettes, when a man appeared who could apparently help me.

'The bellhop is taking his morning break and will be back shortly. He is the only person who has a key to the storage room.'

'But I have a ship to Japan that boards in 45 minutes and I have to get a taxi to the port.'

'I do not have a key; you'll have to wait till the bellhop comes back.'

I smoked another cigarette. Then another. I was pacing the floor in a sweat now, and the spindly clerk was peering over his glasses looking at me contemptuously. Finally I'd had enough.

'Look, I gave my luggage to you people for safe keeping, and you knew full well I had a boat to catch at midday – where's my fucking bag!'

The last syllables were delivered with such force the clerk nearly jumped out of his skin. Other tourists who were checking into the hotel turned their heads disapprovingly. I was making a scene. A friendly Western bystander tried to help, but I shrugged off his well-intentioned efforts and lit another cigarette off the one I was smoking. Deciding there wasn't much else I could do, I sat down on the sofa that I'd slept on earlier and ran my sweaty hands through my hair, when suddenly the bellhop appeared. He had a gleeful look in his eyes, a smile on his face and was holding my rucksack in his arms with the guitar bag strapped over his shoulder. I grabbed both from him and stormed out of the door without saying a word of thanks. Within seconds, a cab drew up and I threw my luggage onto the back seat. Behind me, a pleasant-looking Chinese lady who bore a striking resemblance to my mother attempted to sell me some postcards. I swung round and told her to fuck off as I slammed the cab door behind me and ordered the driver to take me to the port. Looking out of the back window of the cab, I could see the poor woman looking bewildered as the cab pulled way. Further back, the bellhop was standing in the doorway of the hotel with a concerned look on his face. I turned around again and didn't look back.

Shanghai's port area had a desolate air about it. Enormous cranes like gigantic Meccano creations could be seen on the horizon picking up huge containers and plonking them unceremoniously onto waiting ships. From a distance the docks seemed to have been abandoned, and I wondered whether the cab that had just left me on the quay with my luggage in my hands had got the wrong place. Aware of the diminishing time, I walked quickly towards the entrance to the Japan-ferry terminal and glanced nonchalantly at a few customs officers milling about in the doorway. The sight of uniforms had ceased to represent any kind of authority to me in China. There was nothing intimidating about their standardised dress and their role seemed more managerial than repressive. I strolled into their domain oblivious to any sense of danger, as if I had some kind of diplomatic immunity.

Ahead of me, I saw a family being searched. It was bad news. These were respectable, well-dressed Japanese people who'd probably been visiting relatives working on the mainland. The officers were rummaging through their stuff as if they'd been tipped off about some impending terrorist outrage planned for that very day by a gang matching their description. Meanwhile I stood in the customs hall like an ice cube in a sauna, only vaguely conscious that my world was evaporating. A man in a blue suit drew me aside to a beige-coloured Formica table. He immediately opened the top of my rucksack and within seconds found the bag of dope. I smiled and tried to look uninterested as he began to unravel the layers of cling film, and when he turned to ask what the packets contained I pointed to my mouth, implying it was some kind of foodstuff.

He held the sticky piece of hash in his hand and lifted it up to his nose. I got the impression he had no idea what he was holding, as a perplexed frown fell across his face. He grunted to a colleague who was inspecting another passenger across the hall, and the man sauntered over and held the hash up to his nose.

'Dama?' he asked. I had heard this expression many times in Kashgar and knew it was the Chinese name for marijuana.

'Yes, that's right. Is there a problem?' I tried to look genuinely surprised that they should be asking me about the substance.

'In China, this is forbidden.'

'But it grows wild all over the country, how can it be illegal?'

A small crowd of officers surrounded me, and I was ushered into a side room and told to sit on the sofa. In front of me, the contents of my rucksack and guitar case were laid out onto a large table, and I was asked to remove my clothes. I continued to try to look puzzled with the situation, smiling at the officers and pretending I was oblivious to the law I was supposed to have broken. After a few minutes, a film crew arrived with a video camera and I was allowed to put my clothes back on. I'd seen Westerners paraded on the news in Bangkok and Singapore having been busted with large amounts of heroin and wondered how my 400-gram dope bust could be considered newsworthy. There must have been 15 to 20 uniforms in the room, while a crowd was building up around the door. I lit a cigarette and took a can of Coke out of my bag. Three officers were trying to look inside my guitar, and I offered to loosen the strings so they could get their hands inside without breaking it. Having circled me a few times, the cameraman put the camera on a tripod and asked the officers to lay the dope out in front of me so they could get a full live-action mug shot.

An English-speaking officer started to ask me where I'd bought the stuff from, and I said I'd bought it from a guy in Kashgar market. I continued to feign ignorance, talking about how I'd seen the plant growing all over the country. If I'd known it was illegal, why had I not hidden it? I had no answer to this question myself; my failure to repackage the hash before leaving the hotel was such a monumental error I was unable to comprehend what was going on. I started to feel detached from the reality of what was happening, as if I were watching the proceedings through the video camera that was recording my every move. A great foghorn blew through the building as the ferry prepared to leave for Japan, and I asked, half jokingly, if I could get on the boat before it left. My interrogator shook his head and smirked. I lit another cigarette and cast my eyes down to the floor. The film crew started to pack up and the uniforms started to drift out of the room. I sat on the sofa in a trance-like daze, inhaling deeply.

'What will happen to me?' I asked the English-speaking customs man.

'Don't worry,' he said. 'They won't shoot you.'

After customs had finished with me, I was taken up to a room in the same building by three plain-clothed police officers. The good cop/bad cop routine began to unfold between one of the men and a woman. She was fairly attractive, almost sympathetic, whereas he was aggressive, with a sinister ice-cold veneer to his cratered, pizza-like complexion. His gaunt face, bad teeth and sunken cheeks betrayed the classic symptoms of amphetamine abuse, especially *shabu*, the euphoric strain of Methedrine popular in Japan that would later turn up in the West as Ice. The policewoman spoke basic English and acted as a translator. I repeated my story about buying the hashish from a Chinese-looking stranger in Kashgar market whose name I'd somehow forgotten. There was no real opposition to this version of events, but the process was unbelievably slow and tedious, with hours going by and very little being said.

Like the customs officers before them, the police were convinced I had an accomplice. They invented scenarios in which my partner(s) and I had split up before boarding the ship, and said I'd be treated with leniency if only I told them the truth. What they could not understand was that I was acting alone. The truth was inconceivable. Having lived in Japan for some years and visited the surrounding countries, I understood the problem they had accepting this. There is very little freelance crime in the Far East. Wayward teenagers are inducted into gangs at a young age, and later into larger organisations like the yakuza or the Triads. Additionally, such independent enterprises would be considered foolish since the solo criminal would not have the benefit of the cosy relationship between the authorities and the gang bosses that helps to maintain the status quo in countries like Japan. Two years later, I would still have trouble convincing trusted Chinese friends that I'd entered and left the country alone, so entrenched was the notion of crime as a group activity.

The interview lasted several hours and I had one overriding thought all the time. I'd bought a small lump of opium from an Afghan guy in Peshawar, with which I'd been spicing up my spliffs from time to time. There remained about a gram of the piece in cling film, wrapped up in tissue in my briefs with a small quantity of leftover hash I'd planned to smoke on the boat – a daft idea, but hey, so was everything else. I asked to go to the bathroom, which they accepted, but the third officer was despatched along with me and watched me like a hawk. I put my fingers inside the zip and started rummaging around while taking a piss, as the cop leaned forwards like a pervert in a public toilet. I could just about feel the two lumps, but the cop tapped me on the shoulder and grunted to get a move on. Realising it was not the moment to dispose of the additional contraband, I was led back to the interview room, where I was informed I was being taken to Shanghai No. 1 Detention Centre.

I was hustled down the stairs with my rucksack on my back and my guitar in my hand, and marched across a large car park to an unmarked police car. After putting my luggage in the boot, I was handcuffed and prodded into the back seat. The policewoman sat beside me as the driving officer put a magnetic flashing light on the roof and switched on the siren. If I'd suspected my interrogator was a speed freak before, I was convinced now. He drove like a maniac through the bustling streets of Shanghai, screeching at the other cars, running red lights, cursing the pedestrians in his way. I felt I was playing a part in a surreal Chinese version of *Starsky and Hutch*. My mind was racing too; I couldn't take in the sights, sounds and smells around me, but I sensed my life was sliding out of view. I was going to jail.

2

Into the Dragon

Shanghai No. 1 Detention Centre is situated in the middle of the city and serves as both a police station and a remand prison. Like the many other police interrogation and holding centres in China, it is a feared and dreaded place. A large police compound with its own jail, it is the first and sometimes the last destination of many of the city's newly arrested inhabitants. I say the last because some convicted prisoners get to serve their sentences in these awful places. Remand prisoners are never allowed visitors, and their families often spend months tracking them down. Hapless miscreants from far-flung corners of China can spend years in these places while being presumed dead in their home towns. Once the families are aware of the fate of their loved ones, they're able to send monthly food packages from the jail shop, but are forbidden any contact by mail.

Most of the prisoners arrive in a state of abject terror, well aware that only absolute submission to the awesome powers of the police will save them from being crushed by the repressive state apparatus. Since torture is de rigueur in Chinese police custody, and lawyers are distant figures you may or may not meet hours before your court appearance, the average detainee arrives resembling a trussed turkey. Hog-tied, petrified and dumb. Those considered dangerous wear heavy shackles, as do those destined for death row. All the prisoners squat; few have the defiant swagger of the classic Western criminal, from the tough-guy celluloid incarnations of James Cagney to the belligerent strut of the Kray brothers. Instead they walk respectfully, solemnly and, above all, humbly.

My own walk was somewhere in between, I'd guess. I was not obliged to squat like a Chinese prisoner, but neither did I put on any airs; the shock of the moment precludes such grandstanding. Before my first interview, I was taken to a small room to be searched. There was a single chair bolted to the floor in the centre of the room, which they told me to sit on. The chair was made of wood with leather straps at the wrists and ankles. At no point were these restraints applied to me, but their presence was a constant reminder of the countless prisoners who'd come before me. Although at the time I had not read the numerous Amnesty International reports on these contraptions, it did not require much imagination to guess their popular usage by the Chinese police during interrogations.

A couple of police officers started to examine my luggage as a small crowd of uniforms gathered in the doorway. It was difficult to tell the difference between the People's Liberation Army and the police. They had a similar shade of olive-green uniforms and members of both resembled the bored teenagers seen hanging around the bus shelters of small English towns. Few were equipped with boots and tended to wear shabby plimsolls with their toes protruding. They all had Second World War-era rifles, but you got the impression they were not yet trusted with carrying live ammunition. The guards seemed to have no particular responsibilities other than drinking green tea and chain-smoking cigarettes. A constant stream of uniforms with Nescafé jars of tea took turns to look at me, with those at the back of the queue yelling for those at the front to get a move on.

Outside, the sun had set and it was getting dark. I sat watching my belongings being strewn across the cell floor; the door was open and I could see the whites of eyes bobbing eagerly in and out of the darkness. It seemed like every cop in Shanghai had come to see what was going on. I felt like a fallen celebrity. Yet they were affable enough and many were smiling at the exciting discovery, and had their superiors not been around, I believe they would have been eager to shake my hand.

I was gnawing what was left of my fingernails, still harbouring thoughts that I'd be sitting in a hotel room in a couple of hours telling fellow travellers about my lucky escape from the Public Security Bureau.

It was a fantasy, but at such times dreams trump reality: the best-case scenario seems the most likely, however improbable.

In another twist of the good cop/bad cop routine, a new batch of officers arrived to take over. If the first lot had resembled the ramshackle urchins of Shanghai's answer to Dad's Army, these were the Green Berets. Immaculately dressed, with pistols and shoulder badges, they glared at me disapprovingly and told me to strip. Each item of clothing was inspected closely and passed to another officer, who did the same: digging for strands of fabric and dirt from the recesses of my pockets and holding them up to the light. It was as if they thought I was a spy and were looking for a microfilm, and within seconds I was down to my underpants. At first it seemed I would not be asked to make a complete strip as they motioned for me to sit down, but after a couple of minutes I was told to stand again and remove them. I did so and carefully slid my pants, and the small tissue-wrapped lumps hidden in them, to my ankles, hoping the contents would not be noticed. One of the officers flicked his truncheon at the sagging briefs and asked me (via a translator) to step out of them altogether. As I did so, the small package fell onto the floor in front of the officer in charge, who began to unravel its contents. He held the lumps up to his nose, sniffing suspiciously while comparing the two pieces.

'This is *dama*,' I said, using the Chinese name for marijuana.

'*Dama?*'

'Yes, for smoking on the ship.'

'And this?' he said, pointing at the opium.

'That's *dama* too, just a different quality.'

'Why didn't you tell us about this?' he replied, as if I'd personally let him down with my omission.

'I'm sorry, I forgot I had it.'

'Do you have any more doping?' he asked, meaning drugs.

'No, I don't.'

And then I knew I was really in the shit!

Marijuana has never been considered a major social problem in China, and its abundance on the side of countless railway tracks around the country confirmed this for me. Its mild sedative qualities have doubtless been integrated into the myriad medicinal potions in the country's

5,000-year-old history of traditional medicine. Opium, on the other hand, though widely used as a painkiller, has been a constant threat to Chinese civilisation for hundreds of years and was seen as a sinister tool of Western imperialism. Prior to the Communist victory of 1949, the epidemic had been so widespread that thousands of 'hole in the wall' injection points had sprung up all over Manchuria where addicts would drop a coin through the hole and get a shot in the arm. After the founding of the People's Republic, Mao Zedong's Communist Party had made the eradication of opium's pernicious influence on Chinese society a priority, identifying its proliferation during the later stages of the Qing dynasty (1644–1912) as a key element in the West's strategy to colonise China.

He was right, of course. The attempt by the (principally British) colonial powers to turn the inhabitants of the world's most populous country into junkies in order to secure favourable trading rights by shipping in vast quantities of cheap Indian opium from other parts of the Empire was one of the most scandalous episodes in Britain's imperial adventures in Asia. Although I had no intention of selling or giving it away, I realised I'd tipped the scales out of my own favour. Was I in fact a neocolonialist myself, plundering the Orient for my own gain? Perhaps. But in the meantime I tried to tell myself there was little chance they'd ever discover my opium was anything other than a different strain of marijuana. While I was thinking this through, another officer took the laces out of my shoes and the belt off my jeans. It occurred to me that I was considered a suicide risk, though nothing could have been further from my mind. The day's events had sent a massive shot of adrenalin through my veins. I was petrified and electrified, but I was too excited to be depressed.

Since my arrest at eleven that morning, I'd been kidding myself that the authorities would not bother to hold me for very long. I'd never heard of foreigners being given custodial sentences in China; on the contrary, I'd heard of people being held for short periods of time before being deported. I decided the best thing to do was to be diplomatic and convince the authorities I was ignorant of their rules and regulations, which was pretty much true. I'd been giving them a cock-and-bull story about how I'd bought the hash from a 'Chinese-looking' man in Kashgar market, but after a few hours of this I began to wonder whether I was digging myself into a deeper hole than I needed to be in. What's more, they were clearly having trouble believing me, and as I sat with another interrogator going over the story yet again, it occurred to me the true story (with a few modifications) was better than the story I was telling them.

It was pitch dark in the courtyard now, and most of the crowd that had gathered outside the interview room had gone away. I was asked to follow another policeman across the yard to what I assumed would be a cell for the night. I had to hold up my jeans and drag my feet as I was led into a much larger room on the other side of the compound. This room was like a mini courtroom, with a small stage and three very important-looking police officers sitting solemnly staring at me. The room had two doors: the first a sturdy lockable one, while the other, inside door was about four inches thick and made of light cardboard and felt, which seemed to be largely for the purpose of soundproofing the room. There was a blood-red carpet on the floor, at least two inches thick, and in the centre was another solid wooden chair bolted to the floor with wrist and ankle straps. To the left side of me, a dozen or so police officers sat both in uniform and plain clothes. They looked like a jury, and I wondered whether my case had been fast-tracked and I was to be arrested, tried and convicted all in one day.

In the far-right corner of the room, a screened-off area prohibited the accused from seeing the face of a witness that was visible to the rest of the courtroom. I later found out from Chinese prisoners that this had been a Cultural Revolution-era courthouse and that the screen was still used for hiding witness identities. How many people had been tried in this room, I wondered. Probably thousands, and without even knowing who was testifying against them. I was bewildered by why so many police officers were being summoned to witness such a minor offence. Had I been caught at Heathrow, I'd have got a customs evasion ticket and been back in London within hours, as had happened to friends of mine. Instead, I was to be paraded on national TV as an example of foreign decadence and every cop in Shanghai wanted a piece of my fame.

The head officer sat judge-like in the centre of the stage and began to talk to me through a plain-clothes interpreter to my left. After introducing himself as Inspector Wong, he immediately started to quiz me about my reasons for being in his country.

'Why did you come to China?'

'I came to China as a tourist. I have had a long-held interest in your country and recently had the opportunity to visit. I've always wanted to see the Great Wall and to travel the Silk Road from Kashgar to the eastern seaboard.'

After quizzing me for some time about my travels, he finally got to the point.

'Why did you get involved with criminals in our country?'

I'd been waiting for this question and decided it was the best chance I was going to get to change my story. I realised I'd have been much better off telling the truth about buying the hash in Pakistan since passing through China with hash would be looked upon less seriously than dealing with local criminals. It would also make my trail much more vague. Earlier they'd been asking me if I'd recognised a picture of the guy I'd bought the hash from in Kashgar market, and I didn't want to spend hours looking at mug shots of people I'd never met. I finally came clean.

'I didn't get involved with criminals in China. I brought the drugs from Pakistan. I had no intention of breaking the law in your country.'

The change of story caused all sorts of problems, not to mention reluctance on the authorities' part to believe anything else I'd previously told them, but it proved a good move in the long run. I'd been able to show them how clever they were to have disbelieved me in the first place. It showed that their diligent interrogations had paid off and that I had opted to tell the truth in exchange for leniency. A smug, self-congratulatory air hung over the proceedings. Everyone was happy; everyone except the officer to Inspector Wong's left, who climbed down from the stage and began wagging his finger at me and shouting. He made no secret of the fact that he detested me for no other reason than that I was a foreigner, which was not typical of most of the officials I met, who were respectful and even friendly. I looked to the translator, who did not bother to inform me what his colleague was ranting about. In fact he looked embarrassed, and he told me to tell the story again from beginning to end.

It was about 10.30 and I'd been talking constantly for 12 hours. The number of police hours the whole fiasco was taking up over a minor hash bust seemed absurd. Was it really necessary to have 20 high-level officers in the room with me? I took the opportunity to chat to the translator while the rest of them talked amongst themselves and found him to be a genial enough man. I was impressed by how well the translators spoke English. None of them had ever left their country, but they spoke with strong American accents that they'd learned from language tapes. Every question took ages to be processed, as the various parties would talk between themselves and then via the translator.

Like the customs people and the earlier police interviewers, these officers found it virtually inconceivable that I'd been acting alone and were eager to get me to tell them about my accomplices. Since there were none, I didn't have to lie as much as I'd feared. This put me in a better frame of mind, but they were suspicious, reasoning that since I'd lied about the place I'd bought my hash I was probably lying about my co-conspirators. In time I would be vindicated by the fact that hotel staff closely monitor foreigners' movements, and after checking my records the police would smile knowingly and say, 'Yes, we know you were travelling alone.' It wasn't until much later that I discovered the extraordinary lengths the Chinese go to to watch each other, let alone tourists.

By midnight the police were ready to go to bed, and my back was beginning to ache from all the hours I'd spent sitting on uncomfortable hard wooden chairs. I half jokingly asked the translator if I could go home now, but he looked almost embarrassed as he smiled and said I would be taken to a cell for the night.

Two guards led me from the room, back across the courtyard to another part of the compound and into a tunnel that opened up into another courtyard with a large gate manned by armed guards, who were preoccupied playing chess. Seeing us coming, they jumped to their feet and unbolted the gate, and above me I could see dozens of square windows with steel shutters across them. The place smelled of an unhealthy mix of stale vegetables and chlorine, but was not dirty. Doors clanged and creaked, and I could hear prisoners yelling to each other across the courtyard. Once inside, we walked up a concrete-and-steel staircase to the first floor, where some more officers were waiting, and after changing personnel the new guards led me down the block to the last cell on the left.

As the large wooden door was unbolted I could hear the muffled voices of the room's inhabitants, and as it swung open two Chinese guys stepped forward to check out the new arrival. The guards said a few words to them and the door was closed behind me. I barely had a chance to look at the cell before they were offering me hands to shake and smiles to share. I felt immediately relaxed in their company and heaved a sigh of relief after so many hours with the police and customs people. One was a large man in his mid-30s, I guessed, who spoke very little English and introduced himself as Liu. He was a typical-looking Han Chinese with pale skin and jet-black hair. He wore a blue tracksuit and trainers and had overlapping teeth and a gummy smile. The other guy was short and stocky and wore jogger bottoms with no top. He was muscular, with a blurred home-made tattoo on his arm. His skin was much darker and he spoke no English whatsoever. I guessed he was in his early 30s. His name was Yen.

They were eager to know what crime I'd committed, so I gave them a brief description of how I'd been busted at Shanghai's main port on my way to Japan. Neither of them had ever tried smoking dope and were barely aware of what it was, though they'd heard there had been other foreigners in the detention centre for the same thing. I was intrigued to know more about this, but they said they didn't know the details. The room was larger than I'd expected, about ten by sixteen feet, but there were only two beds. Liu said the bed on the left would be mine, and I wondered who would be on the floor. Yen pointed to a pile of linen on the floor and said he was happy to sleep there, but I felt guilty and offered to change places. He seemed almost offended at the suggestion, pretending he preferred to sleep on the wooden floor.

As I began to relax, my mind drifted away from the traumatic events of the day to Rosie. Where was she? Had she experienced some kind of psychic awareness of my situation? We'd often talked about such things. Our parting on the platform of Kyoto station had been sad and disconcerting, coming as it did at the end of the happiest years of my life. We'd met in the warm, balmy tropics of India, where we'd forged a rambling gypsy life for ourselves buying crystals and jewellery to sell in Japan. We'd ventured off into the unknown together and the world had fallen at our feet. Life had been good, as if the love we had was a magic carpet that would carry us for ever. Neither of us had known such happiness, and for a while the joy of each other's company kept coming, as effortless as sunshine. But it wasn't enough for me: perhaps it was too good to be true, and in time a tiny cloud appeared, which grew bigger and bigger until every day was dull again and I couldn't understand what had happened. So I did what I always did at such times: I bought a one-way ticket to somewhere else. Some place far away, and China seemed as good a place as any. So that's where I was going, and don't ask me why, because I didn't know myself.

That day in Kyoto, an uncertain future lay ahead of us as the immaculately dressed guard in dazzling white gloves and shiny black shoes blew his whistle. The train slid out of the station as if in slow motion as we lip-read each other's assurances that we would meet up soon. In three years we had not been apart for more than a week, but this time I had a one-way ticket, which carried with it the curse of endless freedom and the possibility of a final separation.

Yet travel has its own consolations, shifting the mind from its selfish obsessions into a fresh perspective with the promise of new experiences and diversion from the old. I sat on the train surveying our latest twist of fate. And then I found a bar on the train and smoked a pipe out of the loo window, and an old Bob Dylan song, 'It Takes a Lot to Laugh, It Takes a Train to Cry', ran round my brain, and as the bullet train hurtled through the rice fields, I fell asleep smiling to myself.

The *Kanjiro* pulled out of Kobe harbour at midday. My economy-class ticket meant I had to share a large dormitory cabin with some 20 or so mainly Chinese passengers, who sat huddled round Calor gas camping stoves eating noodles, playing card games and yelling at each other in a manner that would make a Japanese wince. I made use of the one Chinese phrase in my vocabulary and said *ni hao* (hello) to the gathering, who glanced up momentarily before returning the greeting and slapping another card onto the deck. There were beer machines on each deck of the ship and I sat guzzling a can while eating the sandwich Rosie had made me earlier that day. A cloud of heavy fog hung in the air, suspended a few feet above the waterline, and I wondered how the captain managed to navigate the huge vessel, which cut through the water like a great iron on a steaming damp shirt.

On the deck I spied an elderly Korean couple I'd noticed at the immigration checkpoint in Kobe. They were sharing a bento box of fish, pickles and rice, taking care to leave the best till last. We'd made small talk about the trip ahead, and I'd congratulated them on their youthful looks when they'd told me they were retired and having a second honeymoon after 40 years of marriage. Had I just arrived in the Far East, I'd have guessed their ages as being somewhere in the mid-50s; neither had a grey hair on their head and they had barely a wrinkle between them, but I'd long become used to the way in which the people of the Orient managed to slow down the ageing process. Some said it was the ginseng, traditionally believed to be a cure-all elixir promoting longevity, while others said it was the diet of raw fish and seaweed washed down with copious quantities of green tea. Perhaps it was the sobering influence of Buddhism, with its tranquil acceptance of life's uncertainties. I couldn't put my finger on it, but I envied the cheerful resignation of Asian people. Rosie had been my link between the East and the West, and without her I was stranded in my occidental prison. The elderly couple made me reflect on the choice I was making. Was I closing the door to happiness? And if so, what would I replace it with?

I lit a cigarette, cracked open another bottle of beer and wandered along the deck gazing out across the ocean as numerous small islands appeared in the distance, jutting out of the sea as if they'd come to spy on us. Peering over the edge of the railing I could see dolphins gliding beneath the surface of the water, their grey backs like new-age submarines traversing the side of the ship. I'd last seen the fresh-water round-nosed species with Rosie from a small dinghy on the Ganges river, where we'd made vows to each other under the auspices of a Hindu ceremony known as a pooja. Now my mind flashed back to revisit that sacred river, the lifeblood of millions, where bodies were burned and babies were born and dreams came true. On an earlier trip to India, we'd watched their salt-water cousins frolicking around in the Indian Ocean and from that day on had seen our romantic fortunes linked to those creatures. Now, as I glanced across the water, dark thoughts of sadness and loss overcame me.

One of the dolphins came up for air and I felt an inexplicable urge to take its life. I imagined myself hurling a harpoon into its side and watching the poor creature writhe spastically in the pink-tinged phosphorous surf, its tail lashing the water in a deadly dervish dance before rolling onto its belly. The image sickened me almost as much as it shocked me, yet I was momentarily engulfed with bloodlust, like some crazed Ahab coming face to face with my own white whale. I'd left the woman I loved and could now feel myself being sucked into a whirlpool in which only pain and suffering could redeem me. But the fleeting picture I'd conjured up in my head represented far more than the termination of the loving bond we shared; its connotations were signs representing an ominous glimpse into the descent into which I was taking myself. I was flirting with disaster and I knew it. Looking out across the grey-blue cusps of the waves, I could see the earth's curvature on the horizon, and sensing I might slide off the edge of the world, I returned to my cabin and slept.

Now I lay on my prison bed and felt engulfed with emotions. I'd managed to keep my cool and stay calm throughout the ordeal, but now I felt overwhelmed and within seconds I was in floods of tears. I rolled over onto my stomach to shield myself from my cellmates' gaze, but the tears turned to convulsive sobs and I felt a hand on my shoulder. Rolling over, Yen and Liu were smiling kindly at me, and Liu told me not to worry. I felt a sudden desire to laugh and did so, which made them laugh, too. It felt good to be amongst criminals: they helped me relax, they didn't have the baggage that people in uniform carried, they were themselves, and I could be myself. We talked for hours, with Liu's bad translations and my sign language, squatting mosquitoes against the stained brown walls of the cell.

3

Killing the Rooster

I woke early. At least I think it was early – the 24-hour lighting gave the impression of being in an airport lounge, with its permanently illuminated sanitised glare. I could hear the clatter of mess-tins down the corridor and the yakking of voices moving down the cell block until the bolt on our door rattled. Liu leapt out of bed and took three tins of rice from the trustee behind the door. A small group of prisoners gathered in the doorway to look through the hatch at the captive foreigner. A guard barked down the hall and they scuttled off as he took their place and gawped at me before slamming the hatch shut again. My first meal in the cell arrived in a rectangular metal mess-tin. The container was half filled with rice, with a thin veil of something resembling cabbage on top. My cellmates ate theirs as if it were the last meal of their lives, hoovering up the contents in seconds, encouraging me to do the same. I peeled back the slivers of snot-yellow vegetable with trepidation, revealing a gluey white brick. By chance, my rice had a millipede lying on the surface. I guess it had to really – it was one of those Third World jail clichés. There was something almost cinematic about it. The other guys found it particularly amusing, and after a brief retch I saw the joke too. As a kid, Henri Charrière's prison memoir, *Papillon*, had been one of my favourite books. Now I was spending my days pacing the floor of my cell, picking insects out of my rice bowl. I began to imagine myself as Steve McQueen, teeth falling out, riding a sack of coconuts to freedom through shark-infested waters.

I'd barely eaten a mouthful when the hatch of the door opened again and my cellmates leapt to their feet and stuffed their washed bowls through the door. I was ordered to do the same before Yen pointed out I'd barely started. A small commotion ensued before it was agreed I needed more time to eat. Later in the day, it was decided that since I was suffering from a contagious disease I should have my own bowl that never left the cell. I would get a tin like everyone else and empty it into my 'personal' bowl, and from then on I was free to eat in my own time. But during that first meal, after a couple of mouthfuls I lost my appetite and left it. Yen bounced over and asked for my ration, which I gave him. He seemed to swallow it whole.

After breakfast, I took time to check out the cell. At one end of the room there was a toilet and washing area with a bath and a white-tiled three-foot-high wall. I climbed onto the wall and lifted myself up to the level of a steel-barred window with heavily shuttered panels that restricted the view to a small gap at the bottom and top. Below was what appeared to be a flowerbed; above, a slim band of sky. The steel mounting plates that bolted the shutters to the window obscured what could be seen from the sides, leaving a letter-box view of either the sky or the muddy ground.

At the other end of the cell was a red door, its paint chipped by the rectangular rice tins that were slipped through a ten-inch-square hatch three times a day. The first was at 5.30 a.m., when one of us had to leap out of bed and hold a plastic bowl under the opening to receive a bowl of hot water. A trustee stood at the other side with a metal watering can. A different prisoner would use this bowl each day to wash himself. With three in our cell, we were able to wash twice a week in the freezing winter months. In the summer, we were at the mercy of the frustratingly sporadic cold-water supply. When water was available, the bath was used as a storing space. No one ever got in the bath; it would have been considered the height of bad manners.

I could hear doors opening down the landing. Liu said it was prisoners going to work. There were extra cells with machinery in them downstairs, and opposite our block there was another identical building. The jail held around 500 inmates, but the population fluctuated depending on the time of year and how many were waiting to be transferred to work camps and other prisons. A guard opened the door and took Liu and me into his office. I noticed that a large wooden rack with straps on it was standing against the wall outside our cell. I shuddered to think what it was used for, but it resembled some kind of medieval torture instrument. The corridor was a dimly lit row of identical doors with numbers on them, with a shuttered-steel window at the end. Bare light bulbs hung from the ceiling just above head height, and the waft of ammonia drowned out any natural smells. One of the rooms turned out to be an office, though it was indistinguishable from the cells apart from the presence of a small wooden desk. The guard sat opposite and began to ask Liu about my health, which I'd made well known to the police the night before. He spoke no English, but with Liu's help we managed to have a conversation of sorts. The captain, as I was told to call him, had a kindly, sympathetic face, with greasy jet-black hair and thick-lensed spectacles. He'd been in charge of the wing for 20 years, and it showed on his drawn, worn-out face and pockmarked complexion. The room began to fill up as a stream of trustee prisoners and guards took turns to stare at me. I was feeling like a freak-show exhibit in some dystopian carnival when the captain grunted for everyone to leave.

Now it was just myself, Liu and the captain. I began to sweat and shake, as if the ground beneath me was about to open up and suck me in. My muscles atrophied, tears began to stream down my cheeks, my nose ran and I stuttered for the first time in my life. I felt as if my mind had become disconnected from my body and I was momentarily paralysed. Weightlessness came over me and I imagined being suspended in mid-air looking down at myself. I'd heard torture victims recall out-of-body experiences, but I was in no physical pain. The psychological strain was enough to bounce me out of my body, and I worried I was going to shit myself or throw up as I felt more and more detached from my physical being. Liu told me not to worry; the captain was a good guy and wanted to help me. I asked if he knew anything about the charges against me and the sort of jail time that I might expect if convicted, but he said he knew nothing about my case. Liu and Yen had attempted to cheer me up the night before by saying 'short time' whenever I looked on the verge of another emotional outburst. Now the captain chimed in with the only English words I ever heard him say.

'Short time, short time.'

He gave us both a cigarette and told me a doctor would come and see me soon. Another prisoner turned up at the door and the captain invited him in. His English was much better than Liu's and I could talk to him quite normally, without referring to a dictionary. He was in for some kind of thieving, but didn't elaborate, and had opted to do his six-year stretch in the detention centre rather than a prison. I started to relax, and after ten minutes we were taken back to our cell, where a jealous Yen asked Liu to breathe his tobacco breath over him as compensation for missing out on the treat.

Liu was happy to have got out of the cell for the first time in many months, and we spent some time chatting in pidgin English. He was serious about wanting to learn the language, and I lent him the English–Chinese phrase book the police had allowed me to keep when I was arrested, which he read every day for hours on end. As his English improved, he began to tell me about his home town, which I'd only seen for a brief couple of hours before my arrest. To many Shanghainese, anyone born on the wrong side of the Huangpu River was a second-class citizen; to be from another province meant being condemned with the term *bazi*, or peasant. There were exceptions to this rule, with people from Beijing or Guangzhou being given grudging respect as residents of the country's cultural and business centres. Traditionally, anyone from outside the chief domains of Han culture was considered a barbarian, their cultures and traditions sneered at by the dominant group. China has 54 ethnic minorities, all of whom have been – to a greater or lesser extent – sledgehammered into submission by the relentless hegemony of the Han majority. Only the Tibetans have elicited much sympathy from the West, who've long since been seduced by their serene, moon-like smiles and mystical interpretation of the teachings of the Buddha. In truth, the whole of China had been terrorised for much of the twentieth century, and the Han Chinese had been expected to lead the way in the succession of disastrous campaigns the Communists had foisted on them. In the 'new' China of Deng Xiaoping, a burgeoning urban middle class was eager to draw up boundaries between itself and the peasant masses, and Liu knew which side of the fence he wanted to be on. Yen, on the other hand, with his darker complexion and illiteracy, was content to remain a part of the working classes, and was often mocked by Liu for being a *bazi*. Liu would become incensed in conversations with Yen and hold his finger up to his brain to signify to me our cellmate's stupidity. Nonetheless, I started to warm to Yen, finding his simple ways more appealing than Liu's, whom I decided was a smartarse.

As a foreigner, I was by definition dirty. My cellmates were fastidious in the washing of both themselves and their clothes. They took great interest in how I washed myself, offering expert advice on the tiniest aspects of cell hygiene. Within a few weeks I was copying them in every detail, squeezing out the standard-issue mini towel provided by the jail in exact accordance with cell protocol, and folding it meticulously in an identical manner to them. They observed every move I made, chattering between themselves, chuckling incredulously at my alien eccentricities.

Of particular interest was my body hair, especially my chest. Compared to the Chinese, with their sparse, wispy, bum-fluff beards, I was a gorilla, and I quickly acquired nicknames such as 'King Kong' and 'Monkey Man'. Although they had very little facial hair themselves, Yen and Liu spent much of their time plucking the small hairs they did have by binding two toothpaste-tube tops together with cotton and ripping out the offending growth. They would squint with pain as they did this, and their faces often bled. I never understood the point of it all and within months had sprouted a bushy, Marx-like beard that helped me stay warm in the winter months.

It was decided that I would be in charge of scrubbing the floor every night. Yen was already doing the morning clean, and I would relieve Liu of his evening duty since he was the most senior prisoner, being both the oldest and the longest-serving inmate amongst us. My job was to take a piece of damp rag and wipe the floor with it, but as usual there was a particular way of doing it and my circular wipes were immediately criticised by both Liu and Yen, who insisted I copy their lawnmower-style method of pushing the rag in straight lines while crawling on the floor. My other chore was to collect the hot water at 5.30 every third morning. The trustee prisoners who performed the water-dispensing duties on the other side of the door tended to be those who'd opted to do their sentences at the detention centre rather than move on to the main prison at Ti Lan Qiao. It seemed strange to me that anyone would want to stay in this place of his own choice, and it made me apprehensive about what the main jail would be like. Liu said that people with shorter sentences (fewer than five years) often stayed on at the detention centre because they could secure a better place in the hierarchy of the system. The big jail at Ti Lan Qiao had so many long-term prisoners it would be unlikely that a short-term inmate would get any of the benefits or privileges. At the detention-centre jail, it was easier to be a big fish in a small pond and thus receive maintenance jobs like cooking, cleaning and gardening. Also, there was little 'ideological guidance' at the detention centre, and prisoners had more time to themselves. Once sentenced, Liu was hoping to stay on and work as a trustee at the jail and use the time he had off to learn English. My arrival in the cell suited his studies, and for the first few weeks at least we got on well with each other.

Liu was from the 'right' side of the Huangpu River. Like so many middle-class Chinese, his family had lost everything during Mao's decades of perpetual revolution. To his credit, he'd managed to salvage something of his family's affluent past by working as a junior officer for a Shanghai shipping line. The job had enabled him to travel to countries like Japan, Cuba and Chile, though he was rarely permitted to go ashore. He spoke a very basic pidgin English and after some difficulties managed to tell me how he'd landed in Shanghai's No. 1 Detention Centre.

In addition to their usual cargo, the ships' officers often brought back goods from the countries they visited and took kickbacks for their services, sometimes unaware of the goods' contents. One such package had turned out to contain almost ten kilos of pure amphetamine. I had no idea whether Liu had known what he was carrying, and I didn't blame him for not confiding in me. There was a good chance he'd be executed for such a crime. The captain of the jail assured him that he'd only be charged with smuggling, as opposed to drug smuggling, which seemed to cheer him up a bit. As time went on, I realised the captain always told people what they wanted to hear.

Liu had been in the detention centre for about 18 months. Like the rest of us, he'd been denied access to a lawyer and had not been permitted to have any other visits since his arrest. His family were aware of his predicament, but any contact, even a letter, was forbidden. There was no mention by any official of when he might conceivably get to court, since other members of the ship's crew had fled and his case couldn't proceed without them.

Many prisoners found themselves in this legal limbo, which was compounded by the time-honoured tradition of 'killing the rooster to frighten the monkey'. This Chinese idiom refers to making an example of certain criminals to admonish the others. If, for example, there had been a high incidence of bicycle theft in Shanghai district and the authorities felt a crackdown was needed, local bike thieves would be stockpiled in the region's various lock-ups until the police could claim to have cracked a major ring. A large gang of hapless petty criminals would then be dragged into court together and presented on the evening news as enemies of the people before being handed down unusually harsh sentences. Someone charged with a similar offence either before or after one of these dragnet operations usually found their sentences significantly shorter. It was pure luck – or misfortune – that decided who would get to play the rooster in the Chinese roulette of the People's legal system.

It was well known by everyone that one noisy prisoner down the corridor had been waiting for many years to get to court. He made regular howls of protest, which fell on deaf ears, but they served as a reminder to the rest of the inmates that they too were going nowhere fast. Yen and Liu told me the record for time served on remand in this place was 17 years. The unfortunate holder of this record had been lost in the system, and when he eventually got to court he was given 17 years and promptly released. Many petty criminals would not waste the courts' resources at all due to a law that permitted the police to imprison minor offenders for up to three years in police-run sweatshops.

Yen's case was more cut and dried. He'd been convicted of stealing scrap metal from a disused railway line after being grassed up by a member of his own family. His brother had been charged and convicted with two other men of one of the grisliest murders of recent years. The three men had killed a business rival and chopped his body into small pieces before throwing it into the river. During his interrogation, he'd been forced to inform the authorities of any crimes his family members might have committed, so he fingered his brother for a completely separate offence.

A couple of months later, Yen was reading the local paper when, out of the blue, he started pounding the wall with his fists. Liu eventually translated to me (with a wide-eyed smile, as if he was reporting on a friend's engagement announcement) that he'd just learned of his brother's execution. Nobody was surprised. In a country where thieves are routinely put to death, his had been an extraordinarily brutal crime. It would not have occurred to the guards to inform Yen in advance, and besides, executions are only newsworthy in China when the state wishes to 'frighten the monkeys'.

After breakfast on the second day, the hole that the food had come through opened again. A guard grunted, and Yen and Liu leapt to their feet and stood to attention as the big door was opened and an officer asked me to step outside. The police wanted to interview me again. I was led downstairs, along a corridor and out the back door of the jail section into a small courtyard, where they left me. I stood around for a couple of minutes as a handful of young guards smiled and stared at me. I was getting used to my celebrity status, relaxing into the idea that wherever I went heads would turn and mouths would gossip. When someone saw me, they'd nudge the person next to them until everyone had a good look. I'd smile and say *ni hao*, which they appreciated, and I liked to think I was a breath of fresh air in the dreary place.

'Please come with me.'

A young man in civilian clothes appeared and led me into another building. It was a long, poorly lit corridor of identical cells, each containing the standard-issue bolted chair with straps, situated in front of a three-man desk. There was shouting coming from one of the cells and police with sticks milling around outside, and the young man ushered me into one of the spare rooms.

'Please sit down,' he said, pointing at the chair in the centre of the room.

He took his place behind the desk and started talking to his colleagues in Chinese. There were no windows in the room, just nicotine-stained walls with some Chinese characters stencilled on them in red paint. A gekko scuttled along the ceiling to steal a fly from a cobweb that stretched across the top corner of the room. I had my eye on a packet of Chinese cigarettes on the desk in front of me. In the middle of the desk sat the detective in charge of my interrogation, with a female secretary to his right who was writing everything down. The detective introduced himself in Chinese and looked to the young man, who, it turned out, was the translator. Neither the detective nor his assistant spoke any English, so every time he spoke he would pause to let the young man translate. The translator introduced himself as Alan and said he'd been involved with other foreign dope-smuggling cases. Most English-speaking Chinese give themselves English first names that have no relation to the translation of their own names. I think they just like to have an identity in the language they have chosen to learn. Alan spoke excellent English and dressed in stylish Western suits. He was friendly in a rather smarmy kind of way, but I decided it would be a good idea to get on friendly terms with these people and made a point of chatting about anything other than my case.

'What music do you like, Alan?'

'George Michael – do you like him?'

'Sure. "Guilty feet . . ."' I said, wangling my legs around the concrete floor with a distinct lack of rhythm.

'Yes,' he laughed, 'and "Careless Whisper" is my favourite song.'

'Can I have a cigarette please, Alan?'

He spoke to the detective, who quickly pushed the packet across the desk as if he felt guilty for not offering me one already.

We were getting along: a good start under the circumstances. Alan's ambition was to visit England or America one day, but like most of his countrymen he had no passport, let alone a visa, and few policemen had the money to buy a plane ticket. I felt more relaxed with these people than I had with some of the ghouls I'd met the night of my arrest; they seemed more human, less intimidating and quite excited to have a different kind of criminal to pass the working hours with. It's always a good idea to get policemen on your side if possible, and in a country like China, where the police have powers far beyond those in the West, I knew that being liked by them would be a great help. They could make my life hell if they chose, and there was nothing to be gained by being arrogant. My future was in their hands, and it was crucial that their overall opinion of me was positive.

'She's very pretty,' I said, pointing at the detective's assistant.

Alan laughed and translated the compliment, which made the detective laugh and the girl blush.

'Do you like Chinese girls?' He was translating for the detective, and I nodded.

'Chinese girls are beautiful.'

'I like foreign girls better,' said Alan.

After the pleasantries we got down to the details of my case, which I thought had been pretty much exhausted already. How wrong was I? In Britain, I doubt whether terrorist suspects are given the kind of grilling I got with my half-kilo of hash. The endless attention to the smallest, irrelevant details went on and on for hours. A typical conversation went as follows.

'In your earlier statement you said that on arrival at Shanghai railway station you took a yellow taxi?'

'Yes, that's true.'

'And yet today you said the taxi was brown?'

'Well, it was yellowish-brown, sort of beige, I suppose.'

'Beige?'

'Yes, that's a sort of light-brown colour.'

'So why did you say it was yellow?'

'Well, it was the middle of the night. Does it really matter what colour the taxi was?'

But it did matter, and hours would go by without anything of any real importance being said. This suited me fine, because as long as they stuck to such trivial questioning I could smoke their cigarettes (which no official ever denied me) without having to answer any awkward questions. After weeks of this, I came to the conclusion they actually quite enjoyed it, especially Alan, who was effectively getting free English lessons. I picked him up on his pronunciation and introduced him to new vocabulary, and I knew my stuff, having taught English for several years. Occasionally a tricky question would catch me off-guard and I'd have to invent a name for someone and make a point of remembering it later. We talked for hours about Pakistan, and I decided the guy I bought my hash off would be called Abdul. I found this easy to remember because whenever I told a Pakistani my name was Dominic they would say:

'Abdul Malik?'

'No, Dominic.'

'Abdul Malik?'

'No, Do-Mi-Nic.'

'Yes, Ab-Dul Mal-Ick?'

'OK, fine, Abdul Malick it is.'

Japan was trickier, but I never gave them a surname so it was just Jack and Bob and Sally and so on. The secret was to keep it simple, because you knew they'd bring it up later and everything had to match up. Some days there would be shouting and cries from down the corridor, when it became obvious that the locals were not sharing my relatively civil interrogations. I felt mildly guilty at being given an easy ride by the police, but my story was fairly straightforward and verifiable. I *had* been to see the Temple of Heaven, the Great Wall and the Terracotta Warriors; consequently, I fell into the classification of dumb tourist rather than international drug baron. I didn't have to tell too many lies, and when I did they were only slight variations on the truth. Best of all – with the exception of a few brief spells with the odd backpacker – I'd spent all my time alone in China. In spite of what the police imagined, there were no accomplices. I was what I said I was: a stupid tourist with hepatitis and a bit of dope.

The illness that had plagued me on my travels along the Silk Road brought me unexpected benefits now. After a few days, I succeeded in getting a pot of ink and a dipping fountain-pen head on a stick into the cell. I wrote a poem called 'The Dragon' on the back of a cardboard toothpaste box for something to do. Then I asked the police to give me some of their writing paper so I could keep a diary. It was then decided that for health reasons nothing should be allowed to leave the room, that our cell was effectively quarantined. Consequently I would be able to keep the pen for the duration of my stay. This pleased my fellow inmates (or Liu at least; Yen could not write); however, they were less happy to be sharing a cell with a sick person. Speculation immediately started about whether I had the 'foreigners' disease', AIDS.

A blood test and reassurance by the doctor eventually put their minds at rest, but things took a turn for the worse when the doctor said I should not exercise. This deprived me of my one source of relief from the boredom of lying on my bed. I had spent my first few days pacing the floor endlessly, much to the annoyance of my cellmates, who complained that I was making them feel dizzy. I already felt like a wild bird in a cage; the doctor's latest order was the wing-clip I'd been dreading.

Unable to walk about, I devised a new game to amuse myself, which involved rolling a few socks into a ball and throwing them at the wall. The cell was not dissimilar to a small squash court and the sock-ball had as much bounce as a red dot ball. I would catch it and throw it back as quickly as possible. For the next few weeks, I would spend more hours doing this than I'd spent playing racket sports in my entire life. This, of course, was how Steve McQueen had amused himself in the POW classic *The Great Escape*, but sooner or later my increasingly sulky living partners decided this too was unacceptable, and my languid existence became virtually bedridden.

As I began to settle into the routine of the jail, the captain told me I had a visitor from the British consulate. The room the meeting took place in was the most comfortable I'd been in yet. There was a sofa in the corner and the windows were not barred. Seated in the centre of the room was a casually dressed man who introduced himself as the junior vice consul, Jim Short. He told me he had already seen duty in several international postings around the world, and I guessed he was about 40 years old. After enquiring about my health, he pointed out that as a representative of the British government it was his duty to ensure I was not being treated worse than the local villains, which struck me as odd in a country not famed for its human rights. What would the British government have to say if I were sent to a labour camp for three years without a trial, I wondered. He also pointed out that I had yet to be formally charged, which made me feel a little better.

We started with small talk on the day-to-day trivia of his diplomat's life before getting down to the more sombre issue of my own situation. I asked if there was any chance of a smoke, and Inspector Wong, who I'd met on the first night, offered me one of his. The main question on my mind concerned other foreigners who'd been arrested on dope charges. What kinds of sentences had they received? Short's reply was both shocking and reassuring:

'One got four years, a couple walked free and, er . . . one got fifteen years.'

'Fifteen years? For heroin, right?'

'No, hashish.'

My mind started to reel at the thought of what such a sentence would do to my life, not to mention Rosie and my family. Even four years felt like an eternity, and I quickly enquired about the ones who'd got away.

It turned out they were the sons of the guy who'd got the 15 years. The police had decided to throw the book at their father and let them go. I asked about the guy who'd got the four-year term, how much dope had he had?

'About eight kilos, I think.'

'So what could I expect to get for less than half a kilo?'

'It's impossible to say. They may just kick you out of the country.'

This was music to my ears. I began to imagine myself waving goodbye to Inspector Wong and co. as I headed off in a cab to the airport after the short sharp shock of incarceration in a Chinese prison.

'But don't get your hopes up,' he said, sensing my brief elation at the prospect of imminent release. 'There's a long way to go yet.'

Inspector Wong, who'd been glancing at his watch for the duration of the meeting, finally muttered something to the translator and the visit was over. Mr Short asked me if I'd like the Foreign Office in London to inform my relatives of my situation, adding that he recommended I give him permission to do so. I thought for a moment before agreeing it would be a good idea, since there was no way of knowing how long I'd be here and Rosie would start worrying, having not heard from me. I shook the consul's hand and tried, unsuccessfully, to get some cigarettes off Wong to take back to my cell. Walking back to the cell block, I had the misfortune of seeing the cop who'd made no secret of his distaste for me on the night of my arrest. He sneered at me and made a comment that amused Wong.

Inside the building, I noticed for the first time what the conditions were like in some of the other cells. In one there were more than a dozen shaven heads peering back at me like Buddhist gargoyles. Another was full of what appeared to be teenagers folding napkins, while the third was so full it reminded me of the scene in the Marx Brothers' *A Night at the Opera* when the waiter opens the door of a cupboard-sized cabin and 25 people fall out. It occurred to me how lucky I was to have only two cellmates in a similar-sized room, and I wondered what my own roommates had done to warrant such favouritism.

The day after the consul visit, I was back in the police interrogation room, where I was officially arrested. It had been ten days since my detainment, and by law the police must arrest suspects within ten days. I'd assumed I'd been arrested at customs, but it turned out I'd only been detained. I asked the interpreter, Alan, about other foreigners he knew of in Shanghai. Particularly the one who'd got fifteen years.

'He was from Liverpool. An American also got 15 years,' he smiled.

I tried to dig more, but he was vague, as he hadn't personally dealt with all the cases. It was depressing and so I changed the subject. I asked him about the Cultural Revolution, but he said he'd been too young to know much. His boss, who must have been about 50, remembered it well.

'Did you wave a Little Red Book?'

He laughed and nodded.

'Were you a Red Guard?'

He looked down at his desk, as Alan butted in.

'It was a long time ago,' he said, bringing the conversation to a close.

After the police investigation had finished, weeks would go by between consul visits. During my time in the cell, I tried to keep myself busy as best I could. I was invited to take part in the daily card game after Liu had made some papier-mâché playing cards out of newspaper and rice gruel. Now we had a pen it was possible to draw the numbers and suit icons on the cards, whereas before small bits of relevant newsprint were glued to the front to identify the cards. Card-playing was forbidden due to the probability that it would lead to gambling – a ubiquitous Chinese vice – so we played close to the wall adjacent to the door to keep out of view of the peephole. The games would invariably end in an argument, with Liu calling Yen a dumb country bumpkin who didn't understand the rules. It was an absurdly daft game that made snap look like bridge, and I soon got bored.

Over the weeks, the relatively tranquil relations between the three of us slowly deteriorated. Liu decided to stop his English classes, and before long days went by without my having so much as eye contact with the two people living just feet away from me. Although he no longer wanted to study with me, he hung onto the phrase book I'd lent him and continued studying English by rote. He'd sit cross-legged with the book in his lap, mumbling under his breath like the Koranic students in the madrasas of Peshawar. It occurred to me that even if these guys were my best friends, we'd still have fallen out with each other by now, and I tried to stay positive and not allow resentment to build up between us.

The situation worsened one sunny day when Yen decided to block out the miniscule ray of natural sunlight that occasionally crept into our cell by hanging his freshly washed bedding over the window. I was furious and protested, but the washing had to take priority. In retrospect, they were probably right; in wintertime there were few opportunities to launder the bedding and even less time to dry it, but I'd become almost obsessed with catching what sunlight I could in the increasingly gloomy environment by positioning myself on the floor at an angle to catch the rays. After long periods of time with bad food and no natural sunlight, the skin turns an ashen grey and any ray of light is welcome. I also felt that Yen and Liu were jealous that I was lapping up the little sun that came into the cell. Of course, they could have done the same, but it hadn't occurred to them, and if they couldn't have it, neither could I.

As the chasm between the Chinese and myself widened I became depressed and lonely, and even a brief connection with the smallest natural phenomenon took on supernatural significance. Having made a stand about them hanging out their washing, I made a point of not doing the same with mine, thus reinforcing their prejudice towards 'dirty foreigners'.

The freezing winter put an end to the mosquito problem, but for months we were bedridden. The bath had a thin layer of ice on it now, and we slept in thick socks and padded jackets to keep out the cold. Though we no longer spoke, to their credit Liu and Yen continued to share any treats they got hold of with me. They'd get tangerines their wives had bought from the prison shop, strips of dried mango and small candies like the Fruit Salad variety I'd eaten as a kid. Even on the worst days we shared what we had, even if they were thrown across the room disdainfully.

As my external world took a darker turn, I became increasingly absorbed in books and writing. Along with the phrase book the police had allowed me to hang onto, I'd had the good fortune to be arrested with a couple of excellent books, which had been returned to me after the first couple of weeks of my incarceration. The first was *Robinson Crusoe*. Although I'd been an avid reader for many years, books took on a whole new significance in my present surroundings. I found I was constantly underlining sentences that seemed to strike a chord with my own situation. It seemed that the books I read had been written explicitly with me in mind, and I was easily transported to the places they were set. As a free man I'd sometimes found it hard to concentrate on novels, and my past was littered with unfinished books. Now I found the world on the page was more real than my own; in fact, there seemed to be a correlation between the characters and my own life, as I found myself identifying with them more and more. I began to imagine myself on Crusoe's island, diving for seafood and hunting wild boar. I could taste the coconut milk and guavas described in the book, as well as feeling the loneliness that the protagonist endures. Crusoe's predicament reminded me of how lucky I was to have cellmates, even if we didn't like each other. A friend of mine spent 13 months in solitary confinement on remand in Japan with no connection to anyone at all. He'd done jail time in other countries, but had never experienced such cruelty before. He told me the fear of insanity was worse than any cellmate could be and that long-term solitary could destroy a person completely. I tried to remind myself of these wise words when Yen and Liu were getting me down.

The second book I happened to have in my possession when I was arrested was Yukio Mishima's extraordinary *The Temple of the Golden Pavilion*, in which a stuttering, inarticulate student of Zen Buddhism becomes obsessed with the most beautiful thing in his world: Kyoto's magnificent Golden Temple. Unable to attain the beauty and purity that the temple symbolises, the tormented student destroys it, burning it to the ground. I'd been to the rebuilt temple on several occasions while living in Kyoto on and off since 1985, but I'd never heard of the tale behind the original building's tragic demise. Mishima, one of Japan's greatest writers, is widely respected by foreigners, though less so by my Japanese friends, who often seemed mildly embarrassed by his association with right-wing politics. In 1971, the writer committed hara-kiri after a failed coup attempt in which he and a small group of followers took an army general hostage and tried to instigate an uprising at a Tokyo barracks. Standing in full military regalia on the balcony, haranguing the troops with a megaphone about the loss of Japan's imperial past, Mishima was considered by many to be an anachronistic crackpot, out of touch with modern Japan. When his calls to reinstate the emperor and his godlike pre-war status fell on deaf ears, he performed the classic Japanese act of humility and ripped open his abdomen with a knife, before his assistant decapitated him with a sword.

The 1956 novel is particularly interesting in its depiction of the changing face of Japan's religion and what Mishima saw as its corrupt hierarchy. I'd often been surprised how commonplace it was to see Buddhist monks in the more upmarket bars in Gion (Kyoto's largest nightlife district), often outrageously drunk, cavorting with hostesses and geisha girls. There seemed few earthly pleasures these custodians of the nation's faith were expected to abstain from, but I liked the way they reconciled the placid, meditative monastic life with a good night on the town, and made some friends among them. Kyoto even had a Rastafarian monk who played reggae music at a local radio station and was a friend of the legendary Jamaican record producer Lee 'Scratch' Perry.

The Chinese were not permitted to have books, but did get the odd newspaper and comic that they enjoyed. I was allowed books simply because I was a foreigner, and it struck me as appalling that they were not otherwise permitted in such a place. If prisoners were expected to educate themselves, it seemed natural to at least allow educational reading matter into the prison. In truth, the powers that be had no interest in education, but rather wanted to break the inmates through boredom and ideological brainwashing. Each cell had a copy of the rules painted on the walls, which the Chinese were expected to know by heart. Among the rules was a reminder that all inmates were expected to inform the authorities of any crime they knew about, particularly regarding their own families. This kind of paranoid self-policing has become associated with Stalin's Russia or Mao's Cultural Revolution, but in 1993 the idea of shopping your own family members was still being actively encouraged by the authorities. Later I would learn much more about Chinese-style surveillance, but for now I was unaware and assumed the paperwork I saw Liu and Yen write was to do with their legal cases.

Yet before that long winter, there were some rays of light. One day, after I had been officially arrested, the cell door opened and a guard called me out and walked me down the corridor to the captain's office. There was good news: I had a visit later that morning, and he asked me if I'd like to have a shave. I jumped at the chance and was led to a spare cell where a guy stood with a pair of clippers, shaving the heads of other prisoners. The clippers took off about 95 per cent of my growth and left me with a little stubble, but I looked less like a caveman now and would hopefully look attractive to Rosie. She'd written to say she was coming with my dad at some point soon, but I had no idea quite when it would be.

The guards led me out of the main block and across a courtyard towards the building where I'd previously met Jim Short, the British vice consul. I walked into the room and my dad was sitting on a sofa with Rosie, who jumped up to give me a hug, before stepping back to give my dad his turn. Dad was never much of a hugger, but he did his awkward best. He was wearing a tie and jumper as always, being from a generation where a man without a tie is only half dressed. Inspector Wong had come along for the visit, but left to smoke outside after a couple of minutes, and I lit up one of Rosie's Camel Lights. She brought news from friends and family, while my dad wanted to know more about my case. Since there were no lawyers involved I had no answers for him, and he put his hands together and pushed them towards his lips, staring into space while pondering the situation.

We asked a guard to take a picture of the three of us – which later proved to be out of focus – and he obliged after clicking the wrong button several times, much to Dad's amusement. There was a good-sized pile of books, too, but I'd have plenty of time to look at them later, and anyway, there was so much to say in the little time we had.

Unfortunately, at times like these it's hard to think of anything to say at all. Nervous laughs punctuated the silence as I smoked another 'ghastly weed', as my father called them. Rosie and I spent most of our time gazing into each other's eyes while holding hands. We were grateful to the Chinese for allowing us to have such a 'hands on' visit, and yet there might be something to be said for speaking through glass like you see in the movies. Being able to touch and even kiss makes the eventual parting even worse, and one could argue that contact-free visits are cruel to be kind.

These thoughts crossed my mind as Wong appeared in the doorway, looking at his watch. We were down to the last five minutes, but I think we'd all had enough. Since parting is the worst bit, it makes sense to make it as brief as possible. There was little to be gained from a tearful farewell, and I was quietly confident – or, rather, suffering under the delusion – that I'd be deported when I got to court. We hugged again, and I was surprised how much my sense of smell had improved since I'd been off the cigarettes. I could smell every scent on Rosie's skin, from the familiar specialist soap she used for a skin ailment to Tiger Balm. My dad hugged me too, rather closer than before, as if the meeting had thawed him out a little.

Wong led them to the consul car as two guards escorted me back into the cell block, and I turned one more time to see them wave. A bird flew past – a Chinese blackbird, perhaps – the first I'd seen in months, and it settled on the wall that led to the outside world. I climbed the now familiar stairs with a box of books and letters in my arms, and the captain was standing at the top. He sent the guards away and walked me down the corridor to the cell at the end where Liu and Yen were standing to attention. Yen took the box from me and put it on my bed, and when the captain had locked up and left, I climbed up to the slit in the window in the hope of seeing the bird again, but it was long gone.

Memories of the visit soon faded as I got to read the new books. First up was Ben Okri's *The Famished Road*, which I loved. Its magical, spiritual view of life and its astonishingly surreal imagery made it the perfect prison read, lighting up my inner world and making the 'real' world more bearable. It was the first – and last – book to make me cry. Another favourite was Malcolm Lowry's *Under the Volcano*, which appealed to the boozer in me, with its vivid portrayal of alcoholism. The book charts the tragic decline of the British consul in Mexico, who drinks himself to death on the Mexican Day of the Dead. Lowry creates a delirious, hallucinatory world that is as much about the protagonist's mescal-fuelled fantasies as it is about the 'real' world. I was struck by the character's insistence on destroying his life at all costs as he stumbles drunk around the small Mexican town with a 'hideous pariah dog' on his tail. The book is not easy to read, but it is a sprawling masterpiece that reminded me of my own downward spiral.

The week following the visit from Rosie and my dad, I was called downstairs to what I assumed was another police visit only to be met by a different official, who introduced himself as Mr Song. My first thought was that he looked like Stan Laurel from Laurel and Hardy. He even scratched the top of his head with a vacant look on his face, like the film legend's classic pose. He had a translator with him and a pretty assistant, and they told me they were from the prosecutor's office. I'd expected a prosecutor to be intimidating, but he was a surprisingly amiable, laid-back character. He handed me a packet of Marlboros, which, oblivious to the prison regulations, he told me to keep. His assistants were friendly and a pleasant change of company after the dozens of hours I'd spent with the police. We went through my case and he sounded sympathetic to the idea that I was a foolish tourist rather than a criminal. The girl smiled a lot and made me horny. She wore a blue uniform with shiny buttons and a red and gold Communist Party lapel brooch. I couldn't take my eyes off her. Before leaving, they asked if I'd like them to get me anything. I asked for a carton of Marlboros and told them they could take the cash out of the money of mine the captain had. They walked me back to the bottom of the cell-block stairs and the girl waved and said goodbye with a smile. It made my day.

The cigarettes went down well with Yen and Liu, who started jumping for joy and patting me on the back. The only problem was we didn't have any matches. Liu came up with an idea to rub a soap brick with a bit of fabric, a method he'd seen former cellmates using. We were given a block of gritty soap that looked like a horse lick. I couldn't see how on earth we'd generate enough friction to warm this thing up, let alone set it alight. Apart from anything else, the soap was damp. Liu must have spent two or three hours rubbing this thing, trying to work out how his former cellmates had ever got it to work. Yen and I were doubtful it would ever catch fire and started to think of different ideas. Yen came up with one that involved using the electricity from the light fitting on the ceiling. If Liu could hoist him up onto his shoulders, he might be able to do something. Liu, who liked to think of himself as vastly more intelligent and sophisticated than the country peasant, wanted to soldier on with the silly soap-brick idea, but Yen found a tiny piece of tinfoil that he rolled into a wire and proposed to use as an element. Suddenly the idea sounded possible, and after a quick listen at the door to check no guards were coming, Yen jumped up onto Liu's shoulders and got to work. Within minutes, we'd lit a cigarette and everyone was ecstatic. Even Liu admitted Yen's idea was smart, and we still had 16 cigarettes left in my packet. When we got to the end of the butt we lit another one off it and so shared two cigarettes and kept the rest for tomorrow. Thanks to Mr Song's generosity and Yen's resourcefulness, everyone had a smile on their face in the cell that night, and for the time being, at least, I was popular.

4

The Company of Men

After the prosecutor's visit, I saw no more of the police. My case had been fully investigated and solved on the night of my arrest, and the subsequent investigation had been an absurd waste of police time and resources. Five weeks' worth of three senior police officers' time had been spent chatting about a half-kilo dope bust, but Alan's English had improved steadily and I'd got to smoke cartons of free cigarettes. The door of the cell rarely opened now, and I went back to throwing my rolled-up socks at the wall until Liu got pissed off and told me to stop. The jail diet was terrible and I was beginning to regret telling the police I was vegetarian, which I wasn't. I'd turned my nose up at a sliver of fatty pork belly in my first week, since I was not used to eating a lump of fat, but now I began to have second thoughts. In fact, it was the only tasty dish we got. Along with the rice, there was either cabbage, boiled cucumber, pork, hard-boiled egg, tofu or occasionally chicken. I was getting tofu, hard-boiled eggs or cabbage while my cellmates had more variety. I don't much like hard-boiled eggs, and the cabbage was vile, but tofu can get pretty dull after a while, too. I got a meeting with the captain and told him I'd decided to take up a meat diet again, but I don't think he passed on the message as they never gave me pork again. Funnily enough, pork belly has since become one of my favourite dishes, which I cook regularly.

I started to cast my mind back to how it had all gone wrong, and how the trip designed to 'get my head together' had become such a disaster. It was in the mountains of Amdo Tibet that I'd first decided to make the Silk Road trip from Pakistan back into China. At that point I'd still not made a decision to buy hash once I was there, but I knew it would be cheaper and easier to fly to Pakistan and come back overland than make a return trip from China. Besides, I knew it would be a long and gruelling trip, and I didn't want to do it twice along the same route. Pakistan had been high on my list of countries to visit for some years, and I'd hoped to be able to cross the border into Iran while I was there. At that point my health was still good, and while staying at a guesthouse in the mountains I'd written a folk song called 'Peshawar', based on a meeting I'd had a few weeks earlier with an Afghan refugee. Writing the song had filled my head with romantic notions of the famous border town, and I wondered how I might integrate a visit to the North-West Frontier into my Silk Road trip. I knew I could fly from Hong Kong to Karachi quite cheaply and then make my way overland through Pakistan, along the Indus Valley and over the Khunjerab Pass back into China.

The next morning, I took a long walk into the hills above the town of Xiahe, a Tibetan hill station a day's bus ride from Lanzhou in Gansu Province. The high pastures around the town had been populated by Tibetan yak herders for hundreds of years and had been generally left alone by the Han Chinese who tended to occupy the lowlands. The people spoke a different dialect of Tibetan from those from the Autonomous Region, but pilgrims came from far and wide to the lamasery on their way to Lhasa. Some made the gruelling trip on their hands and knees, prostrating themselves as they went, which would take literally years to achieve. It was an absurd challenge from an agnostic Westerner's point of view, but the elderly lady I saw embarking upon her ordeal was oblivious to the hardships of her chosen path, and I felt an awkward combination of awe, envy and pity that she could derive such peace and happiness from the bizarre undertaking.

My own mission was less noble. I didn't really believe in anything, nor was I searching for any kind of union with God or a higher state of consciousness. I liked to think I was a vaguely spiritual person – cherry-picking my way through various belief systems as long as it didn't require undue sacrifice – but I'd never taken the plunge into religiousness. At boarding school we'd been forced to attend both morning and evening prayers, but I'd sat upright in my pew as the rest of the school bowed their heads. Now, 15 years later, my religion was a swashbuckling mix of adventure and daring that put me in the same frame as the fugitive heroes of my favourite folk songs and movies. I identified with the loveable rogues and lucky losers, the riverboat gamblers, the chancers, the hustlers. I wanted to be out on the high seas flying the Jolly Roger, rustling cattle across the Mexican border. What I lacked in religion, I more than made up for in personal mythology. My guides were the renegade prophets of popular culture, from Joe Strummer to Johnny Cash, though I was yet to realise the significance of the latter's prison songs to my own journey. And the promise of this idyll drew me towards the mountains of the Afghan–Pakistan border, the nearest I was likely to get to the Wild West of my beloved cowboy songs and films. The modern world had lost its magic. You could tell as soon as you walked out of an airport, where every street was lit like a garage forecourt and no one spoke to strangers. And so I made a plan, sitting in my room at the guesthouse, guitar in hand, to seek out the best dope in the world, from the oldest growing region, and take it by hand all the way to the centre of the modern world. There would be money to be made – a few grand, I guessed – but it wasn't just about the money; I could just as easily get the Afghans to pack it into a parcel and post it. No, it was vindication for a way of life, testimony to my quixotic verve; it would be the apogee of the picaresque existence I'd chosen. It was dangerous, even foolish, but the myriad dangers would magnify the excitement. It would be the mother of all scams, and in just a few weeks I'd be sitting on tatami mats in Kyoto drinking cold beer as my friends got to smoke the best dope in the world.

The next morning, I took the bus back down to the sweaty lowlands of the Yellow River basin. Halfway down the mountain Tibetan culture gave way to a mild strain of Islam, where men and women mingled in the streets. I found a friendly restaurant with tasty stew and naan bread. After lunch, the bus meandered down through the valleys into Han country, with its ugly concrete blocks and police sirens. The Yellow River was soupy brown with silt, but Lanzhou was not a bad place to hang out. I got a dorm bed in a large government-owned hotel that accepted foreigners. A young Chinese girl came into the hotel. She was a student and spoke poor English, but was eager to learn more. Her name was Xiao-Lian (lotus cloud), and she was skinny with long hair and big eyes.

I liked her and she asked me if I'd like to walk into town together. We ate delicious garlic-and-peanut noodles at a stall by the river, and she talked of how she'd love to go to the West. I got the impression she wanted to do more than just visit. She was a sensitive, delicate girl and looked out of place in her often crudely harsh surroundings. China is a tough country for such dainty souls. She was different, and people who stand out in the crowd need to be tough, as Chinese society demands uniformity and standardisation before happiness. I was surprised when she asked if I'd like to go to her room and was concerned about whether there would be any bad repercussions for her. I had never been invited into a Chinese home before, let alone a single woman's, and felt nervous for both of us.

I said yes.

She lived on the sixth floor of a nasty grey tenement block. The room was small, drab and cramped, but she'd made the best of it. There were rolled-up piles of futon bedding on the floor, and I learned she shared the room with two other students. Through a barred window I saw another horrible concrete block opposite. Washing hung from its balconies in a patchwork of colours that took the worst out of its dreary facade. She stood close behind me, and I could feel her body heat as I spied a bunch of jasmine dangling from the window frame. I turned as she took a shy step backwards. She was attractive rather than pretty, with a downtrodden but resilient demeanour. An awkward silence hung in the air, and it was almost a relief to hear a key turn in the lock of the room's door. One of her flatmates, a dumpy girl in a polo-neck jumper, walked in and seemed oddly uninterested in what must have been an uncommon sight. I said *ni hao* and she nodded back before collecting a satchel and leaving. We were alone again. I looked across at Xiao-Lian; her eyes were sad but hopeful, as perhaps were mine. Then the door creaked open and we both turned towards it and left. At the bottom of the lift she gave me a book of Chinese poems with English translations, and I took a rickshaw back to my hotel. I never saw her again, but rewrote the events of our meeting in my head, lying between the sheets in my prison cell, for many pleasant nights after.

I booked a train south to Guangzhou. There was time to kill scouring the nearby streets for dried noodles to eat on the journey. I bought a large hot-water flask and a small bag of Dragon Well tea from a hunchback and his dwarfish wife who'd set up shop inside the station. They were happy for my custom, still beaming their waifish grins across the lobby as I queued for my ticket. I was fortunate to get a second-class sleeper, but the berth was cramped all the same. My co-travellers turned the occasion into a picnic and were more than happy to include me in the festivities. The men chain-smoked throughout the meal, gnawing on chicken drumsticks, with smoke puffing out of their nostrils. Large bottles of beer appeared out of a plastic cooler box, and I got my mini dictionary out and attempted to communicate with my hosts as the women filled my glass. I asked one of the men what he thought of the late Chairman Mao, and he waved a chicken foot dismissively while gobbing a lump of gristle out of the window. These were middle-class Chinese who were probably happy to see the back of Mao and his Iron Rice Bowl. The new China was giving them a life their parents and grandparents could only have dreamed of, and they had little nostalgia for the bad old days.

The train journey became a nightmare. I had the most painful headache of my life, and for the 54-hour journey it got worse and worse. The other passengers in my carriage were very kind, giving me whatever medication they had to relieve the pain. There were red pills, blue pills, green-and-white capsules, sachets of white powder to slip into my green tea: I tried them all, and none of them worked. As night fell, I lay on the fold-out bed and balanced a piece of milky-green jade on my Third Eye, in the centre of my forehead, as recommended by the writers of Rosie's New Age crystal books, to no avail. The Chinese found this hilarious and giggled amongst themselves as I writhed in agony. Eventually a girl from New Zealand got on the train and gave me a couple of ibuprofen, and the pain went away, at least for a while.

The train pulled into Guangzhou late in the evening, but there were no spare beds at the foreigners' hotel and the shops were shut. Some tourists gave me some more headache pills, and I found a pleasant park with a comfortable bench. I chained my guitar bag to the bench and used my rucksack as a pillow. Mosquitoes arrived in squadrons for a sustained attack, and there I lay with a coat over my head like a tramp. I woke to the sounds of birds singing and the sight of pensioners doing t'ai chi. They looked ghostly, gracefully pushing the air around themselves as they stared at me. I felt hopelessly clumsy just watching them, scratching incessantly, having been bitten all over by mosquitoes. As the sun came up, I found a guesthouse by the river and drank a cup of coffee. I got talking to some tourists who overheard me coughing and recommended I see a doctor as soon as possible. Although it cost considerably more than the ferry, there was a hovercraft leaving the mainland for Hong Kong every hour, so I took a taxi to the port and was in Kowloon for lunch.

At the hospital in Hong Kong, a doctor told me I had Chinese flu without bothering to examine me. He said I'd be fine in a couple of days, but I wasn't so sure. I lazed about in Chungking Mansions smoking some weed I'd bought off an Iranian guy I'd met while having a cheap beer outside a 7-Eleven store. He was on his way to Japan, and I gave him some good advice on where to stay and go out at night. All the time I was coughing and spluttering; he felt sorry for me and encouraged me to fly back home, meaning the UK. I didn't consider England home any more, and the Hindu Kush was as good a place as any to recuperate. I decided I'd rather find a tranquil mountain retreat and get my strength back, so I booked a flight to Karachi for the following day.

The Philippine Airlines flight was packed, so the girl at the airport apologised and asked if I minded being upgraded to first class. I was not used to such luxury. We flew to Manila first, even though it was in the opposite direction, and I was pampered all the way by a bevy of beauties in batik gowns and silk slippers. It was one in the morning when we got to Karachi, and I bought a connecting flight to Peshawar for fifty quid that was due to depart at seven o'clock that morning. I got chatting to a taxi driver outside the airport, who gave me a small piece of hash that we smoked together as I fanned myself with my boarding pass.

The flight to the north of the country took about an hour and a half. A young Pakistani guy in Western clothes sat next to me and tried to make conversation, but I had no energy. He was in the Pakistan Air Force and spoke excellent English, which he was eager to practise. I felt I was being rude, but I could barely keep my eyelids open while he talked about himself. The 'Chinese flu' had got worse, and I began to feel that whatever was wrong with me could not simply be a bout of flu. My muscles ached and I couldn't stand up for more than a few seconds before I collapsed onto the nearest seat. I was angry, too. This was a trip I'd been looking forward to for a while, yet I couldn't even muster the energy to look out of the window of the plane. At the airport my rucksack and guitar turned up on the carousel, but I could barely lift them onto the trolley.

'Here, let me take that.' It was my co-passenger smiling sympathetically. He got a cab with me and dropped me off at a guesthouse on Saddar Street in the centre of town before leaving me his phone number.

'Call me when you're feeling better.'

But I felt a lot worse. The hotel manager pointed me towards a doctor's surgery that was a stone's throw from the hotel. Dr Khan greeted me with a warm smile before announcing cheerfully: 'Got hep, have you?'

I looked in his mirror to see the whites of my eyes had turned piss yellow. He said there was no treatment except the 'three plentys': 'Plenty of rest, plenty of water, plenty of fruit. Don't worry, you'll be fine in a few weeks.'

I figured I had just enough money to get back to Japan overland as long as I didn't hang out in Pakistan too long. This news was a serious blow, but Pakistan was so cheap I could stay as long as I liked within reason. My room at the guesthouse resembled a small prison cell, but it was on the roof with a small communal garden, which I appeared to have all to myself. There were other guestrooms across the way with shutters on their windows, which I took to be empty, so I made myself at home. I took off my shirt and sat drinking water from a plastic bottle when two immaculately dressed men with tightly cropped beards approached me.

'Excuse me, sir. Would you mind putting your shirt on while our wives pass on their way to the mosque?'

Iranians are the most courteous of people, and I was embarrassed. I apologised for my slobbish behaviour and quickly put the shirt back on. Seconds later, a group of women spanning four generations shuffled past me, averting their eyes from mine. A couple of young children took a peep out of their veils to reveal eyes as blue as Kashmiri sapphires. They were Shia pilgrims from Mashhad who'd come to celebrate the martyrdom of one of the Imams. Loudspeakers trumpeted the call to prayer, and looking over the wall of the roof garden into the street below, I saw lines of riot police closing ranks to separate the pilgrims from Sunni protestors who'd come to torment them. It was my first experience of the Sunni–Shia schism that had divided Islam since the death of the prophet, and I sat entranced as the two factions attempted to drown out each other's cries, like Celtic and Rangers fans at an Old Firm derby.

The hotel receptionist asked me if I wanted any hash. It's usually a bad idea to score from the place you're staying, so I said no thanks and wandered down the street to buy my own. I didn't have to wait long, as a guy sitting on a moped yelled 'hashish?' from across the road, within spitting distance of the hotel. He spoke a little English and told me to hop on the back of his bike. He seemed a nice enough young man, so I climbed on and off we went. His name was Babur, and he was an Afghan refugee from Herat, in the west of Afghanistan. We drove along the main drag of Saddar Street before taking a sharp turn down a long road lined with poplar trees out of the town.

'Where are we going, Babur? The town is that way, no?'

I was a little nervous. I'd imagined he was going to take me to some family shop and get a commission for his trouble, but we were heading out of Peshawar now. Every few hundred yards there were army checkpoints, which waved us through, but if I was buying dope I'd have to come back along this road and run a gauntlet of uniforms.

'No problem my friend, we will go to my family's house. They have very good hashish.'

It was too late to argue and I was under no obligation to buy any dope, so I just sat back and let him take me where he liked.

We drove a good ten minutes outside of Peshawar and off the road into a maze of mud-walled compounds. It was a refugee camp, but not as I'd always imagined them, with sky-blue UN tarpaulin tents and corrugated-iron huts. These refugees were here for the foreseeable future and had built sprawling shanty towns alongside the Pakistani cities. It occurred to me I was lost and that I was entirely reliant on Babur to get me out of the place. I had little money on me and had left my passport at my hotel so I wasn't really worth robbing, but I'd probably been foolish to get on a motorbike with a complete stranger.

'I'd like to go back to Peshawar now, Babur. I can't buy hashish here anyway.'

'No problem, my friend. We will get you hashish. Here is my family's house.'

He pulled over to the side of the road beside a green door built into a brown wall and banged on the door. An old man appeared and was clearly shocked to see me, but Babur spoke to him in Afghan and ushered me in. The house was dingy and badly lit, and we sat on a tattered piece of carpet in a medium-sized room with a cow-shit floor and a large loom along one side. A young man was working at it while several small boys looked on. A door opened and several men walked in and sat down. One of them was very old, while the others were in-between. It occurred to me I was sitting with at least four generations of the male members of the family. Apart from the small boys, everyone wore a beard except me. Nobody spoke English except Babur, who, I was discovering, only spoke a handful of words himself. The men started asking Babur questions about me, and he did his best to translate.

'How many kilograms you want?' said a stern-looking uncle with a saffron-coloured beard.

'I don't want any kilos, just a small piece to smoke.'

'You want heroin? How many kilograms?'

'No thanks, just a bit of hash to smoke, please.'

'You want boy?' said one of the other old men, running his hand through the hair of the youth who sat in his lap. 'Afghan boy very good.'

'No thanks.'

'Carpet?'

'No carpet, thank you. Too big.'

They were disappointed and started talking amongst themselves. I wanted to get out; there was no way I was buying anything off these people, and I got up to leave when tea arrived. They looked offended and I began to feel I was being rude, so I sat down again as another man with a huge silver beard came through the door with a kilo of hash in his hand. I broke a tiny piece off the corner and gave the man 50 rupees and the rest of the hash. He looked puzzled and handed the brick back to me.

'Babur, you must tell them I can't take this hashish away with me. There are police everywhere, and I don't have any money with me anyway.'

When they discovered I didn't have any cash, they relaxed. Now I was a family guest, and a large, round naan bread arrived. I tried to eat some but I wasn't hungry, so I tried to take an interest in the carpet-making. The wooden looms looked a hundred years old and were worn out. The carpet being made looked cheap and nasty, and I wondered how these people earned a living. I felt guilty that I wasn't spending money and asked if they had any stones. I was thinking of lapis lazuli or some other semi-precious stones popular in the area, and I showed them the lapis stone in my ring as a clue.

Once they saw the ring, one of the small kids was despatched to find some lapis. Five minutes later he returned looking pleased with himself, carrying a small handkerchief, which he opened before me. None of the stones were blue; in fact, I think he'd just grabbed a handful of gravel from the side of the road. I'd had enough; it was clear that there were no stones here. Drugs, young boys and carpets, sure, but I'd have to find my lapis elsewhere.

I said my goodbyes, and after a lot of hand-shaking managed to get back onto Babur's bike for the trip back to Peshawar. I was stoned at least, and I'd got a little smoke for later, but the massive police and military presence around the refugee camp made me paranoid. I wrapped the bit of hash in a handkerchief and stuffed it down my underpants for the ride back to town.

An American junkie from New York called Arty (or 'Ardy', as he pronounced it) was staying in the room next door to mine on the guesthouse roof garden. He was around 50 and had had a habit since his 20s, but looked pretty good on it. Like many addicts with access to high-quality drugs, his skin looked remarkably youthful, presumably due to the lack of stress involved in being out of it for decades. He offered me some smack, but my flirtation with the stuff was long behind me and I declined. Like me he was doing a dope scam, and like me he was looking for lapis lazuli. Peshawar bazaar was an Aladdin's cave of the stuff. I'd put aside a hundred dollars or so to buy some and enjoyed haggling with the Afghan traders who sold everything from beaded necklaces to carved figurines in the lovely blue stone. Many of the simpler items were sold by weight, and I ended up with a good-sized collection of the stones. Arty bought several mini pestle and mortars as gifts for friends to use as 'coke crushers', and I bought a bead necklace for Rosie.

Arty loved the North-West Frontier Province and had been coming to Peshawar for years. In the '70s he'd visited Mazar I Sharif, but now Afghanistan had been ravaged by war and Peshawar was the next best place. He had many tales of his dope escapades in the old days, when hippies drove VW camper vans from Kabul to London and borders were less heavily policed. Terrorism had put an end to that, as had the War on Drugs, and you could no longer pay a fine to have your vehicle pass through the green channel unsearched. The tribal area was one of the last places on earth where the old rules still applied, since the Pakistani law had no jurisdiction there and a Pashtun version of sharia law was enforced. Rather than jail time you'd be more likely to get sentenced to lashes, which could be overturned in favour of a fine, but since drugs were sold openly anyway you'd be unlikely to be arrested in the first place.

'How many kilograms do you want?'

I was sitting in a shop on Saddar Street drinking tea with a middle-aged Afghan man. He had a kid of maybe five sitting on his lap, with almond eyes and a blue plastic aeroplane in his hands that he whirled around in circles while his dad talked business. The father reminded me of the English actor Brian Blessed, with a booming voice and a jet-black beard. Before taking his flight to New York, Arty had introduced me to the guy, whom he'd been dealing with for years, and suggested I ask his wife to sew it into the lining of my guitar bag for me.

'Inshallah, you will have a safe journey,' the Afghan reassured me.

I was running low on cash, so we settled on 600 grams and that I'd drop off the bag the following morning. That night, I sat on the roof of the guesthouse smoking a spliff in the moonlight. I'd always been interested in visiting Peshawar, but my health was so poor I could barely move from my room. I was drinking mineral water by the litre, but it was dripping through the pores of my skin at a faster rate than I could swallow it. Now, on top of everything else, I was about to embark on a dangerous dope scam across several highly policed borders. I must've been mad.

The building shook. There was a slight pause, and then the whole thing seemed to jump a foot in the air. I staggered into the doorway of my room, which is supposed to be the best place to be during an earthquake. The Iranian pilgrims came out of their rooms, too, and we all stood staring at each other, waiting for a follow-up tremor. It never came, but I was superstitious enough to take the event as a shot across my bows. Of all the days to have an earthquake it was the day I'd bought my dope, but now I couldn't afford to go back to Japan without it. Everything was going wrong, but I was determined to carry on regardless.

The following day I had a visitor. I was strung out on the roof terrace drinking mango juice when a giant with a small briefcase arrived in a *jalaba*. I'd been complaining to the hotel manager about my illness and he'd offered to help. 'My uncle is a doctor, he will make a massage for you,' he'd said. I wasn't convinced a massage would help, since the doctor had already told me there was no cure for my condition, but it couldn't do any harm. Now a huge turbaned man had turned up at the hotel to give me a massage and 'cure' my hepatitis. He looked like one of the mujahideen guys I'd seen fighting the Russians on the TV news. His hands were calloused and hairy, like grizzly bear paws, and it wasn't long before I asked him to stop. I doubt the man had ever massaged anyone in his life before, but had simply got the job because he was the manager's uncle. I'm not sure what I was expecting, but it seemed a good idea at the time.

The Iranian pilgrims were returning from evening prayers and saw me topless, lounging on a mattress with the man on top of me. The father looked embarrassed and quickly hustled his women into their room. I can't imagine what they must have thought. I gave the guy some rupees and, as a parting shot, he gave me some 'medicine', a small piece of opium.

I tried not to let my illness stop me from making the most of my time in Peshawar and booked a one-day tour into the tribal region around the Afghan border. By the time my cab arrived, the temperature had become unpleasantly hot. It was a dry, dusty heat, and yet water streamed down my neck as I sat glugging on a bottle of mineral water. There was no air conditioning in the taxi, so I wound down the window and hung my head outside like a drunk waiting to vomit.

We stopped at a roadside cafe for tea, and the owner got out a water pipe, loaded it up with sticky hash and handed it to me. I took one puff and went into a coughing fit. My lungs had packed in completely and every puff left me convulsing, so I had to blow the smoke out immediately. I'd come all this way to find the best dope in the world and I couldn't even inhale it: my body had had enough. The owner of the shop took over and smoked it himself, and I sat back on the cushions looking at the purple peaks in the distance. It was a beautiful place that had barely changed in a thousand years. Only the weapons had been modernised, and they'd produced little more than death, destruction and millions of refugees. The Afghans were war-weary even then; little did they know that 15 years later things would be even worse.

The Khyber Agency is the last outpost before entering the no-man's-land that borders Pakistan and Afghanistan. Every visitor to the region must first submit their passport and pay for a bodyguard. Mine was to be Hasan, a mountain of a man with a black turban that brought his height to around seven feet. He had to slide down the seat with his rifle between his legs to accommodate the headwear that identified him as a member of one of the local Pashtun tribes that ran the border region. A photocopy of my passport was handed to a security guard on the edge of Pakistani government territory, and the cab was waved through.

There was a monument commemorating the British soldiers who'd died fighting the Pashtuns. Finally they'd given up, and instead drawn a line through the region known as the Durand Line separating India and Afghanistan. The idea was that this Pashtun area would eventually be seceded to Afghanistan, in much the same way as Hong Kong was returned to China. More than a hundred years later the conflict remains, as Pakistan grows increasingly embroiled in a conflict between the Afghans and Western forces.

Ramshackle shops lined the dusty road, their contraband displayed for all to see. Old men sat dozing lazily in shaded corners while young men and boys dawdled about, stocking the shelves with the latest gizmos from the Gulf. A minibus hurtled by with Afghan men dangling from the sides, a loudspeaker on the roof blaring out an exotic mix of sounds reminiscent of Ravi Shankar's sitar compositions and John Coltrane's snake-charming music. The women inside wore the family's wealth in gold rings, necklaces and bangles while children slept on their laps. The men huddled together wearing long white tunics, holding hands and chewing betel nut, pausing only to squirt the red slime onto the roadside. A seemingly endless caravan of trucks lay on the hard shoulder of the road to Kabul, while their drivers haggled with the various border guards and tribal chiefs in makeshift customs shacks. Barefoot Pashtuns with Kalashnikovs and bullet belts rummaged through the cardboard stacks of microwaves and video recorders as cartons of Marlboros changed hands over cups of mint tea. A street kid grabbed hold of my sleeve and directed me towards his family's barber shop, and I didn't resist. A cup of tea arrived as the lather foamed up around my sprouting beard.

'You want heroin?' whispered the barber as he slid a switchblade from my chin to my throat, expertly navigating round my Adam's apple.

'No thanks, just a shave, please.' The barber shop was packed, but I'd jumped the queue, probably because I was prepared to pay twice as much for a head massage than the price of a shave. My face was smooth for the first time since leaving Hong Kong and now he set about my head, pouring coconut oil into my tightly cropped hair and jerking his cupped hands backwards and forwards over my scalp. In the mirror I could see a row of men and boys waiting their turn patiently, all looking at me with interest as the barber kneaded the back of my neck with his knuckles. All the adult customers waiting had beards, so it seemed a lousy place to earn a living shaving people, but the men were fastidious about their beards and liked to keep them trimmed regularly.

Outside, a group of five or six men stood brandishing Kalashnikovs. I took them to be the bodyguards of one of the men getting a shave. In a country rife with land feuds and intertribal vendettas, a visit to the barber's could be dangerous. Then there was the civil war raging a few miles away in Afghanistan. The border region was the main staging post for the war, with various mujahideen militias passing through at any given time. After the Russians had been driven out in the 1980s the country had descended into chaos, but the North-West Frontier Province, with its burgeoning arms manufacturers and smuggling routes, benefited from its lawless liminality. The Pakistanis used the area for transporting vast quantities of tax-free electrical goods from the Gulf states, while the Afghans made use of the region's ancient smuggling routes to get their opium to the West. As the middlemen overseeing these clandestine activities, some of the tribes of the North-West Frontier Province had prospered, and the modest-looking mud-walled compounds that dotted the landscape concealed an independent, relatively affluent society between the two poor nations it straddled.

I paid 50 rupees for the shave and head massage and wandered aimlessly on my own around the town, killing time until the taxi was ready to take me back to Peshawar. The border town was famous for its gun shops and so it came as little surprise that arms were the main commodity on sale. The shops had almost no visible security arrangements and were little more than shacks, with men and boys sitting in workshops at the rear, polishing barrels and filing down pieces of metal.

There were no women to see in the town, just hundreds of men lounging around without much to do. I started to feel uncomfortable as shop owners began to hustle me into buying guns, as if I could simply put a shotgun in my bag and drive across the border. I started to dislike the town and looked forward to meeting up with my cab driver and getting out. Pariah dogs patrolled the alleyways, growling menacingly at me, while gunshots rang out from rooftops, giving the town an almost tangible air of violence. The place was like a Wild West town without the saloons or horses, and I found the atmosphere oppressive. But most of all I hated the complete absence of women. Of course, they were there, shuttered off behind compound walls running the households and bringing up the children, but there was not so much as a chador in sight. I felt as if I'd landed in some macho, post-apocalyptic dystopia where half the human race had disappeared. The men looked bored and frustrated, marooned in their stifling masculinity. I began to see some correlation between the lack of women and the surfeit of guns, as if the men had traded their womenfolk for weaponry and now had to live out their days as overgrown schoolboys playing soldiers.

A shop owner succeeded in coaxing me into his store for no other reason than that his was identical to all the others and I felt I ought to have a look at one. A pot of tea dutifully appeared from behind a black curtain that hung at the back of the shop, and I sat down on a cushion, listening to the shopkeeper's spiel. For three hundred rupees, I could go up onto the roof of the house and fire one magazine from a Kalashnikov. For a thousand rupees, I could fire a bazooka at a battered cave entrance on the edge of the town. I declined both offers, feeling there were better ways of spending my money, and walked out, leaving the shop owner standing in the doorway cursing. I'd travelled all over Asia and had often been off the beaten path, but this town gave me the creeps.

The taxi drove quickly to the border and I reclaimed my passport at the Khyber Agency. Back at the guesthouse, I lay on my bed and lit a cigarette beneath the whirling blades of the ceiling fan. My mind drifted back to China, whose border was just two days away, and how Chairman Mao, standing on the steps above Tiananmen Square in 1949, had proclaimed that 'women hold up half the sky'.

The next morning, I woke early and went to the bus depot to buy a ticket up to the Chinese border in the north. It was time to move on.

|5|

Going to Court

Chinese New Year came with a bang. A million bangs, in fact, as the area around the detention centre was submerged in a deafening torrent of firecrackers. Through the slit at the top of the window, we took turns looking up at the sky above. It looked like a war zone, with tracer rockets flaring across the sky followed by massive booms. The Chinese loved fireworks, especially firecrackers, used as part of an ancient custom to ward off evil spirits. In recent weeks, my relationship with Liu and Yen had slowly disintegrated. It was inevitable, I suppose; there was nothing left to say to each other, so we didn't even try. But tonight we could at least share in the festivities, and my cellmates had decided to make an effort to be nice for the first time in a while. Both of their wives had sent in food from the prison shop, which they shared with me, and the captain let me buy some packets of noodles, melon seeds and tangerines. Liu was having his third New Year in jail on remand with no knowledge of when he might get to court or see a lawyer. He wasn't even sure what he was being charged with. The captain decided that he'd let all three of us into his office for a smoke, and Liu took the rare opportunity to enquire about his case. As usual there was nothing to report, since the captain was basically just a screw with no information on prisoners' cases, but he did have a photo that Liu's wife had handed in with his Christmas food hamper. It was of his wife and young son, and he burst into tears the second he saw it. I felt sorry for him. Although we'd grown apart, there were still times when a sliver of camaraderie remained, and the New Year had shown me a side of the Chinese I'd not seen before.

The festive season brought about major improvements in the kitchen, too, as the cabbage and rice were replaced with a new and much improved menu. The dry, stony rice was replaced with fluffy, glutinous kernels, while various dishes involving such delicacies as chickens' feet and heads came through the hole in the door. Yen and Liu sat gnawing on the claws for hours, sucking the soggy eyes out of the birds' heads, while I got a variation on the tofu menu. There was even an old black-and-white TV passed from cell to cell for a couple of hours a day, and I got to see my first Chinese propaganda movie, a sprawling epic about an industrious peasant's trials and tribulations during the calamitous Great Leap Forward. Afterwards, I brought up the familiar discussion about Chairman Mao and got the standard Party verdict:

'He made some mistakes.'

'Seventy per cent good, thirty bad.'

I'd lost count of how many times I'd heard these words. When I told them I thought Mao was a disgusting tyrant, they gave the other favourite response: 'You don't understand China.' This seemed a reasonable enough point to make, except it was only partly true. The majority of mainland Chinese are not well informed regarding their country's recent history. When Deng Xiaoping and his cronies reassessed Mao's dictatorship, they kept in mind that the Party's fortunes were inextricably linked to the deceased despot. To reveal the truth about the rise of the Communist Party in China would have undermined the movement that Deng presided over. Even today, the central myths of the revolution – and Mao's glorious part in them – go relatively unchallenged. Of course, the people who had questioned the myths were dispersed swiftly to the Chinese gulag (*laogai*), so it wasn't surprising that most people were happy to repeat the official version of events.

But if Liu and Yen were unsure about where their country had been, they knew exactly where it was going. The Party was more than happy to spread the good news – even the country's critics acknowledged the inevitability of China becoming the largest economy in the world. Liu often liked to remind me of this and also of the pioneering achievements of the nation's diaspora, the countless millions who'd been leaving the Middle Kingdom for new lives around the globe for thousands of years. When I was pissed off with him, I decided to wind him up on the subject.

'The Chinese are very successful in the West, yes?'

'Not really,' I said, 'they run the laundries and work on the railroads.' I was thinking about the stereotypes in films and TV shows like *Thoroughly Modern Millie* and *Kung Fu*.

'But they do many other things too, don't they?' He looked hopeful.

'No. They just dig holes and wash clothes.'

It was my silly way of getting my own back for the bullying I got. Sometimes I'd attempt to build bridges by expressing an interest in pre-Communist China. I had some poems and folk tales from the book Xiao-Lian had given me, with corresponding pages in Mandarin, and asked Liu what he thought of them. He said the characters belonged to some arcane form of Chinese that nobody understood any more. Perhaps it was like reading Chaucer, or else he was just embarrassed to admit his limited vocabulary.

When I'd first arrived in China, Beijing was in the midst of Olympic fever. It was 1993, but the Chinese had already decided that the 2000 Games would be hosted by their nation and that foreign tourists would help foot the bill. Consequently, the capital city was levying an Olympic tax that extended to hotel rooms, which made the once cheap accommodation a struggle for backpackers. Vast billboards embossed with the Olympic logo and portraits of President Deng Xiaoping were strewn across the city, proclaiming China's entry into the international community. No one I spoke to had the slightest doubt that their country would host the games, which ultimately went to Australia. The once beautiful city had long since been disfigured by Soviet-style architecture, with its colossal granite state buildings and boulevards like aeroplane runways. There's something unsettling about cities that are designed to facilitate the movement of tanks and heavy artillery through their streets, and Beijing was still haunted by the ghosts of Tiananmen Square, in which thousands had lost their lives while many more 'disappeared' into the labyrinth of prisons and work camps. Apart from taxis and police vehicles I saw few private vehicles on the roads, yet top-of-the-range Mercedes-Benzs with their blacked-out windows sped through the streets as emblems of the two-tiered society that was Communism's legacy. Mao had succeeded in airbrushing the middle classes from the Middle Kingdom, leaving in their wake a state-controlled mafia of officials whose grip on the power and wealth of the nation was absolute.

Across from the dreary concrete box that was my hotel, a few restaurants served Western food and catered for the tourists passing through the city. I made a point of sitting with some Pakistanis who I rightly believed would sell me some hash, and within minutes we sat smoking at the table, oblivious to the State Security vans that chugged up and down the streets.

'The Chinese don't care about hash,' said one of the Pakistanis, slurping on a bottle of Tsingtao beer. 'They don't smoke it and they don't care what we do. We never offer it to Chinese and they leave us alone. The police don't speak English, let alone Urdu, and anyway, they'd rather not get involved with foreign devils.'

Friends who'd visited the country before me had told me the same thing: that tourists were off-limits even to officials in China, who looked bewildered if you went near them. The Pakistanis were traders from Lahore who had come overland through the Khunjerab Pass along the Karakoram Highway, a trip I'd often thought of making myself. Though they were Muslim, they drank with the determination of errant public schoolboys, as I had in my teens, getting plastered on Woodpecker cider on Sunday afternoons and crunching packets of Extra Strong Mints to disguise the toxic fumes on my breath. Amongst them was an Afghan man, and we got into a lengthy conversation about his reason for being in China. His story was a familiar one, shared by millions of his countrymen who have been sent packing from their beleaguered land. His family were staying in one of the sprawling refugee towns around Peshawar that have served as a base for fleeing civilians after decades of invasions and despotic feudalist tyrannies. He'd left the relative safety of the North-West Frontier Province to find work and had ended up in Beijing in a stateless limbo, unable to get back to his adopted country or return to his civil war-stricken homeland. He had no idea how long the Chinese would allow him to stay, but in the meantime he'd found a niche for himself selling dope to tourists while anaesthetising himself with the cure-all potion that his religion forbade. Though I was unaware of it at the time, the conversation would act as a catalyst for my own adventures, and Peshawar, with its itinerant population of war-weary exiles, would be the town that changed my life.

I found my own refuge in the jade markets of the capital city, where I spent many hours haggling with the street vendors over tiny pieces of the milky-green stone that had enchanted the Chinese for thousands of years. Many of the stalls in the antique markets appeared to be full of family heirlooms, and I felt mildly voyeuristic pawing over trinkets that had probably been sold by the poor to keep pace with the skyrocketing prices of the new China. Every stall had old copies of Mao's Little Red Book, but now they looked less like the tyrannical musings of a despotic ideologue than quaint relics from an era that the young could not remember and the old chose to forget. I picked up a copy that stood out with its scarlet cover and gold star stamped on the front. Inside were glossy pictures of the Great Helmsman greeting peasants, commanding soldiers, rubbing shoulders with heads of state and standing on a hill with a red sunset behind creating a pink halo effect around his head. In the last of the pictures, he wore a long, flowing tunic that reminded me of a childhood image I'd had of Jesus with a shepherd's staff, but the lambs were replaced by the angelic faces of adoring children who gazed up expectantly towards the fatherly figure, with copies of the book I was holding in their hands.

At sunset, I made my way to one of the city's main tourist attractions, the Temple of Heaven, a beautiful complex of Daoist buildings constructed by a Ming Dynasty emperor in AD 1420. As was often the case with my visits to shrines, the grounds around the temple held more interest for me than the building itself. An elderly couple were standing next to a tree, taking turns to rub their backs against a protruding stump. I sat on the grass near the tree and watched as their faces contorted pleasantly as they moved from side to side, wedging the stump between their shoulder blades. After a minute they wandered off, and I got up to take a closer look at the therapeutic tree. A round swelling about three inches wide stuck out of the trunk: its curved growth reminded me of the head of a walking stick my grandfather had when I was a child; its contours blended from one shade of brown to another as if it had been worked on a lathe and polished.

Turning round, I saw two tiny old women with minute rounded feet that I took to be the result of childhood foot-binding. They hobbled towards me like ageing ballerinas and motioned me to take my turn against the tree, allowing its healing lump to slither across my vertebrae, as countless others had done for decades. A giddy sensation tiptoed down my spine and made me chuckle as the women burst out into toothless grins. More elderly people gathered to practise t'ai chi, the supreme boxing exercise the Chinese had performed for thousands of years. Loudspeakers from the Temple of Heaven played classical harp music that rippled across the gardens as hundreds of silhouetted bodies glided between the trees. I sat on the grass marvelling at the sights and sounds around me, absorbing the atmosphere of this magical place, feeling privileged to witness the timeless ritual before me. I took a jade tortoise I'd bought at the market out of my pocket and rubbed its curved shell and belly between my fingers, its leathery back patterned with tiny bottle-green tombstones, its head peering quizzically at the world from the safety of its mobile home. An old man with a hunchback came over to the tree with a cricket in a square wicker basket dangling from his wrist. He hung the insect from a branch, closed his eyes and groaned as he kneaded his back muscles against the massage tree, as the forlorn cricket droned in the background. This was the China of my dreams.

It was almost pitch dark now, and I began to feel tired and hungry. I wandered out of the temple grounds and found a small noodle shop, where everyone stared at me. Everyone, that is, except a girl who sat opposite crying into her soup bowl, her lips quivering as the noodles slithered through her chopsticks back into the bowl. I wanted to talk to her and find out what the problem was when a man walked in and led her away. Her half-eaten noodles were taken away as mine arrived, and I sank a bottle of Tsingtao beer while trying to outstare the other customers, who gawped at me across the room. Most of them cast their eyes down into their soup bowls, looking mildly embarrassed, as if I were sitting naked in front of them. A young girl of maybe four with rosy-red cheeks and hair in bunches stood glaring at me, her mouth agape as if she'd seen a ghost as a mixture of fear and wonder came over her tiny face. Her mother called out to her, but she was entranced, paralysed before me like a living doll. I winked at her to break the spell and her face lit up into a cherubic grin, revealing her gapped teeth as she giggled and ran back to her mum.

The next morning I took a minibus to the Great Wall. The long, straight road was lined by poplar trees, punctuated every hundred yards or so by watermelon stalls that spilled onto the asphalt. The road was not particularly busy and it seemed like a ridiculously competitive business, with few of the vendors having any customers at all. Stallholders squatted next to pyramid-shaped piles of the dark-green footballs, waving slices at the passing tourists, as their kids sat munching on the succulent wedges, which dribbled down their chins.

I'd half expected to be disappointed by the fabled wall, which is said to be the only man-made landmark visible from space. Its main role, to keep the barbarians out of the Middle Kingdom, had been a failure from the start, but foreigners were fascinated by the sheer manpower that its creation had involved, seeing it as emblematic of the Chinese worker-ant ethos. I thought of the hundreds of thousands who'd lost their lives building something so useless, but at least it was still around as a tourist attraction. Architecturally, Mao's legacy bequeathed little to future generations and robbed them of much. Ironically, Mao had been a great admirer of the Qin emperor who in the third century BC had united the warring states and started building the Great Wall. He'd also given the country its name in the West, where Qin is spelled *Chin*. Like Mao, he was a megalomaniac disposed towards genocide, and his subjects paid a grim price. Where Mao used Marxism to advance his personal power, Qin had used Confucianism, which he banned, burning its books and burying its scholars alive. He was also responsible for the Terracotta Army, which I had visited in Xian, and the huge mausoleum became his shrine when he eventually died of mercury poisoning, given to him by his physicians as an elixir of everlasting life.

Many of Mao's more hare-brained schemes resonate with the Qin emperor. Like his forebear, Mao was fond of mobilising vast numbers of people to carry out largely meaningless tasks. Just as Qin had ordered hundreds of thousands to leave their villages to build the Great Wall, Mao had the masses toil for years on canal-building and other gigantic planning enterprises that rarely served any real practical purpose. These tasks were usually cloaked in the dogma of 'ideological purification', and those ordered to do the work were known as 'volunteers'. Yet not all the epic plans Mao made were wasted; the railroad that I travelled from Urumchi in Xinjiang to Shanghai is a remarkable feat of engineering. The number of tunnels along the route is staggering, and it is, in some ways, an achievement on a par with the Great Wall itself.

I enjoyed sightseeing in China, though generally I'm not that bothered. Traipsing around tourist attractions has never held much attraction for me; I'd sooner find a street cafe and watch people go about their daily lives. My visit to the terracotta warriors in Xian was a typical example, in which three different sights on the day of my visit managed to eclipse the ancient clay tombs. On the minibus to the shrine, I saw a fight. We were driving along a street in town, and out of the corner of my eye I saw a commotion going on down a side street. A man was attacking another man with a meat cleaver, and I could see blood splurging out of his neck. It only lasted a flash as we drove past, but I'll never forget the sight. After visiting the famous shrine, I had to go to the train station to buy a ticket. I got caught short and made it to the nearest public toilet beside the station. As soon as I walked in the door, the stink hit me: the acrid stench of ammonia. I jerked back out of the door for fresh air, but I was bursting and couldn't wait, and taking a deep breath I ran into the dreadful place and did my business. There were hundreds of concrete stalls with holes in them and a dividing wall at shoulder height: you could chat to your neighbour, and many people were doing just that. I'll never forget that loo.

Opposite the station were dozens of noodle shops, and being a noodle aficionado I took my time to wander and find the best one. The men who made them were acrobats: throwing them over their heads, between their legs and slapping the doughy strands against stainless steel boards. I sat marvelling at the sight, thinking how much more interesting it was than the dreary Terracotta Army. Perhaps I'm a philistine, but to this day I remember the noodle-makers as if it were yesterday, as I do the man with the meat cleaver and the ghastly public toilet. The Terracotta Army has long since faded away.

* * *

After the relative high of New Year, the winter turned mean, and we spent our days in bed trying to stay warm. My mum sent a parcel of books from friends and family so there didn't seem much point in trying to communicate with my cellmates at all. They played cards and chatted amongst themselves and I immersed myself in books. I read Victor Hugo's *Les Misérables* in three days and *Moby Dick* in four, as well as various historical tomes by James Michener about South Africa, Iberia and Israel. I wondered why I'd been sent so many Michener epics and thought of friends scanning their shelves for books they probably would never read, but I enjoyed them nonetheless. I particularly liked Milan Kundera on living in a Communist state, though the books were too short and soon came to an end. The boozy ruminations of Charles Bukowski were fun, but barely kept me busy for an afternoon. I tried reading *The Lord of the Rings*, but abandoned it after the first volume of the chunky trilogy left me cold. What do people see in that book?

Of particular interest was Colin Thubron's *Behind The Wall*, in which the travel writer visits Shanghai Municipal Prison at Ti Lan Qiao, a place that I could well end up knowing intimately. Liu said that if I was sentenced that was where I would go, since that was where the other foreigners were. I tried to picture what it would be like. My references were movies like *Birdman of Alcatraz*, *Midnight Express* and *Papillon*. Would there be a Mr Big like Grouty in *Porridge*? Would the warden be a bastard who wanted to see me get a longer sentence? Would I have to take care not to drop my soap in the shower? Could I escape? The celluloid clichés of incarceration ran around my brain, but after six months in jail I'd yet to see anything that I'd ever watched in a movie.

My mother sent me a copy of the guide to the I Ching, and it became a constant companion. I fashioned a set of hexagrams out of paper and consulted the 'Sage' on all matters that came into my mind. The book had some sixty-four chapters, but one recurred with uncanny regularity: Chapter 36, 'The Darkening of the Light'. The book advised me that 'the light has sunk into the earth' and that the light is always threatened when we engage in looking at a difficult situation from the viewpoint of our ego or childish heart. I'd read many spiritual books and they all spoke of the need to dissolve one's ego, but putting it into practice is something else. Every time Chapter 36 appeared, I took it to be about coming to terms with my surroundings. 'Discontent with slow progress, we lose our inner independence,' said the Sage. I decided that it was crucial not to look forwards or backwards if at all possible. Yearning for things I couldn't have only made me unhappy, and allowing my mind to dwell on the past or the future would only make it worse. I needed to get happy, and I couldn't rely on anybody other than myself to achieve it. After all, it was only a state of mind, and I discovered that I could indeed be happy, and that just as many 'free' people are unhappy. I could liberate my mind in this or any other situation.

After six months in jail, I got called out of the cell to meet my lawyer, a tall, sinewy-looking man called Xue, and his assistant, who spoke half-decent English. Choosing myself a lawyer had been a tough decision to make. My predecessors had all opted for an English-speaking private lawyer and had paid for the privilege. When I heard about some of the sentences his clients had ended up with, I decided to take a different path and asked the judge who was presiding over my case, Mr Shen, to choose a lawyer to represent me. This was the probably one of the smartest moves of my life.

'Don't you want to have the same lawyer as the other foreign prisoners?' Shen was surprised by my request.

'No thanks. As the judge in this case, I have absolute faith in you to find the best person to help me defend myself. I'm sure you know many good lawyers, Mr Shen.'

There was no doubt in my mind I was doing the right thing. I'd lived in the Far East for years and was well aware of the power these people had. Even in countries like Japan, acquittals were virtually non-existent. If the police sent you to court, it was all over. The best you could do was ingratiate yourself with the court by showing you had total respect for the system. By requesting that the judge dealing with my case select a lawyer for me, I was showing my high opinion of his judgement and the system as a whole. I reasoned that by doing so I would gain the respect of the court and thus be shown leniency in return. I'm quite sure that this decision saved me from a much harsher punishment.

The meeting with Mr Xue and his English-speaking sidekick was brief. Xue was a nerdy kind of guy who seemed to know his stuff. He was tall and slim with a short back and sides and a parting. He wore a pinstriped suit and wire glasses. His assistant was a smooth, casually dressed man wearing a fashionable brown leather jacket and slicked-back hair. His English was reasonable, and he and Xue raised some good points I'd overlooked. We went through the details of my case and agreed that he would represent me as a naive tourist rather than a criminal. I hoped he might be a pal of Shen's and that between them they'd do a deal that worked in my favour. At the end of our meeting, he informed me I'd be going to court the following week. Back in the cell, Yen and Liu wanted to know how things had gone, but I'd learned not to trust them any more. I was suspicious of the monthly reports they'd been writing to the police and thought it wise not to give them any more information than necessary. I'd made an effort to get along with them in the beginning, but now my days in the detention centre were numbered I didn't care what they thought of me and closed myself off.

I suspected from their letters that my mum and Rosie would come to the hearing, which meant I'd probably have a visit, too. The problem with having anything to look forward to in prison is that time suddenly slows right down. Ordinarily time flies, like those old movies where you see the pages of a calendar turning, seasons changing or newspapers running through a printing press. The days just melt into weeks, into months. But as soon as some impending date appears on the horizon, the process goes into slow motion, the days drag and a week feels like a month.

I'd asked the captain for a shave before my day in court, and was taken into a spare cell where a couple of trustees stood waiting with a pair of clippers. The room had a hole in the ground for a loo, and I was reminded of the relative comfort of my own cell. I jumped the queue of inmates waiting to have their heads shaved, and the guys made jokes about cutting my chest hair. It was strange to lose my beard, and I felt the icy chill on my fresh cheeks. Liu and Yen told me I looked handsome without the bushy growth, which was the first compliment I'd received in a while. I'd written a couple of hundred words that I planned to read out in court, explaining how dumb I'd been to break the law in China and how sorry I was for my foolish actions. When the Monday morning arrived, I'd barely slept the night before. I'd been reading my speech over and over, making small amendments and then changing them back again. When the door finally opened, my cellmates wished me luck as I was led along the familiar corridor and down the stairs to the waiting minibus. There were five or six other prisoners on the bus, and three guards. One of the inmates wore heavy manacles on his legs, which I found out later meant he might well be looking at a death sentence. I asked one of the guards for a cigarette and he gave me one, to the surprise of the other prisoners. It'd been six months since I'd last seen the streets of Shanghai, but I was more interested in looking at my fellow prisoners. Two young lads sat chatting, while a third was sitting at the back. There was tension between them, and the third boy looked petrified. Another guy spoke a little English and told me the three were all part of the same gang who'd been arrested for theft. They'd been to court already and were now coming back to hear their verdicts.

The van pulled into a large car park in front of a huge Soviet-style concrete building with a red star embossed on the front. We were taken round the side and led through a small door into a corridor with tiny cells the size of telephone kiosks, and our handcuffs were removed before we were given one of the squalid cages each. Opposite, a guard sat listening to the radio, and I called him over and asked for a cigarette, but he didn't smoke. The cell had a slim concrete shelf for a seat, which made my back ache, and I must have sat there for at least two hours before a couple of cops arrived to take me to the hearing. The paint was peeling off the wall, exposing the graffiti beneath, and I thought of the thousands who'd come before me. There must have been times when several prisoners were crammed into these tiny spaces, especially during political purges when people were rounded up simply to fill quotas. As we wound our way up a spiral staircase, it felt like the walk from a dressing room to a stage before a performance. The guard told me to wait a moment, and we stood in the wings for what felt like an eternity. I leaned forward and peered into the huge room, looking round to my left, where I saw Mum and Rosie smiling at me. I felt an overpowering sense of pride and shame at the sight of them: pride at the thought that two people who loved me had come across the world to stand by me in my hour of need, and shame that I'd dragged them through my own selfish drama. They both looked beautiful, Mum in a striking red dress and Rosie in her hippy hemp gear from Vietnam. Alongside them, there were a couple of faces I recognised from the British consul and a handful of Chinese journalists taking notes. At the back of the room, the ubiquitous film crew was hurriedly loading the camera onto a tripod to film my entrance. I was led to a wooden lectern in the middle of the room, as Shen and two other judges walked in from a side door and sat down opposite me. I recognised one of the other judges from a previous visit with Shen, but the third judge was an attractive girl of thirty-something I'd never met before. They all wore navy uniforms with white hats and gloves, which they took off with great ceremony as the proceedings began. To my left sat my lawyer, Mr Xue, with his assistants, and to his left was the prosecutor whom I'd come to call Stan Laurel due to his resemblance to Oliver Hardy's associate. A translator stood between the two camps in front of a lectern similar to mine, except he had a chair to sit on. My lower back was throbbing and I wanted to ask for one, but thought it better to go without.

The prosecution made a long-winded case about how I was the peddler of a pernicious substance, which was a grave crime in China, but he also made a point of saying that my case was less serious than some of the others that had been through the People's Court. I thought that was pretty good of him; he even recommended the court show a degree of leniency in my case, which I appreciated. I'd liked him in our meetings at the detention centre, when he'd given me a few packs of Marlboros to take back to my cell. Now he was helping me out in the courtroom, and this guy was the prosecutor. Things were going well for me. When Xue's turn came to make my defence, he was an efficient advocate, arguing that my time in detention was quite enough considering the small quantity of drugs I'd had, and he recommended I be released without a custodial sentence.

We broke for lunch, and I waved to Mum and Rosie before being taken back to the cells. After about ten minutes, Shen turned up with a huge plate of seafood on rice and a pack of cigarettes. The meal was the first decent one I'd tasted in months, but I had no appetite and chain-smoked the cigarettes instead. I couldn't believe the judge had taken time out of his lunch break to run an errand for a prisoner whose case he was presiding over. I can't believe it would happen in Britain. I'd made an effort to like Shen, because if you like people they tend to like you, and nobody wants to ruin the lives of those they like. The fact that I'd asked him to get me a lawyer had flattered his ego, and I often told him how much I loved China and how sad I'd be if I was unable to return. He reassured me more than once that I'd be welcome to come back whenever I liked and talked of all the places I should visit. I'd convinced myself he was a good guy, joked with him and his assistants about my case, and flirted with his secretaries. Somewhere along the line we'd almost become friends, and here he was taking time out of his lunch break to see that I was OK and had everything I needed.

My strategy seemed to be paying off, and I knew exactly who I had to thank. When I was a kid, my mother was masterful at dealing with officials in a position to make her life a misery. Traffic wardens would write her tickets only to screw them into a ball five minutes later as she flattered and flirted with them. She could charm the birds out of the trees, and people did her favours without even realising it. My father often noticed that I'd inherited this skill from her, and it was true. Since my arrest, I'd done my best to treat every customs man, police officer, prosecutor or judge as my mother had dealt with those traffic wardens 20 years earlier. Whether it would ultimately get the result I was hoping for remained to be seen.

My back was killing me from standing up for hours on end after lying on a bed for six months. When the guards came to take me back upstairs, I struggled to walk up the steps. The second half of the day went much quicker than the first. The prosecution mentioned that the dope I had was of a particularly strong variety, which I felt quietly chuffed about. Why get busted with crap? Best of all, nobody mentioned the minuscule piece of opium, except in the opening statement. It looked like they were not going to make a fuss about it, which they could have done, even though it was unlikely I'd have been charged for that alone.

When my turn came to stand up and say my bit, I was tongue-tied. I forgot the piece of paper I had in my pocket – stuttered – and then remembered it. But when I finally looked at the words I'd written, I no longer wanted to say them. They would have had to be translated anyway, a laborious business that would have rendered the words almost meaningless. Instead, I apologised to the court for breaking the law and said I'd been stupid rather than malicious. I wanted to turn round and look at my family, whose presence I could feel behind me, but the formality of the occasion demanded I look ahead deferentially towards the speakers. Most of the dialogue was in Chinese, and there were long gaps after each speaker. They insisted on reading out my full name – including my middle name – whenever I was mentioned, so every sentence dragged on for ages as the officials kept referring to their paperwork to get my name right.

My spine groaned under the strain, and I cursed myself for not accepting the offer of a chair at the start of the day. Finally Mr Shen announced it was over, and I was led out of the courtroom. I got one last glance at Mum and Rosie, who were mouthing something to me that I couldn't understand, but took to mean 'I love you'. I also knew I'd be seeing them soon, as they'd surely have arranged a visit, so I walked back down the stairs with a spring in my step, feeling lucky to have had them beside me.

In the cell downstairs I continued to stand, only this time I used the bars to yank myself up and take some of the weight off my coccyx. I still had most of the cigarettes that Shen had given me, which I hid in my underwear in case I was searched on my return to the detention centre. Back on the bus, the lads I'd come to court with were talking cheerfully amongst themselves. They'd got twelve years each but you'd have thought they'd got six months. The kid on the back seat who'd grassed them up got 18 months and was crying his heart out as they swore at him. The other guy with manacles on his legs wasn't on the return trip at all.

Yen and Liu were happy to share my latest packet of cigarettes, and this time I had a box of matches Shen had given me. I felt the day had gone pretty well and that Mr Xue had put across my defence well. There was no way of knowing what sentence I would get, but Xue's suggestion that I should not do any additional jail time was the hoped-for outcome that filled my head that night. No date had been set for my return to court, but it was possible that I would be out within weeks and that the ordeal was coming to an end. After scrubbing the cell floor, I did a hundred sit-ups to loosen up my back and then fell into a deep sleep.

Mum and Rosie were permitted an hour-and-a-half visit with Jackie Barlow, the latest British vice consul. Jackie was a friendly woman in her 50s with a long career in the diplomatic service and was new to China, after taking over from Jim Short. Mum had brought books, playing cards (that I was not permitted to have) and Bassett's Hard Liquorice Sticks, a childhood favourite of mine. The visit took place in a kind of hospitality room with a sofa in it, and I was permitted to sit next to Rosie and Mum, chatting about their lives while trying to remain upbeat about my predicament. While Mum chatted to Jackie, I asked Rosie if she'd been faithful in my absence. She said no. 'Why couldn't you have lied?' I said bitterly. But it didn't really matter any more. Our lives had changed so much it was far from certain we'd ever be a couple again anyway. There was still no indication of what kind of sentence I was likely to receive, though obviously I hoped my lawyer would have his way and I'd be let off with just the time I'd already spent in detention. Mum was a huge inspiration, passing on messages from well-wishers back at home, some of whom I hardly remembered. It occurred to me how far I'd gone away from the world she inhabited. I'd been a lousy son in the preceding years, rarely bothering to write home or keep in touch, and yet here she was, crossing the world at great expense to support me when it really mattered. I held her hand and told her how sorry I was for all the trouble I'd caused.

It was almost a relief when the guards took me back to my cell. After lying on a bed for nearly seven months I had been exhausted by the last thirty-six hours, and my back ached from standing up in court the day before. Mum gave me a dried seahorse that she'd had since I was a kid to keep as a memento, and I put it in a small box beside my bed. There were many new books to read, but my back was so painful all I could do was lie in the foetal position on the bed until I fell asleep.

As relations with my Chinese cellmates turned sour, my insides turned hard. Some kind of cabin fever crept into our cell life and my bowels decided to stop functioning, as if my body could not bear to operate under the circumstances. Sometimes several days would go by without success, just hours on the toilet trying to ignore the insults. The worse things got, the harder it was to go. The longer they held their noses, sneering unkindly, the more reluctant my bowels were to let go. A menacing succession of sighs accompanied every sit down, till my stomach ached as if it were filled with cement. I tried to wait until night-time but there was no night any more than there was day. The strip lights saw to that, turning our cell into a 24–7 film set from a scatological B-movie. After four or five days, the floodgates would open and I'd finally deliver a revolting stench that engulfed the cell for twenty minutes while I was bombarded with abuse. Liu would climb up to the window and hang off the bars to get fresh air, and I'd lie on my bed feeling pleased with myself. Purged.

One morning, I'd forgotten to scrub the cell floor and Liu had to remind me. I stuck my head back into a book and ignored him, so he began his usual taunts and threats. I muttered 'fuck off' under my breath and he heard, springing to his feet and punching me in the face several times as I shielded myself with a book. Blood trickled down the side of my mouth and my cheeks swelled up into fleshy red bulges as I got down on my hands and knees to perform my duties. He looked triumphant at first, but after talking to Yen the smiles gave way to fear. Perhaps Yen had pointed out to him that if the guards saw my face he would be in serious trouble, and the ghoulish contraption that was situated outside our cell would be his bed for the night. I toyed with the idea of requesting a doctor's visit, which would bring the captain round to our cell. But I didn't want to get anybody in more trouble than they were already in; after all, in spite of everything we were all in this together. I tried to put myself in Liu's position and consider how I would feel if I'd been in the cell for nearly three years without the slightest idea what the charge was against me or when I would go to court. I told myself that in other circumstances we'd be friends, and did my best to ignore my feelings of hatred and to pretend I was alone in the cell. From that day on, my cellmates became invisible. Days would go by without any eye contact whatsoever. I did my cleaning chores without prompting and absorbed myself in writing letters and poems and reading books. My former friends no longer existed as I buried myself in my own solitary confinement. I was determined not to allow them into my world.

One day, the door-hatch opened and I got to my feet, but it wasn't for me this time. Yen had a meeting with his lawyer. He was back in the cell within 20 minutes and changing clothes to go to court. I'd had a week between meeting my lawyer and my court appearance, while he had about ten minutes. There was no mirror in the cell, so he asked Liu if he looked all right for his big day in court. Liu inspected him and picked a couple of pieces of fluff off his jumper. They looked like a gay couple preparing for an important job interview.

A few weeks later, Yen was moved to another part of the jail to do his sentence. He'd ended up with a three-and-a-half-year stretch and was in pretty good spirits about it. The captain had told him what to expect and his prediction had been correct. Within hours, a skinny new guy of about 40 was moved into our cell. He was gaunt, had bouts of stomach cramps and would lie on the floor in agony, screwing up the sheets around his belly, whimpering. I had no reason to dislike the man, but failed to be moved by his suffering. The prison doctor palmed him off with his 30 seconds of verbal quackery before handing over the usual 'painkillers'. I wasn't hopeful for him. Day in day out he lay on the floor squirming in misery, popping the useless pills, getting up only to try to eat his meals before curling up into a ball on the floor again. One night, Liu banged on the door requesting a doctor and took the opportunity to speak to me for the first time in weeks, pointing out that our cellmate was very ill. He was as shocked by my indifference to his friend's tormented condition as I was unsurprised by the guards' apathy to it as they slammed the hatch back in his face. Deep down I felt guilty: I began to question my own humanity, my inability to empathise with these people – or any people. I could cry for characters in books, but I felt nothing for the people living a few feet away, as if I'd been robbed of the most basic human instincts.

Thoughts of my childhood at boarding school came back to haunt me in the form of an old contemporary from Singapore. He too had stood out for his Otherness, and we let him know it. He worked harder than us and was respectful of the housemaster and tutor, whom we hated. We called him a swot and a Chink and jeered at him for having a study that smelled like a Chinese takeaway. Now I was on the receiving end of a karmic boomerang that would cut me down to size. I began to scan my brain for unflattering memories of myself, convinced I was a terrible person who'd got his just deserts. I pieced together a grim trajectory of misdeeds that had brought me to this place, a misspent life and now a ghastly end in which I'd lost all compassion for myself or anyone else.

My journey had come full circle: ghosts from the past flickered into view, mocking me, taunting me, and holding up a grubby mirror that showed me my life, and I didn't much like what I saw.

The cell door opened for the first time in five weeks. It was the captain, with good news. I was going to court in ten minutes, and was told to get all my belongings together.

'Maybe you go home,' Liu sneered jealously, in response to the guard who'd just muttered a few words through the hole in the door. I was sitting on the end of the bed in a purple tracksuit the police had brought me and a prison-issue padded jacket. Liu thought the fact the captain had told me to get all my belongings together could only mean one thing: I was going to be deported. He seemed pissed off at my good fortune, as if I was somehow the cause of his own bad luck. Even so, he began to start helping me pack, throwing my possessions into a blanket on the floor, which he tied up into a knapsack. A moment later, the door hatch opened once more. False alarm: I could leave my stuff behind, which meant I'd be coming back to the cell after my court appearance. Liu smiled as he translated the happy news, clearly relieved that we'd be seeing each other again. Would he miss me when I was gone? I shrugged my shoulders, feigning indifference, and waited for the door to open.

A police minibus waited in the courtyard, and my right hand was handcuffed to a metal handrail on the empty seat in front of me while a couple of officers got in the front. I leaned forward, tapped one on the shoulder and held two fingers to my mouth, and he passed me a lit cigarette. It was my first cigarette for some time, and the smoke rushed to my head as the city crawled by the window outside. It was an ugly city, and seeing the neon signs in daylight just made it uglier: miles of dull plastic tubes trailing down the sides of grey buildings waiting for the night to bring them alive again. Street urchins in padded coats like mine were rifling through garbage cans at the side of the road. Liu had talked of his home town many times. He loved the place: it was the centre of his world, the epicentre of the Middle Kingdom, but it was also, for generations, the home of many Europeans and Americans, whose colonial parks had been off limits to 'dogs and Chinese'. I thought of the tiny piece of opium I'd had in my briefs and tried to lie about: one and a half grams of 'medicine' given to me by an Afghan 'doctor'. A chill ran down my spine. Of all the things to get caught with in this town, with its history. Jesus! They could throw away the key.

I walked up the same stairway to a different, smaller courtroom. In front sat three judges in blue uniforms, with their hats on the desk in front of them, beneath a red star. There were a couple of people from the British embassy and a handful of Chinese I didn't recognise. Mr Shen, the head man whom I'd come to know fairly well over the last couple of months, led the proceedings through a translator. The charge was read out and the sentence was pronounced: '*Liang nian ban.*' My eyes flashed across to the translator as he called out 'two and a half years'. It was a fair result, I thought, and the woman from the embassy congratulated me on my relative good fortune. Mr Shen came over, and I shook his hand and smiled. It was an oddly surreal moment, but I knew things could have been much worse and didn't feel any bitterness towards anybody. I knew that at one point I'd been on a charge that carried a minimum sentence of seven years, but I didn't know who had been responsible for downgrading the charge to a maximum of seven. Maybe it was the judge Mr Shen, or perhaps Mr Song the prosecutor, or even the police. Either way somebody had decided to show leniency, and in China two and a half years is a slap on the wrist.

Two guards ushered me back down the staircase to the cells below. There would be several hours to wait before I'd be going back to the jail as we had to wait for the other prisoners to go through the system. The guard on duty asked me how long I'd got. I held up two fingers and bent a third, and he smiled in recognition. An English song came on the radio: it was the cheesy love ballad 'Just When I Needed You Most'. I'd brought along a poetry book by Robert Browning because it fitted in my padded-coat pocket. I opened on a random page and read a poem called 'A Light Woman'. I was back in the mini cells that had given me chronic backache before. My knees touched the bars of the narrow cell, so I started doing pull-ups. After a while I asked to go to the toilet, and the guard opened my cell door and pointed down the corridor to the loo. An old man with grey hair sat in the cell next door to mine, sobbing. When I came out of the loo, I noticed the door to the outside world was wide open. It was a clear, sunny day and the sky was a deep electric blue. I could see passers-by walking down the street beyond the fence surrounding the courthouse. I fantasised about escaping, running through the streets of Shanghai with sirens blazing behind me. With no money, passport or friends I wouldn't last long. Walking back to my cell, I stopped outside the old man's. His anguished cries distressed me. Turning to the guard, I held up my hands and wiggled my fingers to ask what the old man had got. He held his index finger up to his temple and pushed down his thumb with a throaty hiss. I looked back at the condemned man, tears streaming down his wrinkled cheeks, and thought of giving him the cigarette I still had from earlier. Instead I reached into my jacket and pulled out a packet of tissues and handed them to him. He nodded gratefully and wiped the snot and tears off his face. Then I went into my cell, pulled the door behind me and heard the click of the iron bars. Next door the old man went quiet as he waited for the end to come.

Later that night, I sat on my bed and thought about the old man. I felt bad for not giving him my last cigarette. It seemed mean to have kept it for myself, and I started to believe that somehow if I had given it to him, he would have taken my addiction to his grave with him and I would have been rid of the vice I'd had since adolescence. Instead I'd take the habit off to jail with me, and he'd have a tissue to wipe away the tears on his way to the killing ground.

Everyone told me I'd be transferred to Ti Lan Qiao any day now, but two weeks had passed since I'd been sentenced and I was still lying on my bed in the detention centre. My attention span had gone and I didn't feel like reading books. I was on tenterhooks and sleeping badly, and every time there was any noise outside the cell I thought they'd come to take me to the prison. Liu appeared to be disappointed with my relatively light sentence. He'd made an estimate of around eight years when he'd seen my original indictment. He said that since I'd only have to do half my sentence, I'd be going home in less than a year, which, including the eight months I'd spent on remand, was less time than he'd already spent waiting to go to court.

At around ten o'clock at night, there was a rattle on the other side of the door. Liu and our other cellmate, who seemed to be in better shape, rushed to look out as the hatch was opened.

'Pachistan! Pachistan!' cried Liu, standing aside to let his mate take a look.

A new prisoner was outside, presumably a Pakistani. Then Liu's face dropped.

'Africa, Africa.' They both turned with looks of utter disgust on their faces. Both were holding their noses as they repeated the unhappy news. 'Africa, Africa.'

They were still holding their noses when the poor guy was led in. He was in his late 30s, with short cropped hair. He'd been arrested at the airport with an American passport that the Chinese were saying was fake. He said he was from New York, but he sounded like he'd never left Africa. I told him not to worry about it because the Chinese would probably kick him out of the country as soon as they verified where he was from. Liu and his pal were still waving their hands around their noses to drive away the imagined pong. I felt vindicated by their behaviour. If this was how they treated a complete stranger on the grounds that he was black, they weren't really worth the trouble I'd gone through to make them like me in the first place.

The new arrival's English was poor. He said he'd lived in America all his life, but he didn't have even the mildest accent. I thought his story was nonsense, but didn't blame him for sticking to it. Liu kept asking me to translate what he was saying, but I ignored him. When the guy eventually went to the loo, he got a torrent of abuse about the smell. I told him they were a couple of ignorant pricks and not to let them get him down. Chinese bigotry towards blacks was nothing new. Not long before my arrest, there had been riots in Beijing after a black student had gone out with a Chinese girl. The army had been brought in as hordes of irate Chinese went on the rampage, horrified at the thought of one of their kind cavorting with a 'monkey', as Liu called them. Later, a Chinese friend who should have known better explained the Chinese view to me, as if he spoke for the entire nation.

'You know *this*.' He was pushing his index finger in and out of his clenched fist to simulate intercourse.

'Yes.'

'In China we say that African is chimpanzee and human together.'

I heard this view of Africans echoed by many Chinese I met, and they all said it in a very matter-of-fact way. They weren't trying to be rude or obnoxious; they seemed to actually believe it. The Chinese had always considered their country the centre of the world, the Middle Kingdom surrounded by barbarians. In fact, they considered China to be less a nation state than an empire, like Christendom or the Islamic world. The country had been on its knees for decades, but now, under Deng Xiaoping, it was on the rise once again, as was Chinese chauvinism.

The next morning, I was chatting with the African when the door opened. The captain had come to say goodbye. We shook hands and I thanked him for his kindness over the last eight months. He was a good man with a bad job, but he'd made an effort to show some humanity to the people in his care, and I appreciated that. I shook Liu's hand, too; it wasn't a time for grudges; the guy hadn't even been to court yet and who knows what he'd get when he did. But me, I was doing all right; the worst bit was probably over and things would likely be better in Ti Lan Qiao. I took one last look around the room that had incarcerated me for all this time. I'd become used to the smell of the place and the sound of a soap-opera title song echoing down the corridor from the guards' TV at the same time every weekday. The song had become the soundtrack of my life, and I didn't even know its title or the artist who sang it. The room had brought great sadness, but great hope, too. When everything is stripped away, it's perfectly possible to get happy on the side. In fact, it's essential for survival. I'd filled my head with books and exotic thoughts and fantasies to compensate for the banal reality of the situation. There had been many days when I'd found some kind of contentment, even happiness. My inner world had risen to the occasion and lit up the gloomy predicament I'd put myself in. I thought of the endless days and nights I'd spent staring at the walls and ceiling, the hours I'd spent composing letters and poems, throwing my ball of rolled up socks at the walls and gazing at the moon through the crack in the window. Now it was all over. I was on my way to prison, and it felt like freedom.

[6]

The Foreigners' Unit

The drive from No. 1 Detention Centre to Shanghai Municipal Prison takes about 20 minutes, and I had a Public Security minibus all to myself. The handcuffs seemed unnecessary since I had no thoughts of escape and accepted the relatively light sentence handed down by the People's Court. I'd spent eight months on remand and was assured I'd be released after half my sentence was completed. That meant I had less than a year to serve before I'd be free again, and I made the most of the drive to the prison, taking in the sights, sounds and smells of the city that I knew only from behind bars.

It was a warm spring day, and the van driver and his cheerful sidekick kept me furnished with cigarettes as we approached a large iron gate outside the jail. Two young soldiers appeared through a small door to the side, glanced in my general direction and within seconds the gates opened. The van drove a few yards into a holding area and the gates clanged shut behind us, leaving me feeling like a steer waiting to be branded. Eventually a huge steel gate opened in front, and I recalled the opening sequence of the BBC TV show *Porridge* and half expected to see the dour Scotsman Mr Mackay swinging his key chain to greet me off the bus. My first sight of Ti Lan Qiao was of a large courtyard with a hundred or so new arrivals in civilian clothes squatting like bullfrogs on the asphalt. I felt a sense of camaraderie with them as I was led into one of the rooms off the courtyard, some of them grinning as I winked, smiled and said *ni hao*. After eight months in a cell with two other guys, and all the intense emotions that involved, it was good to be part of a larger group – even if we were all criminals.

We walked into a large room with huge piles of grey flannel uniforms and a mug-shot camera set-up. The place smelled different from the detention centre, and I was already feeling tired from the short walk. An officer removed my handcuffs and asked me to put out the cigarette I was still smoking while another appeared with the now familiar fingerprinting apparatus. A friendly officer appeared with a wet rag to wipe my inky fingers, and I was led to a chair in front of the camera. To my surprise I was told I would not be wearing a uniform, so my photograph was taken in a bright-green, yellow and red T-shirt with the silhouette of a spliff-smoking Rasta on the front. The Polaroid was then glued onto a card with the number 10071 printed on it and slotted into a rectangular plastic folder on a piece of cord, which was placed around my neck. Now it was official: my custodial sentence had finally begun and I had a number to prove it. I felt a vague sense of achievement, as if the last eight months had been a trial period and I'd finally been inducted into an exclusive gang of outlaws.

My guitar and rucksack went off into another room to be checked, and I was led across the courtyard into a larger area with huge grey concrete walls and shuttered-steel windows. Prisoners with tightly cropped hair walked around in pairs, pointing towards me and chattering between themselves. Heads crowded round windows to get a glimpse of the new foreigner, while guards' heads turned at the sight of the exotic-looking detainee, and I started to appreciate how a panda from the bamboo forests of Sichuan might have felt in London Zoo.

We stood in the doorway of one of the blocks, and the details from my ID necklace were written down in a large reception book. A couple of officers came down the stairs as the ones who'd escorted me handed me over and returned to the processing area. With them was a smiling, English-speaking prisoner who introduced himself as Mr Yin. We shook hands and walked up the staircase to another landing, and then another, until we reached the third floor of 8th Brigade, which was to be my new home.

I was met at the entrance to the wing by six Western-looking guys in civilian clothes, who shook my hand and welcomed me to the foreigners' unit. There was an American, a Welshman, an Englishman, a Scotsman and two Germans, and before I had a chance to sit down they began to bombard me with questions. How long had I got? What for? What was the charge on my indictment? The last question was of particular interest, as I would later find out, but for now there was an easy, almost fun exchange of stories and anecdotes, particularly with respect to the detention centre, where everyone had spent between six and eleven months. The news that I was another dope smuggler went down well with my new companions, who'd all been involved in hash-related incidents of one kind or another. I spoke at length to Mark, from England, whose mother had got in touch with mine via Prisoners Abroad, a London-based charity that helps the 3,000-odd Brits in jail overseas. He told me that he had less than a year and a half to serve, and suggested that we might be leaving together. The other foreigners exchanged cynical glances with each other before pointing out that I'd almost certainly have to serve my whole sentence. This came as a shock because I'd spent eight months thinking I'd only have to do half of whatever sentence I got. 'They always tell you that,' said the Germans drily.

'The best thing about this place is the food,' said Gareth, the Welshman.

'So it's better than the detention centre, then?'

'That fucking shithouse; I nearly died of starvation. No, really, the food is OK here; it's the one thing they're really on the case with. Apart from Mark and Larry, who are veggies, the foreigners get to eat off the Muslim menu.'

'The Muslim menu?'

'Yeah, there's four menus. The guards get the best, of course, then the Chinese get the stuff in the huge trays you can see over there, and we get the Muslim, pork-free version of that, which pisses off the Krauts 'cos they don't get the fatty pork the Chinks get, but otherwise it's pretty OK most of the time.'

'So what's the fourth menu?'

'Downstairs. You may have noticed a wing on the second floor. That's death row. They get the best food of all the inmates to keep their vital organs in shape so these bastards can make money out of them after they've been popped.' He raised his finger up to his temple and made a gunshot noise.

This ghoulish scandal has become well known in recent years – thanks in part to Mark, who exposed the scandal on the radio and TV, and in Parliament on his release – but at the time it was particularly disturbing. I had noticed the wing he was referring to as I walked up the stairs, particularly the fact that the prisoners, whom I saw handcuffed to benches while being interviewed, had no uniforms. I soon discovered they were having their last chats with their lawyers, who were obliged to go through a mandatory appeal routine before the prisoners were executed. There was also the question of writing wills, since their lawyers were the last civilians who'd see them alive. I wondered if the old man I'd given a packet of tissues to in the court cells was in there. In all probability he was, but I'd never see him again. Neither would his family. There were no visits for people on death row; the next they'd know of his case would be when they received the bill for the bullet that would blow his brains out of the side of his head.

I'd had eight months to build up a mental picture of how my new life might look, and from the first impressions at least it seemed OK. Just being able to speak in my own language and walk for more than five paces at a time was a huge privilege. The prison wing had open windows all along its corridor and you could actually see out of them. The views were of identical buildings with huge concrete courtyards between them, but there were smiling faces and people looking busy. It was a strange place to live, but people had some kind of life here. Families could visit once a month and food was plentiful. Inmates went to work and had close friendships, and everyone knew when they'd be getting out. I breathed in the new smells that wafted through the building and heard the sounds of laughter where before I'd only heard wailing and misery. It was a happy day.

After chatting to the foreigners, I went down the corridor to check out my cell. The first thing I noticed about it was that it had a barred door rather than a solid one. This struck me as a good thing, though I would later change my feelings about this and hang a sarong over the door before being told to remove it. My chief concern was claustrophobia. I've never liked small spaces, and the cells at Ti Lan Qiao were about five by seven feet. I envisaged myself feeling like a battery hen the second the door shut. In fact, I had little to complain about; the Chinese slept two or three to a cell and the door was opened at 5.30 a.m. every morning. Within a few weeks, I was not only accustomed to my new surroundings but also grew to look forward to the sound of my cell door clicking shut at night. The sound came to represent the end of another day, an escape from the stress of prison life, and the beginning of the all-important dream world that so many prisoners long for. As soon as the door shut, the atmosphere changed on the landing. There was a peaceful sense of security, and I felt cocooned in my own world: self-contained, alone, safe.

A bell rang and Chinese began to flood into the wing for lunch. More huge steaming vats of rice and vegetables turned up.

'Not that shit again,' complained one of the foreigners, peering into one of the food containers.

But it smelled great to me, and it tasted delicious. The rice was far superior to the kind we got in the detention centre and the vegetables came with tasty slices of tofu. Better still, I was given various condiments the foreigners had bought in the prison shop, like chilli oil and soy sauce. It was the first tasty meal I'd eaten in eight months. Afterwards, the American, Larry, gave me a cup of Nescafé, my first drug in more than half a year, which immediately sent me off to christen my shitbucket. This small wooden barrel sat in the corner of every cell and was not the kind of thing you'd sit on and read the paper, though some people did just that. First time round it felt awkward, because you had to suspend yourself a couple of inches above in case you slipped in. Someone lent me a roll of loo paper, and when I finished I put the lid on the barrel. This was one of the highlights of my first day, because my problems with constipation and jeering cellmates had plagued me throughout my time at the detention centre. Now I could relax, and in time I too was partial to reading on my bucket.

The first Chinese prisoner to come and say hello was Gao Zhengguo, the head prisoner on our landing. Every wing in the jail had a number one – a prisoner chosen by the guards to represent and discipline the other inmates. Once Gao had broken the ice others followed, until a small crowd gathered round wondering what I'd done and how long I'd got. They all wanted to run their fingers through my chest hair, which didn't bother me, but Gao shooed them away jealously. He seemed to take a bit of a shine to me and was almost overly friendly for my first few days. I was surprised by how few guards there were on the landing. I hadn't seen one since I had been walked up the stairs hours earlier.

'The prisoners run this place,' said one of the foreigners. 'You rarely see a guard outside the office. If they come out here, they might feel obliged to actually do something.'

The office was at the end of the corridor at the top of the staircase, but there were no guards in it. There was a desk outside in view of the wing, but nobody sat at it. I walked over and looked out of a window beside the desk.

'You can be shot for doing that,' said a voice.

I turned round to see Gareth pointing to a line on the floor at the end of the landing in front of the guards' desk.

'See that red line? It's *wei fan chilli* to cross that line, and the guards have a right to shoot you if you cross it.'

'*Wei fan* what?'

'*Wei fan chilli*: it means against the rules. You'll hear that a lot in here.'

The Chinese disappeared back to their jobs and the landing was quiet again. I spent much of the afternoon wandering up and down the corridor. It was about 50 yards long, with 75 cells along its edge. In the middle of the landing there was a wooden island that was removable, opening up the jail to the landings down below. It had been sealed up for years due to accidents, so we were cut off from the noise of the rest of the jail, which was good. At the end of the corridor stood a tall plastic milk urn, which was the urinal. The piss was collected for medicinal purposes, apparently, and everybody seemed to use it. It was a bad idea to piss in the shitbuckets because many of them leaked.

After a few laps of the corridor, I felt exhausted. For eight months I had not been able to walk more than five or six steps in one direction, but now I could walk for fifty yards without having to turn round. I felt like I'd just run a marathon.

'Go and have a kip, if you fancy,' said Gareth.

'Are we allowed to sleep in the day, then?'

'No, but you don't know that, do you?'

Good point, I thought. I might as well make the most of being the new prisoner. The cell had wooden decking about three inches off the ground, with a thin futon-type mattress on top. There was no one around, so I lay down and nodded off quickly. It seemed like five minutes and the Chinese were back from work again. More food arrived and the mealtime hubbub rose as tin rice bowls clattered across the Formica tabletops. I ate my first potato in months and a young Chinese lad at an adjacent table offered me his.

'Is it true people in your country eat this every day?'

He didn't like potato and neither did other Chinese I talked to. They considered it peasant food to eat as a last resort and were mystified as to why anyone would want to eat such a boring vegetable regularly. His name was T'an Ji, and he was my first friend in Ti Lan Qiao. He was around 30 but he looked 20, and appeared to have more status than most of the other prisoners. He shared a cell with the number one, Mr Gao, and ate on the number one table next to the foreigners and apart from most of the Chinese. I thought T'an Ji was gay at first; his friends were very tactile with him, putting their arms around him a lot and holding his hand or stroking his knee while sitting together. He'd taken on a female role on the wing and senior prisoners were protective of him. He was also good-looking, with a boyish grin and long eyelashes for a Chinese. The foreigners told me he was from a well-connected Shanghai family and was favoured by the guards. He was doing 12 years for stealing a load of television sets, and his family had been allowed to come into the wing to visit him when he first arrived to check his living conditions were suitable. We never worked out why he received such preferential treatment, but it was believed that his family were important Communist Party officials. He was brighter than most of the guys on the landing and was said to be talented at fixing electrical appliances. He was one of the stars of his work group, and guards from different brigades across the jail brought their broken radios and TVs to him to fix.

I often saw prisoners giving him massages, though I never saw the favour returned, and when he heard I'd studied shiatsu he asked me to practise on him. His skin was unusually tender for a man, and kneading his muscles with my thumbs gave me a hard-on. Apart from shaking hands I hadn't touched another human for eight months, and for my first few weeks in Ti Lan Qiao I had a bit of a crush on him.

The foreigners were very happy to see I'd turned up with a good selection of books. A spare cell was provided for all our food and personal belongings, while two long shelves were devoted to books. The place was an Aladdin's cave to me, with many great authors from Alexander Solzhenitsyn to Gabriel García Márquez. I started off with *The Executioner's Song*, Norman Mailer's epic Gary Gilmore book, which I loved. The English speakers loved my Milan Kundera books, particularly his brilliantly lucid accounts of Communist police interrogation methods, a subject that was naturally of great interest to us all. There were books by Conrad, E.M. Forster, Flaubert and Tolstoy, and even more Micheners. I had enough books to see me through the rest of my sentence and could afford to pick and choose. When lock-up time came I had a small stack of books by my bed, but was too excited to read any of them.

My mind reeled for most of the night as an endless stream of thoughts flooded my brain. I thought back to my first night at boarding school as a kid, and how I'd cried myself to sleep and felt so alone and alienated by my surroundings. But now, here in my cell on the other side of the world, I felt oddly satisfied with the latest hand my life had dealt me. I lay in bed and thought about how I'd spend the next two years, and when the cell door was opened at 5.30 a.m. I'd barely slept.

The cell block became a hive of activity as prisoners wheeled huge vats of rice gruel down the corridor on sack barrows from the kitchen brigade. Unlike in the detention centre there was no pickled turnip to eat with the gruel, but I was advised by the other foreigners to skip the rice and wait for the *mantou* to arrive. Half an hour later, large trays of piping-hot yeast-free bread buns were brought up to our landing. Because I'd yet to make use of the monthly prison shopping list, other foreigners lent me jars of peanut butter, jam and, best of all, a can of fried dace in black-bean sauce and a jar of fermented soya chunks. This combination of fish and soya became my favourite breakfast from then on.

It turned out that Mr Yin, the English-speaking prisoner who'd helped me carry my bags up the staircase, was the trustee in charge of the foreigners. If we had any problems, he would be the intermediary between us and the guards. All the foreigners dismissed this idea and had a particular dislike for Mr Yin, whom they said was a spy. He was nearing the end of an eight-year stretch for torturing his wife, whom he'd locked in his house and beaten for days on end. Unfortunately for him, her family were well-to-do Party members, and when his violence towards her became intolerable they used their connections to have him put away. Mr Yin was Captain Xu's helper. He cleaned his office, washed his clothes, made his tea and cleaned his spit off the floor. Xu sympathised with Mr Yin, whom he felt should never have been put in prison as his wife was 'no better than a whore'. I had no particular views on Mr Yin, and for my first few days I found him friendly and helpful. I felt that there was no point in adopting all the hatred and animosity that had accumulated before my arrival. Mr Yin was no doubt a deeply unpleasant man, but as long as he was OK with me I'd keep an open mind. Time would tell.

After a week or so my views changed when I got a taste of his sadistic violent streak. I'd been sitting at a chair when he came up behind me and for no apparent reason put his arms round my neck and started to squeeze. It was almost playful at first and I thought it was a joke, but as his grip tightened I started to panic and fight back. Suddenly the American prisoner, Larry, was out of his seat, screaming at Mr Yin to stop. Even then he continued to twist my arm and give me a nasty Chinese burn as Larry was dragging him off me.

'Still think he's a good guy, eh?' said Gareth, feeling vindicated.

'He just attacked me for no reason.'

'So now you know what his wife had to put up with.'

'Don't trust him,' chimed in the Germans, 'this guy is an evil little bastard.'

Larry wrote a rather over-dramatic report to the guards about how Mr Yin had tried to strangle me, and asked me to do the same. I declined, saying it was no big deal and I'd wait and see how things turned out, but it was my first experience of how strained the relations between the foreigners and Chinese could get, and of the mutual hatred between Larry and anyone with authority.

'What's the point of writing reports?' I asked Ludwig later.

'There's no point whatsoever.'

'So why bother?'

'Fun?' He grinned before adding, 'And at least you've got it on record if it happens again.'

I still didn't write the report, but the experience had unnerved me, and while I thought Larry was being over-protective, I could see the logic in ensuring that any negative interaction with the Chinese was worth logging.

'If it isn't written down, it didn't happen,' said Larry later.

For one of my first exercise periods, I was invited to take part in a football game with inmates from another wing. Within minutes I knew I was out of my league, as burly Chinese convicts steamrolled into me every time I got near the ball, leaving me on the tarmac with grazed knees and elbows. Determined not to let them get the better of me in a game that had more in common with rugby than football, I decided to play by their rules. A lanky Chinese had the ball in his possession with his back to me, and I recognised him as the most aggressive player on the other team. Unable to reach the ball, I wrapped my arms round him, put my foot out and hurled him onto the ground. The game stopped instantly, and one of his team members put out his hand and helped him up. Gareth, barely able to contain his amusement at this, sidled up to me.

'You know who that is? It's Captain Ming, who's a top screw on the punishment wing.'

'Oh shit!' I started to imagine myself being moved to the punishment wing under the care of this much-feared officer.

'Don't worry, nothing will happen to you. Anyway, nice one! He's a total cunt and everyone hates him.'

Larry was particularly happy to hear about my minor debacle with Ming, whom he knew better than any other foreigner, having spent some months in the punishment wing for refusing to acknowledge his sentence. His face lit up for the first time in ages on hearing the news, and he recalled various run-ins he'd had with the hated officer.

Larry was three years into his third hash-smuggling sentence in the Far East. The first had been in Hong Kong, where he'd got two years for a kilo of weed at the airport. He'd kept his head down, living in a dormitory with Triad gangs, and served most of the two years. He hadn't been out long before a second dope bust landed him in an American military jail in South Korea. He got a two-year sentence, which he did in relatively cushy surroundings that he seemed to have pleasant memories of. Two years later, he'd been found in Shanghai's famous Peace Hotel with ten kilos of hash and a kilo of hashish oil (a Class A substance) in the roof space of his room. True to form, he'd invented an elaborate excuse for the crime, claiming that a shady syndicate of international drug smugglers had kidnapped his girlfriend and was holding her to ransom, and unless he delivered the dope she would be killed. Needless to say, the Chinese didn't believe a word of the story and the judge sent him down for 15 years.

He was from Colorado and had got into the dope business in the late '60s, running weed from Mexico to Canada. A dyed-in-the-wool liberal and anti-war campaigner, he'd organised draft-dodging scams during the Vietnam War. In the '70s, he jumped bail in Vancouver when a 23-kilo Afghan hash bust was about to earn him his first real jail time, and by the '80s he'd fallen in love with Asia, where he'd got into Nepalese gold-smuggling rackets before realising the profits you could make shifting hash between Nepal, Thailand, Japan and Hong Kong.

He was a sports writer with a legitimate part-time career as a freelance journalist and was an avid basketball fan. He was also an amusing raconteur, and I spent much of my first few weeks in Ti Lan Qiao hearing about his many adventures and prison stories. He had a deep loathing for the guards in the jail, and policemen generally, having been badly beaten up by highway-patrol cops in California some years earlier. Now he looked at every policeman, jailer or judge like something he'd just scraped off the bottom of his shoe.

During his interrogation by the Chinese, he'd taken his wet washing to the interviews to hang up and dry while the police droned on about his case. Had anyone else told me this story I would not have believed them, but I didn't doubt Larry's word: it was typical of his utter contempt for any kind of authority figures. At times, the foreigners thought his relentlessly stubborn attitudes self-defeating – after all, he'd ended up with a 15-year stretch – but he was respected, too. A highly principled man, he never gave up fighting the system, putting himself through endless discomfort and hardship to defend his, or anyone else's, rights. Before my arrival, Larry had attempted to go on hunger strike and had been moved to the punishment wing known as the Young Men's Experimental Brigade. There he'd written reports about the mistreatment of prisoners, resulting in an official inspection from the prosecutor's office.

Whether his efforts had earned him the respect of the Chinese was hard to say, since 'going with the flow' has been the default behaviour of the people of the Middle Kingdom for thousands of years.

If relations with the Chinese could get out of hand at times, disputes between the foreigners were often worse. Nobody chooses whom they're in jail with, but in a 'normal' prison environment there are plenty of people to choose whom to be friends with and whom to avoid. Ti Lan Qiao, with its six foreigners, five thousand Chinese and virtually no exercise time, was a pressure cooker: always simmering, occasionally exploding and often spilling over in a torrent of abusive animosity. People who'd ordinarily keep out of each other's way were thrown in together to get on with it. You could ignore each other most of the time, but sooner or later something would give and a fight would start. At the centre of most of these disputes was Thomas McLoughlin, a friendly but hotheaded Scotsman from Glasgow and, along with Larry, the recipient of a mind-bendingly depressing 15-year sentence.

Thomas's criminal career started early, with successive visits to various borstals and young offenders' institutions. He was destined to follow in the footsteps of his father, a career criminal and regular jailbird. After a tour of British jails, he'd discovered the adrenalin rush of dope smuggling while on a trip to Morocco in the early '80s. Unlike most people, he had no particular fear of incarceration and was unfazed about carrying suitcases full of hash across international borders, and by the mid-'80s he'd moved his operations to the fleshpots of Bangkok and Manila. There, he'd channelled his earnings from the dope scams into various legitimate enterprises, and become a yoga teacher and diving instructor. Along the way, he'd made more than a few enemies and acquired a heroin addiction.

Tommy (as he liked to be called) had greeted me warmly on my arrival at the jail, and over the first few days had been very generous, giving me jars of Nescafé, powdered milk and so on, to be returned when I was 'on my feet'. I was very grateful, but quickly noticed he was segregated from the rest of the foreigners. When I asked anyone, they shrugged and muttered something about it being a 'long story' or 'you'll soon find out'. Nobody really wanted to talk about it, though everyone warned me not to get too close to the Scotsman. For his part, Tommy dismissed the other foreigners without elaborating and said he felt more at home with the Chinese. It was clear he had a good relationship with most Chinese and was always larking around with them, making them laugh. He often liked to impersonate the guards and various prisoners, which they found hilarious, and his cell was at the opposite end of the corridor to ours, so he slept and ate amongst the Chinese.

After a few weeks at the jail we were called out for an exercise period, and Tommy was first in line at our end of the corridor wearing his Scotland football strip. He was a good player and was often invited by the Chinese to play in their six-a-side tournament with other brigades. On this occasion, the prisoners had been held up waiting for a guard to escort us down to the exercise yard and, seeing his precious football time running out, Tommy was getting pissed off. I don't recall what set him off – it was usually something fairly trivial – but in a split second he'd turned into a raving lunatic, screaming and lashing out at anyone close by. His voice changed in tone and the blood vessels on his bald head stood out like pulsating blue worms wriggling under his skin. The foreigners took a step back and tried to look calm as a group of Chinese piled in to restrain him. The number one, Mr Gao, yelled at everyone to get back to their cells as Tommy was frogmarched down the block to his. Sweat oozed from every pore of his head and streams of it flowed down his neck into his football shirt.

I stood dumbstruck as the other foreigners looked at me one by one, saying:

'Now you know why he's down there.'

'He's a nutter.'

'He tried to kill me.'

'He should be in a fucking asylum, not a prison.'

From that moment onwards, the reticence that the other foreigners had shown with regard to talking about McLoughlin's antics had gone. The floodgates opened and everyone had a tale to tell. Gareth said he'd nearly lost both eyes in their first week at the jail as Tommy had attempted to plunge a pair of chopsticks into them after a dispute over a jar of marmalade. Mark had pulled him off and got punched in the face for his trouble. The Germans, Ludwig and Jürgen, had both been spat at and hit during his occasional rages, and various Chinese had found themselves on the wrong end of his fist.

Through mutual friends and dope contacts, Tommy and Larry had known each other for years, and Larry was convinced Tommy had grassed him up with a phone call to the Hong Kong customs. According to Larry, Tommy had seen him packing a bag in his hotel room before flying to the island, where he was busted and given his first two-year stretch. Larry had a long list of former associates he claimed had been violently assaulted by Tommy: one had been repeatedly stabbed after a falling-out over a dope deal, while another guy had been hospitalised after being head-butted by Tommy, who was wearing a crash helmet. Tommy never admitted any of these offences and said Larry was a fantasist who made it up as he went along. I wasn't so sure; I was confused and my loyalties were divided. Tommy had been good to me and I had no personal grudge against him. I also liked Larry but questioned whether he was a reliable witness, given his longstanding dislike of McLoughlin. It wasn't fair to take sides as long as that remained the case. I decided to withhold judgement and try to make peace with everyone until I had enough information to make up my own mind.

Ten minutes after the football debacle, I went down the cell block to get some hot water and Tommy called me over. I approached him warily, as if he were a caged tiger who might pounce any moment, but he acted as if nothing had happened, as if he'd slipped back from Mr Hyde to Dr Jekyll, unaware of what all the fuss was about. We made small talk for a minute, and as I turned to walk away he said, 'Sometimes this place gets to me.'

From that day, I remained cautious of Tommy, although I got along fine with the other foreigners. Gareth's and the Germans' misfortunes were closely linked, though they managed to patch up their differences most of the time. Gareth had been living in Xinjiang Province, in the far-western reaches of China, running a restaurant with his Muslim wife and dealing a bit of hash on the side. The Germans had got busted getting on the same boat I'd intended to get from Shanghai to Japan 18 months or so earlier, and during interrogation the police had figured out Gareth was their supplier. Ludwig and Gareth despised each other and were engaged in an ongoing psychological war that rarely erupted but was never far from the surface. On the other hand, Gareth and Jürgen were good friends and spent a lot of time together, despite Jürgen being partly responsible for Gareth's arrest. I sympathised with Gareth, as his entirely innocent wife had been imprisoned for a year in far worse conditions than any of us in a prison in Kashgar. The Germans had ended up with eight years each, and Gareth had got eight and a half as the 'ringleader'. The case had been covered by the Hong Kong media, which, with typical hyperbole, described Gareth as a 'Drug Kingpin'.

Jürgen was around 40 and had served time in German prisons for dope offences. He was short and turning grey and understandably depressed about the length of his sentence, but he'd made a decision to become an excellent guitar player to compensate. He had the tiniest stubs for fingers I'd ever seen on a guitarist, yet he managed to stretch them to play complex jazz chords through sheer bloody-minded determination. Ludwig was a few years younger, a keen bodybuilder and a Chinese-language student. His head was always immaculately shaven, and his desk and cell spotlessly tidy. He spent much of his time on his noisy typewriter, which infuriated Gareth. All three had been blown away by the length of their sentences, and their trial had been farcical in that the prosecution had claimed they were all part of a conspiracy. It was a classic propaganda exercise to show that China was doing its bit in the international War on Drugs. By making examples of a handful of foreign dope smugglers, China hoped to deflect criticism of its porous borders with the Golden Triangle, through which much of the world's heroin passed. By the time my dope bust came along, they were no longer looking for a scapegoat so I was able to pass through the system as a relatively minor monkey figure. Had I been busted 18 months earlier, I might well have got the rooster treatment, too.

Mark had been derided by all the foreigners for refusing to share the details of his indictment. I couldn't blame him for his discretion as he was frightened that rather than reduce the others' sentences, they'd extend his – not unheard of in China. When I showed them my indictment, they became obsessed with the difference in wording between the description of *dama* (marijuana) on my paperwork and *dama zhi* (marijuana oil) on theirs, assuming they'd been charged with a higher-classified substance. Of course it made little difference what was written on the indictment, because the sentence was the same either way. In the West, such an anomaly might be seized upon by a clever lawyer and used as a loophole to demand a retrial or appeal, but in China it was irrelevant because the legal system could never be seen to have made a mistake in the first place. They were all still pursuing the issue (unsuccessfully) when I left the prison two years later.

After the novelty of having a new foreigner to talk to began to wane, I was left to my own devices. I immediately struck up a friendship with Jürgen, who invited me to join the prison band, the Reformers, and let me have a go on his Yamaha acoustic while my guitar was being processed by the guards. It was a cheap Indonesian-built copy and was difficult to play, particularly since I hadn't touched a fretboard for eight months and the calluses on the tips of my fingers had softened, making every note sting. But the thought that I would be able to play in the jail at all made the news that I was unlikely to get any time off for good behaviour easier to bear. Also, meeting the other foreigners made me realise how lucky I'd been to get off with two and a half years, even though I'd only been charged with smuggling while most of the others had been charged with both smuggling and intent to supply, which carried a heavier penalty. Either way, I had a lot to be grateful for and felt slightly guilty for my relative good fortune, though Gareth made me feel better by pointing out that in many countries I could have walked away with a slapped wrist and a fine.

My arrival at Ti Lan Qiao had been well timed. The previous number one prisoner had been a sadistic bastard Gareth had nicknamed Doctor Death. He'd been a nightmare for the foreigners, whom he loathed, and had made everyone's life a misery. Eventually McLoughlin had got into a fracas with him and spat in his face. When Death fought back, Tommy landed a punch right between his eyes and broke his nose. It was the only time I ever heard the foreigners speak well of the Scotsman.

While waiting for my guitar to turn up, I discovered the blues. Perhaps *discovered* is the wrong word, since I'd owned Muddy Waters's greatest hits for at least a decade and seen many blues acts, from Buddy Guy in Tipperary to Ray Charles in Osaka. I'm not a diehard blues aficionado, though I can appreciate the artistry in the monotony of its simple structures. I'd rather listen to country music, whose lyrical metaphors are often sad and funny. The best thing about blues is that musicians can play along without having to know the song, since the chord progressions are almost always the same. Jürgen, on the other hand, considered the blues the ultimate musical expression and devoted endless hours every day to perfecting his technique in the form. I admired his stamina, being far too lazy myself to bother playing any song more than a couple of times in a row. When my own instrument eventually turned up, Jürgen would get frustrated that I was reluctant to play whatever song we were learning over and over, but for me it's about catching the essence of a song, and the more it's played the more remote that becomes. Besides, Jürgen hated most of the folk and country songs that I loved. Like most people, he thought that country was redneck music and would only play Johnny Cash songs, which even country-haters admit to liking. More adventurous stuff, like the Louvin Brothers and Merle Haggard, left him cold, while Bob Dylan was one of his pet hates. Fortunately, I was happy to play just about anything and would agree to accompany him on a B.B. King tune if he'd help out with a Gram Parsons cover.

Tommy, who rarely listened to music, had a good collection of tapes his brother had sent him, the vast majority being blues compilations. The greatest-hits mixes featured a roll call of greats from the chain-gang ballads of the Mississippi Delta to the Chicago electric blues scene of the '50s. He also lent me a Walkman and I got to listen to my first Western music for eight months. There was Robert Johnson, T-Bone Walker, Lightnin' Hopkins and Sonny Boy Williamson, but the song that really hit me between the eyes, knocked me out and allowed me to *hear* the blues in a way I'd never heard before, was the long, live-in-London version of 'Wang Dang Doodle' by Howlin' Wolf. Its hypnotic voodoo beat seemed to pulsate with the rhythm of the jail, while the wolf man's demonic voice howled through the bars and cell blocks like a demented preacher. This one particular song was such a revelation to me that I spent hours pacing the wing, listening to it over and over again. In a sense it was the first blues song I'd ever heard, and I made the most of my new discovery, wandering around in a trance, pressing the rewind button every five minutes until the batteries ran out. 'Wang Dang Doodle' was the new soundtrack to my life, and I never tired of listening to it.

But for us the jail had less in common with a Louisiana chain gang than a mental hospital. It was more Cuckoo's Nest than San Quentin. Though the wing was eerily peaceful, due to the strict regimen and threat of collective punishments, there were a number of prisoners who clearly belonged in an asylum. One named Dougou Liang spent much of his time trying to catch invisible butterflies, a task he pursued in a waltz, plucking the unseen miscreants out of thin air. He was reaching the end of a 20-year stretch for killing a burglar who tried to rob his house. This was no Tony Martin case; I doubt he would have got a custodial sentence in the UK. A tragic figure, he'd spent more than ten years in a hospital for the criminally insane but had been moved to a 'normal' prison for the last few years of his sentence. One of the more poignant moments of my time in Ti Lan Qiao was seeing this cheerless soul walk free after some nineteen years inside.

Another prisoner acquired the nickname 'Scarleg' due to a number of bloody scratches he had down the side of his thigh. He always looked as if he'd just walked out of a thornbush wearing shorts, but that was the least of his problems. I had no idea how it had happened, but his skull had a hole in it the size of a small melon. The surgeon had made a pig's ear out of the stitches, too, so it looked as if he'd had the top of his head chopped off with a machete. He was chubby and had a robotic walk that made him look like a fat, drunken duck. He was also clearly more than a bit simple. One night he was put on night-watch duties with another prisoner the foreigners liked to call Grumpy. Grumpy was in the neighbouring cell to my own and was disliked by the Chinese, having been convicted of raping his ten-year-old daughter. When Scarleg went to wake him for the night shift Grumpy wouldn't wake up, so Scarleg hit him over the head with a wooden chair. Rather than wake up, Grumpy started to bleed profusely from the wound and Scarleg became convinced he'd killed him. Terrified he'd be executed for murder, he attempted to take his own life by sticking his fingers into an electrical socket – which proved unsuccessful. Eventually a guard heard the commotion and sounded the alarm, and within minutes the whole wing was woken to the sound of Grumpy being taken on a stretcher to the hospital wing and Scarleg to God knows where. A few days later Grumpy was back with a bandaged head, and then news arrived that Scarleg had been exiled to a prison farm in the countryside.

The blurring of boundaries between prisons and asylums were a feature of Communist rule all over the world. Like the Soviet Union, which often sent dissidents to mental hospitals, Mao's China had a similar strategy that reasoned that if you didn't like living in this socialist paradise you must be mad. The endless reform and self-criticism sessions were delivered as a kind of therapy, and the atmosphere this method of reform inculcated owed more to the realms of psychology than criminology.

To the foreigners, the notion of reform was a joke. Nobody felt they'd done anything wrong, other than getting caught. If there were sins to atone for, they were a private affair and certainly not the business of jailers or cadres. And so the Westerners remained outside the apparatus of state ideological guidance and were generally left to their own devices to navigate their own ideas of reform, which suited them. For me it was a blessing to have got this far, and my first weeks in Ti Lan Qiao were a happy time as I came to terms with the last eight months and began to map out what to do with the next two years of my life.

7

Some Kind of Eden

Jürgen and I were learning new blues riffs. A mate of his in Germany had sent over a box of cassettes, so he'd written out the lyrics of a few choice tunes for me to sing. His friend had sent a bottleneck slide, too, so I played rhythm and sang while he did his Ry Cooder thing. Blues legend Robert Johnson's 'Hellhound on my Trail' was a favourite, as was Lowell Fulson's 'Reconsider Baby'. Jürgen was very intense when it came to music and took it extremely seriously. The songs had to be perfect, and he'd devote many hours sitting in his cell getting his lead part right before we played together.

McLoughlin bought a guitar, too: I think he was feeling left out. It was a bright-blue Chinese guitar that he'd got the consul to buy him with some cash his brother had sent. He asked Jürgen and me to give him lessons, so we showed him a few basic chords to practise. I doubt he spent more than an hour and a half practising before he gave up.

Larry was writing his diary, which seemed to be an exposé of the Chinese prison system. He wanted to smuggle it out of the prison up his backside, and I told him he'd better keep it brief. I think he saw himself as more of a human-rights campaigner than a dope smuggler, and if he'd been rich I imagine he'd have worked as a volunteer for Amnesty International, Human Rights Watch or some other organisation. His handwriting was barely legible and the text was interspersed with serial numbers of boxes leaving the prison workshops to go to the West. It seemed like a pointless exercise to me, but it gave some meaning to his life. I think he'd convinced himself that rather than being an ageing failed dope smuggler who'd got caught yet again, he was actually working undercover for some benign organisation shining a light on the dark secrets of the Chinese state.

One day, I'd got a postcard from a friend in Goa and Larry's eyes lit up.

'Maybe you could get one of your pals to send us some trips. You can get at least one hit under each stamp.'

It'd been a while since I'd had any acid, and I couldn't think of any place in the world less conducive to taking the stuff. The thought of walking down the wing watching the bars bend freaked me out. If something kicked off in the jail with the Chinese, it didn't bear thinking about.

The postcard was a picture of the Anjuna Flea Market: a place I knew well. It was shot through a wide-angle lens and you could see the rows of traders amassed on the paddy field, with the palm trees of the beach fading into the horizon. In some respects, Goa had been a key location in my eventual downfall, having introduced me to a new subculture of scammers whose idea of work was to cross a border with a few kilos of dope once or twice a year. The more I visited the place, the more it occurred to me that most of my friends were drug dealers.

I'd arrived in Goa in the middle of Mescaline Ronnie's birthday party. Ronnie was a well-heeled Goa regular from Amsterdam whose parties were legendary. My cab driver took me directly to the party site in a bamboo grove in Anjuna and pulled up beside a sea of Enfield motorbikes strewn across a paddy field. He hooted his horn at a couple of kids trying to siphon petrol out of the tanks, who looked up briefly before continuing with their work. I climbed out of the car and could feel the pulse of the music in the distance as I slung my guitar bag over my shoulder and headed towards the monotonous beat. The sun was coming up but nobody had noticed, and every chai mat had paraffin lamps burning along the pathway towards the dance area. The coconut palms were painted in fluorescent colours, with Day-Glo streamers dangling between them, and plaster of Paris busts of Shiva and Ganesh had been placed strategically beneath ultraviolet lights. The daylight was unkind to these decorations, and it looked more like a Hindu kids' jelly-and-balloon party than a rave.

Jonathon, an old English friend from Thailand and Japan, appeared looking like something from *Lord of the Flies*, with a Technicolor bandana and Errol Flynn-style Robin Hood boots. We hugged, but I could tell he was too out of it to speak as he careered off towards the dance floor with his arms flailing in the air.

I found a shaded spot under a tree where a guy was making sugar-cane juice from an engine-driven mangle, crushing the sticks into a greenish-yellow liquid, with ice cubes bobbing about on top. I sat and drank the syrupy potion, surveying the party from a safe distance. I'd been sitting on a bus all night from Kerala: a bumpy, sleepless journey during which I'd banged my head repeatedly as the back of the bus leapt off its wheels with every hill we encountered. I was in no mood to party and wanted to find a beach and some breakfast. I'd been in India a month and had fallen in love with the place. I'd stopped over in Bangladesh for a couple of weeks on the way, so the culture shock was minimal after that benighted country. From Calcutta, I'd made my way down the eastern seaboard to Madras, where I stayed in the beautiful Broadlands Hotel. There had been some adventures, and I'd overdone the opium and found myself strung out in the fishing town of Puri waiting for the stuff to wear off. After a week of visiting temples and off-licences in Tamil Nadu, I'd made my way by bus and riverboat through Kerala towards Goa.

The beach was deserted apart from a few party stragglers dipping their feet in the ocean while coming down off their trips. I sat in a beach cafe eating grilled prawns and drinking banana lassi with a Swedish hippy from Gothenburg. We shared a spliff as tattooed, suntanned couples on Enfields began to appear, riding down the sandy tracks towards the beach. The party was still going, but the heat of the sun was too much for most, and gurning, Lycra-clad ravers began arriving for breakfast. Riding motorbikes in Goa while on LSD is fun, but you feel like you're going much faster than you actually are. If you're not careful the bike falls over in the deep sand, as happened to one of the party-goers I was watching. I recognised him from his gangly walk and thick spectacles as he left the bike on its side and staggered towards the beach bar.

Alexander, an old South African friend whom I'd met while living in Kyoto, had come to Goa to see what all the fuss was about. He'd been here a week and was just getting into the swing of it, wearing tie-dye Lycra leggings and loud paisley shirts. It took him a while to recognise me, as his trip was still raging and his eyesight was lousy at the best of times. We'd taken acid together many times and had started to have our own Goa parties in clubs on Kiyamachi Street with a small, close-knit group of Japanese drug fiends. LSD was posted in sheets from contacts in California and Amsterdam, or else brought in by 'condom express' from friends who'd been to India. Full Moon parties had yet to take off in Thailand, but Goa was the party mecca in the late '80s, and small groups of party people were spreading the word.

We bought a couple of green coconuts with a straw sticking out of the top and wandered down to the beach for a swim. It was good to be amongst friends after my solo travels, and Goa was much more tourist-friendly than most other parts of India. By lunchtime I'd rented a motorbike, found a room and bought a ten-gram stick of *charas*. All I needed were some colourful clothes. By day two I had the clothes to match and my first 'Goa tattoo': an inside-leg burn from a hot motorbike exhaust, a 'rite of passage' scar that everyone seemed to have.

By day three in Goa, I'd settled in and found myself a place to sleep on a friend's porch in Anjuna. Rather than paying for a room, as I had for my first couple of days, it made more sense to stay in one of the big houses my friends had rented. Alexander was staying in the same bungalow, and we went down to the Wednesday flea market to score some psychedelics. Within ten minutes we'd bought a two-hundred-and-fifty-microgram blotter and a strip of synthetic mescaline of indeterminate strength, with the idea of going halves. The mescaline didn't tear in half, and one piece was bigger than the other, so I had the big half of the mescaline, while he had two-thirds of the acid trip. We wandered around the flea market waiting for the drugs to kick in, looking at the jewellery stalls and drinking warm Kingfisher lager. As is often the case, we started to question whether the stuff was working. It must have been an hour since we'd taken it. Perhaps we'd been ripped off?

Then it started, and the flea market melted before my eyes, exploding into kaleidoscopic fragments. I felt sick, too, and then I lost Alexander and had to go and sit by the beach and get away from people whose faces resembled the characters in Francis Bacon paintings. It was getting dark, and I was getting paranoid. How long ago had I taken this stuff? Was it ever going to wear off? I went to look for Alexander, but the flea market had gone and everyone was staring at me or, worse still, asking me if I was OK. The palm trees all had faces, and they weren't happy with me at all, bending over and wagging their palms at me. I took refuge in a beach bar.

'Drink?' said the owner, whose face I couldn't look at.

Why would I want to drink? I thought. I can't even feel my tongue. I scanned my brain for words for drinks, but there were none there. The owner went to another table, sensing I was lost for words.

'Kingfisher,' I spluttered, finally finding a word.

A beer arrived, and I stared at the green bottle that was breathing in and out as if it were alive. People across the bar were looking at me and giggling amongst themselves.

'Oh dear, look at the state of him,' I could hear one of them saying.

'He's lost the plot,' said another.

I left the bar without touching the beer and wandered towards the beach, which I found less intimidating. I decided I was desperate to go to the toilet, and it couldn't wait. I'd have to dig a hole in the sand and do it there and then. There was no other choice, so I started to dig, and then they arrived.

Dogs! Mangy dogs, rabid dogs, dribbling hellhounds with gnashing jaws, and they were all around me, growling. This is it, I thought. I'm going to be eaten alive by a pack of wolves. I was terrified, and they knew it. They could smell my fear, and I could smell the yellow pus of the sores on their skin. I stood up and bent my knees, trying to see eye to eye with them while walking backwards towards the water. I couldn't see how many there were, but their barks brought new recruits, and by the time my feet touched the wet sand of the water's edge they were well into double figures.

They followed me into the water, and I started to see them more clearly now. The phosphorus in the water lit the scene, and I quickly turned and ran into the deep and belly-flopped as it got above waist-depth. Turning round again I could see they were still coming at me, swimming out of their depth, paws pounding the waves, but I had the advantage now. I was standing waist-deep and I lunged at the first dog in the pack with the full force of my fist, and the psycho mutt squealed and started to swim back to the shore, taking his gang with him.

It was freezing. I must've stood in the water for ten minutes, waiting to see if they had gone, and finally I ventured out and walked along the beach in knee-deep water towards some lights up ahead.

'Your beer is warm. Would you like some ice in it?'

'No thanks.'

I could talk. The trip was finally wearing off, and I was cold from the sea. The beer was foul, with a nasty glycerine aftertaste, but the bottle was no longer alive and people no longer stared at me. I'd survived my first Goa trip, but it'd been pretty hairy. The faces on the palm trees might have been the drugs, but the dogs were very real. They were the hellhounds of blues folklore that Robert Johnson had sung about, and now they were on my trail.

It was my first and last bad trip in Goa. After that the whole place turned into a psychedelic dream, and it was one of the happiest times of my life. I couldn't believe I was so happy; was it all a bit too good to be true? So what: we were having a ball, and the parties just got better and better. Goa in '89 was unbelievable. Perhaps it was akin to being in San Francisco in '69; there was a feeling that you were in exactly the right place at the right time. I'd been into punk music as a teenager, but I'd been at boarding school at the time and was too young to get fully absorbed into the culture. In Goa, however, we'd hit the bullseye. If you were into music, motorbikes, drugs and so on it was some kind of Eden. I'd never experienced anything like it, and still haven't 20 years later.

Everyone was euphoric, and people walked around with giant grins on their faces, as if we were all privy to a well-kept secret. I was aware that the delirious joy of everyone was at least partly drug-fuelled, but the geography and timing of the 'happening' seemed to have a momentum of its own. Some of the older crowd had overdone it in the '70s and had given up drugs altogether, but they still looked like they were on Ecstasy all the time. Many in the 'scene' were intensely fashion-conscious, too, and it took a while for people like me who'd turned up from travelling around the subcontinent to get with it. Different nationalities tended to gather in groups, so there were 'the Italians' and 'the Americans' and, of course, 'the English', who probably comprised the single largest group.

One of the oldest Englishmen in Goa was Acid Eric, a white-haired

Yorkshireman with a furry freak-brother's beard and a single waist-length dreadlock. He'd lived in San Francisco in the '60s, where he'd hung out with such counter-culture luminaries as the Merry Pranksters and the Grateful Dead, and had ended up with a ten-year jail sentence for tax evasion. Eric was something of a local legend and would hold court at parties and dispense liquid LSD to the faithful. At one of my first Goa parties, I made the pilgrimage to a small bamboo shack on the hillside above the mayhem, where he sat cross-legged with a couple of young girls by his side like the Maharishi. He handed me a shot of the fruity potion as a preacher might give Communion, and I felt the strychnine burst into my bloodstream in an instant.

The parties usually took place near the sea, in small bays around Vagator and Anjuna, just far enough from the beach to provide cover when the sun came up in the morning. Local Indians provided huge sound systems that could be heard for miles around, so if you forgot to go to the party, you would likely hear it in the middle of the night and go along later. Sometimes we went around 3 a.m. after a few hours' sleep and took a trip that would peak as the sun came up.

The police often turned up at the parties, haranguing the organisers for baksheesh before disappearing into the night with a wad of rupees. Rumour had it that police officers in Delhi paid bribes to get posted to the area to make the most of this scam, and there were always plenty of tourists carrying drugs who could be threatened with arrest in return for money. Occasionally they would arrest someone and put them through the courts – usually ending with a ten-year prison term, which then involved a great deal of money to secure release. The most I paid was a thousand rupees (around twenty-five pounds), but a friend spent a couple of years in prison and it cost his family many thousands.

Police weren't the only hazard, and one of the biggest problems was people 'flipping out' on drugs. Within days of my arrival a friend of a friend, a young Australian called Baz, lost the plot and appeared to have 'left his body' permanently. He'd shaved his head, covered himself with red paint and was driving around naked on an Enfield. The Goans – who were used to dealing with these kinds of problems – had him sectioned, and his father had to fly out and collect him from a psychiatric hospital in Panjim. Theft was common and was invariably blamed on outsiders from neighbouring Indian states, and occasionally stories of rape would filter through the usually blissful community.

But the darker side of Goa rarely infringed on the general atmosphere of the place, and it was bad form to dwell on such unfortunate events as being burgled by criminals or nicked by the police. Failure to walk around with an almost unreal sunny demeanour was a sign that it was time to go home or, better still, take more drugs.

Ecstasy was all around: I was initiated by a guy called Fast Eddie and promptly threw it up on the side of the road on the way to a party. I was highly suspicious of the drug and have never really changed my mind on the subject. I decided early on that a drug that made you feel deliriously happy while doing nothing in particular was playing tricks on the mind. There seemed to be something fake about its high, though it was unlikely to bring on the kind of trauma that hallucinogenic drugs were capable of unleashing. Sannyasins, the followers of Bhagwan Shree Rajhneesh (later known as Osho), were supposedly making the stuff in Pune, a dusty town between Bombay and Goa, and a kind of finishing school for lost rich kids. They certainly looked as if they were on it much of the time, and their hyper touchy-feely manner seemed to bear this out.

The defining point of my first Goa visit was a Full Moon party that lasted three days. I was 24 years old, and it was the Chinese Year of the Snake: my birth year. Months earlier, in Japan, I'd had many strange premonitions involving snakes and had found myself stepping over imaginary ones in the streets of Kyoto. Hissing cobras became regular visitors to my dreams, where I was both terrified and transfixed. I recall leaping from my futon at the sight of a King Cobra that slithered across the tatami and wagged its V-shaped tongue at me. Shortly after arriving in India I'd visited a snake farm near Madras, and I never missed an opportunity to pay the snake charmers who played their flutes to entice their pets from wicker baskets. Snakes had become my friends.

I climbed up the sandstone cliffs to my motorbike at the end of the marathon party, and there, lying on the ground beside my bike, was a snakeskin. Since drugs tend to heighten one's receptivity to such 'signs', it was a uniquely auspicious sight that convinced me I'd turned a corner in my life. The past was dead and the future beckoned. For the first time in my life I was free, and for the first time in my life I considered making money out of drugs.

It seemed that pretty much everyone I knew in Goa was at the very least a part-time drug dealer and/or smuggler. Scams of one kind or another were always being talked about, and people would disappear for a couple of weeks and fly off to some corner of the world to ply their trade. Since I was based in Japan I was in an excellent position to make the most of my new contacts, and people's eyebrows rose at the mere mention of the place. The yen was still a phenomenal currency and the price of hashish the highest in the world by far. There was a lot of money to be made, but the risks were high and the penalties tough. Friends had been locked up in solitary confinement for long periods of time and had suffered from the psychological ordeal. I had no intention of putting myself through such a situation and abandoned the idea, for the time being, at least.

In an attempt to make some extra cash, Jonathon, myself and another guy called Rich decided to buy a kilo of hash. I'd never seen such a large chunk of the stuff, and we hid it beneath a pot at the back of our house in Goa, in a hole in the ground about a foot deep. Later we went to a party and returned at around 9 a.m. to find the drugs had gone. My first foray into dope dealing had not been good. We'd lost a couple of hundred quid each and assumed that someone had seen us burying it and come back while we were at the party and taken it. I put it down to karma and decided that I wasn't suited to the business, an assessment that I'd have done well to remember later on.

I left Goa in the middle of a beach party, and took a bus up to Bombay. My brain had taken enough battering, and it was time to see more of India. Somewhere along the way I'd gone native and become the kind of spaced-out hippy I'd previously laughed at. I'd seen friends come back from India with beads round their necks, facial hair and a copy of the Tibetan Book of the Dead under their arm. I told myself that it would never happen to me, yet now I was eight and a half stone, with a ponytail and goatee, reading my third Carlos Castaneda book in a row. The first thing I did on arrival at a new hotel was make a shrine with crystals, incense and Hindu deities. I'd given up eating meat and believed myself to be on a new spiritual path: a hotchpotch of astrology, numerology, tarot cards and Eastern mysticism.

It's difficult to say how large a part drugs played in this new mental state. Many people go to India and take no drugs whatsoever and still find the country deeply affecting. I think if you spend more than three months in the place, it works its magic regardless. The pace is so different from in the West that it becomes necessary to shift gears to cope. The traveller who goes into a railway station hoping to leave with a ticket within ten minutes is likely to be frustrated. After you've been in the country a while, you realise that you need a whole morning to buy the ticket and that you should bring along a copy of *Autobiography of a Yogi* to pass the time.

Once the recalibration is complete, many Westerners find the pace of life in India preferable to their home country's. Of course, much of this is to do with economics. Travellers generally don't work and are able to make believe they are sadhus, the ochre-clad holy men renouncing worldly pleasures, or any other fantasy. If they had to carry 25 breeze blocks on their heads in 40-degree heat for 50 cents a day, they probably wouldn't feel they were on their way to achieving nirvana. Travelling in India is a wonderful thing, but keeping your feet on the ground can be tough.

I ended up staying with a sadhu in the Himalayan mountain town of Manikaran. It was an important Sikh pilgrimage site, with a large temple at its centre built on a hot spring. The basement of the temple had a series of large rooms waist-deep in the hot, sulphurous water, which constantly flowed from the centre of the earth. The temple provided free food and shelter for pilgrims, but I stayed with a sadhu on the edge of the town. He called himself Hanuman Baba, and his was the warmest house in the area, having been built on rocks that were scorching from the springs. On my arrival in Manikaran I'd checked into a guesthouse, but it was freezing cold at night and I'd arrived in my Goa outfit of baggy drawstring trousers and T-shirts. I bought a nasty yak-wool jumper that felt like a hair shirt and spent as much of the day as possible in the temple lounging around on the heated stone floors.

Hanuman Baba was no ordinary sadhu and, by local standards, no sadhu at all. We'd met at a party in Goa, where he held court with his waist-length dreadlocks and maroon robes, swinging his head to the

With my sister at home
in Norfolk, 1975
(Richard Stevenson)

Arashiyama, near Kyoto, was a
popular swimming place in the '80s
(Sabrina Rowan Hamilton)

Beneath a billboard in
Kyoto, 1986
(Sabrina Rowan Hamilton)

Visiting a temple in
Kyoto, 1986
(Kelvin O'Mard)

Card players in Beijing, 1987 (Sabrina Rowan Hamilton)

A rave in Goa, 1990 (Kelvin O'Mard)

In Kyoto, 1991
(Sasha Otterburn)

Kyoto's bar district by day
(Sabrina Rowan Hamilton)

Playing the guitar in Goa, 1991 (Kelvin O'Mard)

Smoking on the porch in Goa, 1991 (Kelvin O'Mard)

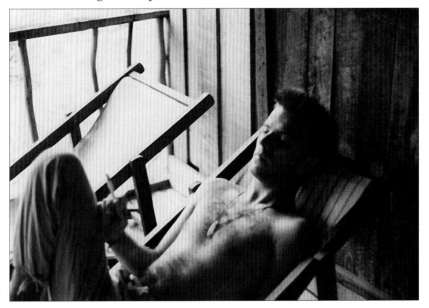

Xiahe, Chinese Tibet, 1993 (Dominic Stevenson)

With Afghan boys at the Khyber Pass three weeks before my arrest,
August 1993 (Dominic Stevenson)

The author in Hanoi, Vietnam,
August 2009 (Andrea Neville)

beat of the music. He enjoyed his drugs and seemed to have money, and spent time hanging out in Italy with friends from the Osho Ashram in Pune. When the heat got too much in the lowlands he moved to the mountains, where he smoked *charas* and played host to a succession of Western hippies.

I had my first Indian dope bust in his little house on the hillside. We'd taken an acid trip and were sitting listening to music and smoking chillums, the clay hash pipes favoured by sadhus. The door to the house opened and in walked the chief of police for the town. He was a tall man with a Colonel Blimp moustache and an awkward Basil Fawlty walk. I'd seen him before, and he'd even greeted me in the street, waving his cane with a smile. Sometimes he wore civilian clothes, but today he was wearing his khaki uniform with his cane under his arm like a sergeant major. He was paying a social visit to Hanuman Baba, but the second he saw me with the dope pipe in my hands he went into a rage. Hanuman tried to defuse the situation and told him to calm down, but he insisted I accompany him to the police station. The acid was a fairly mild trip, and after Goa my tolerance to the drug was greater than ever, and I held my ground when he grabbed my arm and tried to drag me from the room. Realising his words were not going to sway the chief of police, Hanuman presented him with the chillum instead, and this seemed to do the trick, because the policeman promptly sat down and smoked it. Half an hour later we were still smoking together, and he forgot all about arresting me.

Larry and I had been exchanging dope stories, of which he had many, and he was never happier than when he was recalling them. He still believed in the notion of dope smugglers as Robin Hoods sticking two fingers up at the 'establishment', though in reality it was nothing of the sort. If he could throw in a tale about the 'psycho Scotsman' so much the better, and he often talked about McLoughlin's violent past. It occurred to me that I was the only person, apart from Mark, in the foreign group who hadn't known anyone prior to being locked up together. Gareth's and the Germans' fortunes were inextricably linked, and so, in a way, were Larry's and Tommy's. Meanwhile I was the outsider, as

Mark had been before me, and both of us had been given significantly shorter sentences than the others, partly because neither of us had been charged with intent to supply, but also because as individuals we were not viewed as a gang.

None of the other foreigners were Indiaphiles, but for me it had been a second home, after Japan, while England was no home at all. China was a much tougher country to travel in, but it had its charms. Even in jail I held the country in high regard and never felt any bitterness towards the people or even the authorities. I blamed myself for my stupidity and thanked my lucky stars for the short sentence I'd been given. If India had brought on dreams of snakes, China was dragon country, and now they too came into my world. From flames in the fireplace, to mountains and rivers from aeroplane windows, to the outlines of clouds in the sky, they've been with me ever since. My love affair with India had slipped by the wayside, and China had taken its place. I'd lost my freedom, but I'd got lucky on the side. Even in a cage, I felt at home in the Dragon Land.

8

The Monkey House Rules

You had to hand it to the Chinese: they knew how to run a jail. Ti Lan Qiao, Shanghai Municipal Prison, is situated on the north shore of the Huangpu River in the middle of the city and houses some 5,000 inmates, mainly men. Built by the British at the turn of the century, it was later used by both the Japanese invaders and the Nationalists. It was considered a model prison by the local authorities due to its emphasis on Reform Through Labour, a term that I would come to hear like some gloomy mantra.

As well as labour, the jail was the administrative centre for Reform Through Education, which was translated for me by an officer – without the slightest hint of irony – as brainwashing. This was taken incredibly seriously, and the prison had its own TV station that beamed an endless stream of propaganda to the other jails and labour camps across the region. Most officers approached their Reform Through Education duties with the tired resignation of a preacher who's long since stopped believing, while a few came on like TV evangelists, haranguing the bored inmates with fire-and-brimstone speeches that could go on for hours.

The top brass at the jail took great pride in the low recidivism of the criminals that passed through their system, seeing it as vindication for the vapid sloganeering that was their stock in trade. In truth, there was a far more ominous explanation for most prisoners' reluctance to return to crime after their stay in Ti Lan Qiao, chiefly the length of the sentences handed down to first offenders. A burglar, for instance, could expect a sentence of around eight years or more for a first offence, and would serve at least seven of those. On his release, Reformed Through Institutionalisation, he would be sent to a prearranged work unit where he'd work for breadline wages in a government factory. If he had no family to vouch for him, he'd be required to live on the premises in a quasi-Dickensian-workhouse environment. His community leaders would be informed, as would the inhabitants of his neighbourhood, and he might be required to make a public apology for 'letting down the People'. Stripped of the life he once knew, a broken man, chained to the state, he'd most likely have neither the time nor the inclination to reoffend. The system had a brilliantly grim logic to it, which reasoned that if the average criminal was most active between the ages of 16 and 30, such draconian sentences – not to mention the post-prison regimen – would keep them out of circulation for most of the duration of their criminal life. There were no 'career' burglars or 'habitual' thieves, as we say in Britain. In China, a one-time thief stands out in his community like a one-handed Saudi.

As foreigners, we'd missed out on an important part of the Chinese prison experience and come straight to our final destination. All other prisoners were required to spend a month or so being inducted in 6th Brigade, where they had to learn the 'Big Fifty-Eight' off by heart. The prison rule book was the first, last and only book most Chinese prisoners read. The small book had taken on the same significance in prison that Mao's Little Red Book had during the Cultural Revolution, and inmates were expected to be able to quote the rules verbatim. When they got to their final brigades they were expected to know everything in the book, but many couldn't even read and needed help. New arrivals sat around in groups, cross-legged, nodding their heads and repeating the edicts over and over. After a while, they would be summoned to undergo testing by other prisoners and would be slapped every time they got something wrong. Foreigners were exempt from this task since much of the material contained Party jargon concerning ideological reform. However, we were expected to learn an English translation of the 'Ten Don'ts', which were written on the walls of every cell. They read:

Don't sit down in the cell when a captain tours.

Don't eat food in the cell.

Don't spit in the cell.

Don't piss or shit on the floor.

Don't sleep or lie down in the cell unless authorised.

Don't keep the cell untidy.

Don't leave the cell until told to do so.

Don't enter the cell until told to do so.

Don't keep dangerous implements in the cell.

Don't hide contraband in the cell.

Prisoners were divided up and allocated their brigades depending on their skills on the outside. Mechanics fixed cars, chefs worked in the kitchen brigade and so on, while unskilled workers got the really dull jobs, like packaging. Many of the prisoners were serving long sentences, but few had life sentences. If you warranted a lifetime in prison, you would have been shot in the first place. Many prisoners had suspended death sentences, which meant you were on probation for two years and could be executed at any time in that period. Most (though not all) prisoners survived this and were then given a life sentence, which was then changed into a 20-year term. Some were fast-tracked through this process, particularly those who'd been given exemplary sentences for political offences that had subsequently become less serious in the post-Mao era. I met a guy 12 years into a suspended death sentence for a political crime who was hoping to get out within a couple of years, but this was quite rare and most could expect to serve at least 20 years of such a sentence.

The guards wanted nothing to do with the day-to-day running of the jail. This left the majority of the work to the prisoners, who managed to do a remarkable job of keeping the place clean and orderly, even to the extent of doing the guards' paperwork for them. Meanwhile the guards sat around, hunched over Nescafé jars of green tea, stirring only to hawk another ball of phlegm into the spittoon beside their desk. When they spoke, it was usually a disdainful grunt accompanied by a look of absolute revulsion. Captain Xu was our commanding officer, and I was informed early on that he was an arsehole who disliked foreigners even more than he despised the Chinese inmates. He'd been a prison officer for more than 20 years, though he didn't look a day over 30. His teeth were stained with green tea and nicotine, while his uniform was dishevelled and tatty. He had the look of a man whose life had passed him by, and the slim consolation that he was better off than the people in his care failed to elicit even the faintest smile.

If Captain Xu looked young for his age, his deputy Captain Zhu looked about 14. He was small with a round face and wire glasses that reminded me of Joe 90. New to the job, he made a vague effort to look like he had some kind of role in the prison and spent his first few weeks standing around trying hard to look busy. His uniform fitted him and was better kept than his colleagues', but after a few weeks he tired of pretending to have a proper job and settled into the idle routine of chain-smoking and eating sunflower seeds. Unlike Xu, he spoke a few words of English and occasionally managed a smile before checking himself and withdrawing back into his lost-adolescent persona.

Eighth Brigade was one of ten massive concrete cell blocks surrounded by thirty-foot-high walls with gun turrets and razor wire. Each building had six floors with two parallel wings on each landing, which had about forty-five cells each. The cells were five by seven feet, with heavy-duty barred doors that were opened at 5.30 every morning and locked up between six and nine in the evening depending on the season. In the sweltering summer months, the doors were kept open longer and industrial fans were placed between every other cell to circulate the oppressively stagnant air. The whole place was built out of concrete and steel, and in the summer months became like a furnace that never really cooled down. In the winter it was unbelievably cold, and most people got frostbite on their earlobes, which cracked, turned blue and left ruby-red globules of blood like ear studs. We were given prison-issue padded grey jackets that kept out the worst of the cold, but the only warm place on the wing was the shower area, with its huge tanks of boiling water.

The washing area had another attraction. By standing on a water pipe, it was possible to climb up and see out of the window; but this was no ordinary window: it provided a tiny glimpse of the outside world. By looking across the outbuildings and over the prison wall, you could see people going about their daily business down below. It seemed strange that life was carrying on all around you, and less than 50 yards away. The window at the other end of the shower area had an even better view of the city, and you could see Shanghai's famous tower that resembles a spaceship. Needless to say, looking out of these, or any other windows, for that matter, was forbidden. I'd been warned not to climb up on the pipes and look out when Chinese prisoners were around, but before long I was informed someone had written a report about my offence.

Report-writing was the bane of all prison life, and nothing could be done without writing about it first. If you had a complaint, you had to write a report. There was no point trying to talk to a guard unless you'd written one. Even the most trivial matters had to be put in writing. If you wanted a new tube of toothpaste, you had to write a report or you wouldn't get it. Generally the reports would sit around in the guards' office for days before they bothered to read them. Chinese prisoners had to write 'thinking reports', in which they were expected to inform the authorities of their general mental state and that of those around them. These reports were considered crucial to the reform of the prisoners and were expected to be self-critical, personal appraisals about the individual's view of his crime and what he was doing to repent. They were also an opportunity to gain brownie points by grassing up any other prisoner who might, or might not, have shown 'bad' thinking. It was a report like this that had mentioned my crime of looking out of the shower window, and I was called to a meeting with one of my first Chinese friends, San Peiwa.

San Peiwa had decided to call himself John, and was one of the best English speakers in the brigade. He was an articulate, thoughtful, intelligent man in his early 30s, and was well respected by both prisoners and guards. I liked him immediately, and we spent many hours talking in my first weeks in the jail. John was from Sichuan Province, and had done nine and a half years of an eleven-year sentence for what I guess would be called manslaughter. As a teenager he'd been a soldier in the People's Liberation Army, and was part of the ill-fated 1979 invasion of Vietnam, where he'd killed a Vietnamese civilian. Some years later he was summoned to Shanghai to stand trial in a war crimes tribunal, and, assuming it was some kind of formality to improve the frosty relations between the two countries, he went along. Unlike the rest of us, he'd never had to do time on remand in a detention centre; rather, he turned up in court of his own free will, having been told by his former commanding officer that there was nothing to worry about. At the end of his day in court he discovered that rather than taking the train back to his family in Chengdu, he was to start a decade-long prison sentence in the largest jail in China.

The years in prison had been kind to John, and he looked well, with a calm, laid-back demeanour and friendly smile. He was one of the very few Chinese I've met who knew anything about, or had any interest in, his country's Daoist tradition, and we spent many hours talking about the respective philosophies of Laozi and Confucius. Like many Chinese, he was affectionately tactile and would run his fingers through my body hair while we talked. Chinese guys often held hands and walked around in a brotherly embrace, and there was none of the homophobic suspicion that makes so many Western men appear emotionally stranded from each other. They had more in common with men in the Islamic world than in the West.

John sat down next to me and began to explain what the problem was. Somebody had written a report about my climbing onto the water tank and looking out of the window. Because I was a new prisoner, John said, I would only receive a warning this time, but if it happened again he would have to beat me up. I was stunned.

'But you're my friend,' I protested.

'Yes, I like you, and I like the time we spend together, but you don't understand Ti Lan Qiao. This is a Monkey House, and if the captain says you're breaking the rules, we have to discipline you.'

'"We"?'

'Yes, him, him and me.' He pointed to a couple of other guys sitting across the table.

'So let me get this straight. If I look out of the washroom window again, you and those guys over there will take me into a cell and beat me up.'

'That's correct.' He smiled. 'Just don't break the rules and we can be friends.'

I talked about the meeting to Gareth, who was typically cynical about the subject.

'Don't trust any of these bastards. Even the friendly ones will stab you in the back. I'm no racist, but these Chinks are a bunch of slimy, scheming, two-faced cunts.'

I knew Gareth was right when he said he wasn't a racist; after all, his wife was half-Uighur. But prison rarely let you see the best in people and it could provoke these kinds of outbursts. For me, the Chinese guys were the best thing about Ti Lan Qiao, and I was becoming attached to my new friends. Even so, my conversation with John had made the situation crystal clear. If push came to shove, the Chinese – through no fault of their own – could not be fully trusted. They could never side with a foreigner against their own. To do so would be suicide, and after that most of my friendships with Chinese became more superficial, as both parties understood the limits and boundaries of the relationship. Ultimately we were from different planets, and there was no point pretending otherwise.

An exception to this rule would come in the form of a small, silver-toothed hunchback named Zhu Go Hua. His disability set him apart from the other inmates, and he seemed as bemused by the situation he found himself in as the foreigners. Shuffling around in a world of his own, he had no friends and cared less to make any. While most Chinese self-censored themselves in conversation with foreigners, Zhu Go Hua spoke his mind freely, oblivious to whether anyone else was listening. Within weeks I decided to nickname him Xiao Zhonguo (small or young Chinese), after my own nickname, Xiao Yinguo (small or young English), which had now been adopted by pretty much the whole wing. As well as his disability, Zhu suffered from chronic headaches and was often seen slumped in the corner with his head in his hands. I started to give him head massages whenever I saw him in one of these states, which he greatly appreciated, rubbing his head against my chest as I set my fingers to work on his throbbing brain.

My new friend was serving 15 years for manslaughter, having stabbed his former boss on a building site after an altercation over unpaid wages. He claimed that a mob of irate workers had attacked the man, killing him, and when the police arrived he was the only one caught with a knife. Because he spoke no English it was hard to work out the details of his case, and other foreigners had told me that Chinese rarely told the truth about their crimes. I didn't really care what he had done anyway; he made me laugh, had a cheery smile and thought as little of the mindless reform indoctrination as the foreigners did.

Although all the brigades were subject to the same Reform Through Education programmes, some were expected to take part in extra activities, like singing patriotic songs. The lifers' block opposite us had to sing one of these songs every day before supper, and you could hear it booming across the prison, and probably beyond its walls. The song was a typically self-aggrandising Communist Party mantra, which repeated over and over the lines:

No Communist Party,
No New China.

Though we were forbidden to talk to anybody in the lifers' block, there were daily opportunities to make contact during the slopping-out duties, known by the foreigners as 'shitbuckets'. After lunch, a handful of Chinese would carry up to four buckets each down to one of the sewage holes in the courtyard below the brigade, and the foreigners, who specifically requested emptying their own, joined them. The smell was disgusting and made you want to heave, but every bucket's contents looked identical due to the diet we all ate, which seemed to make it more tolerable. Some buckets had much more in them than others, and you could tell how many people there were in a cell from the amount of shit you chucked down the hole. The sewers often flooded and the waste would ooze out of the drains into giant puddles of poo, which unfortunate prisoners in wellington boots would wade into and unblock. The shitbuckets routine was supposed to be done in shifts, with each landing going separately, but they often overlapped because everyone was eager to get the nasty business over with as soon as possible, due to the vile effluvia that it created. This became a daily opportunity to get out of the cell block for a few minutes and made it possible to have a quick chat with some of the other prisoners from different brigades.

I got to know a couple of Pakistani guys who were doing eight years for traveller's cheque scams. One of them, Khalid, a well-spoken middle-class Punjabi, became a friend, and we exchanged books and magazines, which we stuffed up our jumpers and passed through the bars. Khalid's Chinese prison experience was a good deal different from our own, since Pakistanis were not given foreigner status and were expected to blend in with the locals, wearing the standard grey-striped uniform and working in the brigade workshops. The ground floor of his building, 3rd Brigade, was a huge jade-carving workshop where dozens of inmates sat with mini power tools that resembled electric toothbrushes fashioning everything from fire-breathing dragons to bamboo-chewing pandas to sell to the tourist trade. I'd bought many such trinkets myself, and like most naive tourists had imagined they'd been made by elderly craftsman with wispy beards and hand files. In fact, they were being made by prisoners earning less than £1.50 per month, a form of slavery long since outlawed by the international community.

In spite of their government's proclamations about human-rights issues in China, American companies made the most of this illegal exploitation, and workers from the lifers' brigade were often seen slaving long into the night making baseball caps for export to California. Each brigade specialised in a certain trade, and in the daytime the prison resembled a vast live-in factory. There was a whole brigade dedicated to engineering, where officers would get their cars fixed, while others specialised in woodwork, metalwork, textiles and so on. Our own brigade was sometimes called the intellectual wing and specialised in electronics. The workshops were always piled high with fridges, TVs, videos and anything else that needed fixing, and officers from other parts of the prison would frequently arrive with a radio or some other appliance under their arm.

It was strange to think we were part of the intellectual brigade, since many of the inmates couldn't read or write their own language, but upstairs a number of highly articulate and well-spoken prisoners were given white-collar work like translating and copywriting. Many had spent more than a decade inside for criticising the government, though none wanted to elaborate on what this actually meant. Some were called *liumeng*, which meant 'sexual hooligan', and was a catch-all phrase that covered anything from sexual promiscuity to paedophilia. There was still a law that carried the death penalty for anyone caught having an affair with the wife of an officer of the People's Liberation Army, and rumour had it that 'unnatural' (homosexual) activities carried a three-year prison term.

One of the friendliest English speakers the foreigners came into contact with was Mr Sun, a convicted rapist, and in any other situation a nasty piece of work. But in Ti Lan Qiao, Sun's crime set him apart from the main Chinese prisoners and thus made him useful to the foreigners. The genius of the officers was to make disliked prisoners like Sun into trustees who could be relied upon to spy upon other prisoners, particularly the top flight of inmates who effectively ran the jail. The logic behind this clever system was that hated prisoners had no particular friends or allegiances within the general population and so needed protection from the guards. In return they would be the eyes and ears of the officers, and every inmate knew it. This worked in the foreigners' favour when things were heavy with the Chinese, because unlike just about any other prisoner, Sun would not be afraid to side with a foreigner against his own. A thin, wiry man with a sickly smile, he looked like the archetypal snitch in countless prison movies, but to the foreigners he was a useful ally.

While inmates like Sun were the eyes and ears of the guards, the more thuggish prisoners were appropriated by the guards to keep the general population in line. A new arrival prone to fighting and rule-breaking would be severely punished, which usually meant being beaten up by a gang of prisoners and left for days cross-legged, staring at the cell wall with hands cuffed behind the back. Repeat offenders would be sent downstairs to the punishment wing, where they'd be regularly beaten and abused by the guards and trustees, sometimes with hands cuffed behind their backs and the much feared hood over their heads. This resembled a falconer's hood with a couple of nostril holes and an opening for food. It strapped on the back of the head and left the prisoner in permanent darkness, while his friends had to hand-feed him. Larry had come back from his own stint in the punishment wing with horror stories of human-rights violations and brutality. The officer in charge of the landing was a drunk called Peng, who was known to arrive unannounced in the middle of the night and attack prisoners with his electric baton.

Of all the various punishments available to the guards, the most

effective, perhaps, were the group punishments that invari̶̶̶̶̶̶
any kind of trouble. If there was a fight the whole wing
punished, and every prisoner knew it. Consequently, the ̶̶̶̶
responsible would have to make a series of grovelling apolo̶̶̶̶
everyone on the wing for letting down his fellow inmates. This inv̶
writing the obligatory report, followed by a self-criticism speech t̶̶at
both officers and prisoners would attend. Prisoners would be invited to
quiz the wrongdoer on why he'd let down the brigade, and as everyone
sat and listened, he'd have to stand up and be humiliated. The senior
officer present would then inform the whole wing there'd be no TV
for a week, or worse, that family visiting time would be curtailed for
that month. Needless to say the prisoner would find himself deeply
unpopular, and it would be many weeks before he could hold his head
up on the wing. This self-policing system was remarkably effective, and
meant that every prisoner had a vested interest in keeping his fellow
inmates out of trouble. Subsequently, after a fight, the wing was never
more peaceful, as every inmate was on high alert to prevent any kind
of conflict from recurring.

I found this system fascinating. Chinese Communism, with its rituals
of diary-writing and public confession, was acting in the way that the
Church formally did, but had taken on a general, secularised form within
the prison. The guards had adopted the idea of confession in much the
same way as pre-modern Western societies used religion. Individuals
were encouraged to feel guilty for breaking the rules, while their actions
and consciences were determined by their social relationships to each
other and the state, creating a uniquely Chinese form of power. And it
wasn't just prisoners who'd broken the rules who were required to write
self-criticisms. All prisoners kept a diary that was continually updated
to report any new developments in their inner worlds. An inmate who'd
recently discovered a new fault that he, or a fellow prisoner, family
member and so on, possessed was singled out for high praise. If it led
to someone else being incriminated, they might be considered for a
sentence reduction.

'What are you writing about today?'

I was talking to a guy called Zhang, a fraudster from Singapore
serving 12 years.

'When I was a young boy, I stole a piece of fruit from a neighbour's tree. Now I am writing to thank the cadres for their help.'

Zhang was an intelligent man in his 50s with wiry grey hair and plump red cheeks. He was considerably wealthier than most of the prisoners, spoke a little English and was usually friendly to foreigners. He was involved in importing plastics to Singapore from China and had been caught out by bribing the wrong person. Now he was trawling through his past, searching for past crimes to confess to.

'Don't you run out of crimes? After all, you've been writing these reports every week for many years now,' I asked.

'Oh, it's not true,' he said, smiling. 'We just make them up.'

I wondered what my own 'confessions' would be about if I was forced to sit down week after week, year after year, recording every transgression. I wasn't sure I'd have to resort to lying about mine.

With the exception of foreigners, every prisoner had two other numbers on their ID cards. If a prisoner went missing, the person with their number on their ID card would be held responsible; therefore all prisoners were responsible for knowing the exact whereabouts of two other prisoners, which made it easier for the guards to keep track of everyone. This was rarely necessary because with the exception of the number one and a couple of his cronies, no prisoners ever left the wing except for the once-a-month ninety-minute exercise period. The guards had no real work to do, because the minute details of everyone's life – both in terms of their actions and their mental state – were constantly being recorded, not only by their colleagues, but by themselves, too.

Most offenders were sent to the punishment wing for a short sharp shock, and on their return were quickly promoted to their new role of policing the wing. Within weeks, they'd be the ones beating up the new arrivals and would get to eat their meals on the number one table. The week after my arrival, a guy from the countryside came in to start a four-year sentence for theft. He was from Hunan Province, famous for its greasy food and being the birthplace of Chairman Mao. Hunan, as the foreigners nicknamed him, was from a peasant background and like so many of his countrymen had come to Shanghai to find work to support his family back at home. He looked scruffy compared to the Shanghainese lads, and his teeth had a greenish-yellow hue, as if he'd adopted Mao's foul habit of cleaning his teeth with a finger and green-tea leaves. Under Mao, rural people had been favoured over town dwellers, whose education and individuality were causes for suspicion. But under Deng Xiaoping the tables had turned, and men like Hunan seemed a bit simple-minded and out of place in Ti Lan Qiao: like a country bumpkin from the West Country trying to cut it with the Chaps in Parkhurst. Needless to say, the Shanghai boys considered him a halfwit. A useful idiot whose hard work and obedience could be put to good use.

During his first week he was subjected to the usual abuse that most prisoners were expected to put up with. This involved having to sit on a mini chair about a foot high while being 'interviewed' by the top prisoners, who were sitting on normal-sized chairs. Generally, there would be at least one of the more thuggish inmates present who would intimidate the newcomer by kicking him and slapping his face and head while he was attempting to answer the questions. I felt sorry for Hunan, mainly because he was the first of many Chinese I was to see treated this way, but also because I felt guilty that I was not being treated similarly, even though I was frequently breaking the rules. A few days later he was being picked on again, and this time he was confined to his cell for days on end with his head against the wall. I was outraged at this, and every time I walked past the cell I'd throw in sweets and chicken legs to try and cheer him up. We became friends and for the next few weeks had some laughs together.

About six weeks later, I noticed Hunan abusing the latest batch of prisoners in much the same way as he'd been treated on his arrival. A few days afterwards, he was at the forefront of a mob that had decided to take another new prisoner into his cell and beat him up. I'd vaguely got to know the prisoner getting the hiding, and I guessed he knew how to look after himself. He was twice the size of most of the other inmates and wasn't the type to be pushed around. A smack dealer from Shanghai, he'd been caught with sixty grams of heroin but had somehow ended up with a ten-year sentence that was lenient in a country with a mandatory death sentence for possession of more than fifty grams. Had he been from outside the city he would most likely have got the bullet, but there were often exceptions made for local people from the 'right' families. The only English word he seemed to know was Motorola, referring to his phone pager that he'd used on the outside to ply his trade. Such luxuries were rare in China at the time, and may have explained his elevated status in the criminal community and thus the relatively short sentence. After a few weeks, he was transferred to a work farm with a different kind of regime and seemed happy to be getting out of Ti Lan Qiao. As for Hunan, I took an intense dislike to him after that and we spent the next two years avoiding each other.

Not all prisoners were subjected to this kind of intimidation on arrival at the jail. After I'd been at Ti Lan Qiao a few months, a new prisoner arrived called Wang Jun. He was tall for a Chinese, with thin lips and a short-back-and-sides haircut. From the start he seemed to have a higher status than the other prisoners and was immediately promoted to the role of trustee. He'd been given an 11-year sentence for stabbing someone, but like most Chinese he would not elaborate on the details of his case. While the other prisoners he arrived with were going through the demeaning introduction process, Wang sat around looking bored. Rumour had it he was from a well-to-do family with Party connections, and both the inmates and guards treated him with a good deal of respect. When the prisoners went off to work, he was left to hang around on the wing with no particular role. When he got bored with sitting on his arse all day, minor tasks were assigned to him to give him something to do. We came to the conclusion that his main job was spying on us.

Gao Zhengguo, our number one prisoner, became a useful ally when I realised I could twist him round my little finger. He spoke a few words of very bad English, quite liked foreigners, and it became obvious within days that he fancied me. Strictly speaking Chinese were not allowed to talk to foreigners, but the number one and his mates could bend the rules to suit themselves. Gao made a point of watching me shower and telling me I was beautiful, and when I mentioned I'd studied shiatsu massage in Japan he asked me to be his personal masseur. I was quite happy to do this since I enjoyed it and it gave me status with the Chinese, who never crossed anyone who was mates with the number one prisoner. My cosy relationship with Gao would not last, but for my first few weeks in Ti Lan Qiao I could do pretty much as I pleased, and I made the most of it, lying in bed long after the wake-up call and crossing the red line to look out of the cell-block window. The red line was a faded stripe painted on the floor at the end of the corridor, and by crossing it you could make it to a window that looked across a courtyard to 3rd Brigade, where the Pakistanis were. Captain Xu warned me that I could be shot by the guards for crossing this line, as it could be seen as an escape attempt. No one had ever escaped from Ti Lan Qiao. The nearest thing to an escape had taken place months earlier, when a prisoner had failed to return from home leave after a long sentence. He had not even gone on the run, but had simply stayed at home with his family until the police arrived to take him back to jail; nonetheless, he received a three-year extension to his sentence.

Before my arrival the foreigners had campaigned long and hard to increase the frequency of the exercise periods, and eventually the guards had decided we'd be permitted to have a ninety-minute session once every ten days. This involved going downstairs after breakfast and running around a concrete yard while a guard watched over us. Sometimes we'd get a football game going with the Chinese that would get progressively more violent and often end in a fight. Usually I'd take the opportunity to catch a bit of natural sunlight and walk around the yard playing a harmonica. The guards would look down from their watchtowers with bemusement as I traipsed from one end of the yard to the other, blowing bluesy riffs into the air. If it rained the guards would refuse to go outside, so in the winter months these exercise periods were often cancelled and weeks would go by without our leaving the cell block. When this happened, tension grew on the wing and problems between Chinese and foreigners became more common, with Larry and Tommy invariably coming to blows.

Early in my stay at Ti Lan Qiao, I was asked to take part in the jail karaoke contest. I was stunned to hear such a thing even existed. I was still reeling from my time in the detention centre and it would have been unimaginable to entertain such an idea only weeks earlier. Some of the prisoners on our wing had heard me playing their favourite song, 'Jambalaya (On the Bayou)', on my guitar and had put me forward for the contest. Gareth was also taking part so the two of us got to go to the Cross Building, a relatively plush complex across from 8th Brigade. I was confident I'd impress the Chinese, but my self-assurance was misplaced when I realised quite how much my guitar-playing ability and voice had withered away after eight months doing neither. I'd been to dozens of karaoke bars in Japan and always had a good sing-song, but their karaoke machines were state of the art, with excellent microphones and sophisticated software that automatically gauged which key you were singing in and adjusted the machine accordingly. The Shanghai Municipal Prison karaoke machine was rather less hi-tech and didn't even have lyric prompts to let you know when to start singing. I'd brought my guitar along, as I've always felt slightly uncomfortable singing without one, but I still managed to play in a different key from the soundtrack. Even when I got the hang of it my voice was shot to bits, and I started coughing and spluttering my way through the Hank Williams tune, to the amusement of the Chinese, who were pretty good in comparison. Gareth, who was a better singer than me anyway, had had plenty of practice and did a decent rendition of another Chinese favourite, 'Rivers of Babylon', to great acclaim. I felt a complete fool, but it was still fun to get out of the cell block for an hour or so. To my horror, the event was filmed by a policeman with a video camera. Presumably the tape of this embarrassing episode is lying in a drawer somewhere in Shanghai jail to this day.

The karaoke competition was my first meeting with members of 9th Brigade, the women's unit of the jail. A granite-faced female officer led a troupe of 12 girls into the hall to relative indifference on the part of the male prisoners. In a British jail the arrival would have no doubt been heralded with a cacophony of wolf whistles, but in Ti Lan Qiao they were largely ignored. Some of the girls were quite pretty, having been hand-picked to take part in the numerous events that involved visits from local dignitaries. The women's brigade was widely believed to be worse than the men's jail, partly because it had no views of the outside. It was situated in the very centre of the jail, and every window was shuttered like the detention centre I'd been in. Most of the prisoners would spend years without sunshine, and the discipline was said to be stricter than the men's. Rumour had it there was a solitary foreign prisoner in the building, a German girl who'd been busted with five kilos of hash in Beijing. I can't imagine what her experience of Ti Lan Qiao was like. I'd seen their building when walking to 8th Brigade on my arrival and was struck by how depressing it looked from the outside. There were around

500 inmates serving similar terms to the men for various crimes ranging from theft to murder. Some were prostitutes passing through on their way to reform workhouses for fallen women, while many were inside for drug offences. Like the men, the women had access to extra food from the prison shop, but were not allowed to buy bananas or salami sausages unless they were chopped up into small pieces. Presumably the authorities felt such foodstuffs would interrupt the women's rehabilitation.

In October 1994, we were taken across the prison to another brigade for a Reduction Meeting. This was the most eagerly awaited occasion for all prisoners and perhaps the last opportunity Mark would have to be released before completing his sentence. He'd served four years of a four-and-a-half-year sentence, so if he was going to get any time off it would be today. Sentence reductions were loosely linked to merit points, though favoured prisoners seemed to get them regardless. As a foreigner Mark was not involved in the merit system, but had been led to believe he was eligible for early release anyway. Since I'd arrived in Ti Lan Qiao he'd spent much of his time in hospital with pneumonia, and I'd missed having him around to talk to. The hospital sounded like the punishment wing with beds, with many prisoners chained 24 hours a day. He'd become friends with an attractive nurse who worked there and actually preferred it to being on our wing on 8th Brigade.

As the first foreign prisoner to be sent to Ti Lan Qiao, Mark had spent his first year alone with only Chinese for friends. He spoke decent Mandarin and had actually had a much better time in the jail before any other foreigners turned up. Before, he had been left to his own devices and had managed to get by without too much hassle, but when the others arrived the atmosphere changed and relations with the Chinese soured. As a solitary foreigner in a jail of 5,000 inmates he'd been looked after and respected, but the *petit* feuds and threats of violence that came with the new prisoners had made the hospital seem like a pleasant break. Now we sat on our tiny plastic stools waiting to discover if today would be his last day in China. The judge began to read out the names of prisoners who would be getting time off their sentences. They stepped forward and thanked the judge. Within minutes it was all over, and Mark's face dropped to the floor. Out of more than three hundred prisoners, some twenty-five reductions had been handed out, ranging from six months to a year. The lucky individuals received a certificate, but there was nothing for Mark.

I wasn't expecting anything, and Mark was still just six months away from release, but others from our group were bitter. None of the foreigners had reached the halfway point of their sentences and, with the exception of me, had many years ahead of them. Even if they'd got a year each it would have given them something to look forward to, but not one single day off for any foreigners. Yet just as we got up to leave, Mark was called aside and left through another door. By the time we got back to 8th Brigade, he was packing his bags and was out of the door within minutes. I was sorry to see him go. He'd been a good mate to me in the little time we'd spent together and had been the only person who was vaguely neutral in the feuds between Tommy and the rest. From now on I'd have to tread carefully between the two groups and the bad blood that was never far from the surface.

Many inmates kept tiny insects as pets, which they carried everywhere in small plastic boxes that they made in the workshops. No bigger than a small matchbox, some had clear Perspex lids so the pets could be seen munching on the pieces of fruit they were fed. Some looked like very small crickets, while others had beetles. Occasionally they'd get them out and put them on the tabletops to hop about together, and no doubt a few cans of tinned pineapple were gambled on these races. I'd had many pets as a kid, so when Rosie and I got together it wasn't long before we found our first furry friend.

We bought a chipmunk from a guy on the side of the road in Goa. It was our first family pet and we named him Cosmo. He was still a baby, at least we thought it was a he, and we were his mum and dad. I put him in the cigarette pocket of my baggy Balinese shirt and he curled up like a baby kangaroo in its mother's pouch. Being hippies, we couldn't countenance the idea of putting him in a cage, so our house became his adventure playground. We found some branches in the garden and roped them together to make elaborate climbing frames with banana-leaf slides. His paws were quite sharp, with tiny talons that enabled him to hang upside down in any piece of fabric and fall asleep. If we went out to a beach cafe, Cosmo would come along, bobbing up and down in my pocket as we rode our motorbikes through the paddy fields.

Before we'd met, Rosie had planned to go off on a trip to Kerala with her friend Nadia. Since we'd barely been out of each other's sight since getting together, it was a good opportunity to give each other a bit of space. To shorten the time apart we decided to go on the first leg of the trip together, after which I'd return alone before meeting them back in Goa after their jaunt on the backwater riverboats down south. Hampi was a lengthy bus and train ride inland, and had a famous temple where visitors from Goa liked to visit to see the 'real' India. I'd spent many months travelling around different parts of India on previous visits to the country but had never been to Hampi before. It was famous for its ancient ruins and massive, erratic stone boulders that dotted the landscape, as well as its temples to the monkey god Hanuman and other Hindu deities.

It was still dark when it was time to leave, and Cosmo was nowhere to be found. We looked all over the house and shook his favourite sleeping spot – a large green blanket where he liked to hang upside down like a bat, snoozing. We'd made him a little house out of cardboard, sawdust and screwed-up balls of newspaper. We took it to pieces and tossed the contents across the floor in the hope that the little mite was kipping in the debris of the *Times of India*. Nothing.

Finally we gave up. Cosmo had left the building, and that was that. We were gutted, and felt our first attempt at parenthood had been a failure. With the bus departure looming, we took a taxi to Mapusa and boarded the bus to Hubballi, which was the nearest train station to Goa at the time. The bus trip was around six hours and wound through the hot, humid lowlands away from the cooling ocean breeze. After a couple of hours the bus started climbing into the hills and the temperature dropped, so we took out our travel blanket and laid it across our laps. Rosie flinched, and looked at me as she let out a ticklish giggle and pulled back the blanket. Cosmo was lying in it with bleary eyes, looking rather annoyed at the intrusion into his sleeping patterns. We took some fruit out of our bag, and he sat up on his hind legs gnawing the piece of apple in his paws. Other passengers on the bus crowded round to see the tiny stowaway, but being a shy little fellow he scrambled up my arm and into my shirt pocket for another nap.

When we finally got to Hampi the Hindu festival was in full flow, and tens of thousands of pilgrims had descended on the small temple town. After checking into the hotel, Nadia produced a tab of acid with a print of the Buddha on the front, which we split three ways before heading into town. The temple was packed and the people swaying through its courtyards and walkways resembled a football crowd. Our feet barely touched the ground as the heaving masses carried us along with them in their trance-like ecstasy. Cosmo got squashed, too, and leapt out of my pocket onto the floor, and within a split second I heard a terrible squeal. I went into a squat to find the poor little critter, but the crowd would not let up and his squeal stopped. I was convinced he'd finally gone to that great chipmunk heaven in the sky when a woman screamed. Cosmo had his tail trapped under the woman's foot and was desperately trying to claw his way up her leg. I yanked the lady's foot out of the way and put him back in my front pocket, which I shielded with my hand until we could get away from the festival.

'Maybe we should just find somewhere to let him go,' said Rosie wisely. 'I don't think he's going to live long in our care.'

'He's too young to fend for himself and wouldn't last long without us,' I said. 'Looks like we're going to have to stick together.'

We climbed a hillside above the town to get away from the crowds, and the acid was kicking in as the sun set, leaving a gorgeous peachy smear across the horizon. Just then two Indian lads came careering down the hillside behind us, shouting, laughing and waving their hands around their heads. One of them had a long stick with a huge wild honeycomb on the end, bees still whirling frantically around it.

'Eat, eat! Very delicious, very sweet.'

And so we did. And it was the best honey we'd ever tasted, the glistening, treacly goo dripping between our fingers as the sun went down. Even Cosmo came out for the occasion and licked our fingers before climbing back into his pouch for a doze.

The trip to Hampi was short and sweet, and then it was time for Rosie and Nadia to go to Kerala without me. I saw them off at the station, and the week we'd be apart felt more like a month. Cosmo and I took another train back to Goa and arrived in time for a party. I didn't really want to go, but neither did I want to sit around on my own missing Rosie. Tripped-out tourists gathered round to pet my new friend as we sat on bamboo mats at a chai shop under the stars. I had a couple of drinks, but avoided any psychedelics and headed home early, feeling exhausted from my long journey. Before I knew it, it was morning, and I was lying on a futon with all my clothes on. I walked out onto the porch as a schoolboy trundled past along a sandy track on his way to class. Then I remembered Cosmo, and I could feel his familiar body weight hanging in my shirt pocket. I reached in, but his body was cold as I pulled him out and laid him in the palm of my hand. Somehow, I'd rolled over in my sleep and squeezed all the life out of the little guy. I sat on the porch and wept like I hadn't done in years. Later a couple of friends came round to cheer me up, and we buried my pocket-sized pal under a banyan tree in the garden.

The Chinese prisoners in the lifers' block had found themselves a pet, too. A small, furry kitten. Rather than giving it a name and doing their best to look after the creature, they broke its legs and poured boiling water over it.

9

Coming Down From the Mountain

I'd been in Ti Lan Qiao for less than a year, but I'd already reached the halfway point of my sentence. The Chinese called this stage of the sentence 'coming down from the mountain'. The metaphor implied a relaxing stroll back down from the dizzying heights of arrest and incarceration, but it was not to be. Though in private I could consider the worst to be over, the fact that my colleagues had yet to reach their own personal peaks robbed me of my own sense of relief. Added to this was the post-New Year gloom that inevitably set in as the jail returned to normal, and the guards arranged a flurry of meetings to propose new ways of reforming the prisoners. This usually involved a purge of those who'd risen to the top of the existing order: a recurring feature of Mao's monocracy, in which the cream that had made its way to the top of the system was summarily reduced to scum at the bottom. The strategy had served the dictator well, enabling him to scupper the careers of those perceived to be a threat to his rule, replacing them with thuggish lackeys until their own day of judgement arrived and they, too, were sent to 'learn from the masses'. Two decades after his death, and three years after the Tiananmen Square massacre, the Party still employed similar tactics to purge itself of 'bad elements', while the reverberations could be felt throughout society as a whole.

Shanghai radio, which had aired a good selection of Western music, began to play traditional Chinese music after the Party warned against the creeping tide of 'bourgeois cultural imperialism'. There had been an American DJ on most weekday mornings, playing songs from bands like Smashing Pumpkins and many other US indie bands, which we listened to religiously. Suddenly it was replaced with 'wholesome' Chinese music that made our ears burn. Meanwhile the Elvis lookalike and ranting demagogue Warden Lai appeared with greater frequency on prison TV, delivering mordant sermons to his flock about the need for ever greater vigilance in the lofty pursuit of reform. A deluge of fawning missives followed as the Chinese cleansed themselves of barbarian tendencies, singing patriotic songs and marching for hours on end around the concrete compounds of the prison. Even Captain Xu, who was expert at keeping out of the way, had to turn up to work and look like he had something to do.

Given the casual manner in which the judiciary handed out death sentences, and the swift efficiency with which those sentences were executed, it came as little surprise that there were few genuinely heinous offenders in the prison. In a country where cigarette smugglers and fraudsters are regularly put to death, it followed that few murderers made it through the courts without getting a bullet through the back of the head. One such lucky person was Mr Zhao, a factory worker nearing the end of a fifteen-year sentence for strangling his wife. Like Mr Yin, who'd got eight years for torturing his wife, Mr Zhao was respected by the officers, who felt his wife had got what she deserved. While every other prisoner had to make grovelling apologies for their crimes, actively expressing repentance as part of their reform, Mr Zhao talked openly of his lack of remorse.

After our number one prisoner, Gao Zhengguo, was stripped of his title for passing letters to an inmate in the women's brigade, Mr Zhao had been given the job of keeping order on our landing. Though respected by most of the Chinese, the foreigners were wary of Mr Zhao, who made no secret of his dislike for our group and set about trying to bring us in line with the Chinese way of doing things. His first plan was attempting to get us to work alongside the other prisoners, a situation that we all dreaded. Larry refused to have anything to do with working on human-rights grounds. He argued, quite rightly, that the unpaid work was slave labour and contrary to international law. He'd made a point of logging the serial numbers on the boxes of prison-made sports clothes destined for the United States and was using his consul visits to highlight this illegal activity. The authorities were well aware of this, and in spite of Mr

Zhao's efforts the idea was quietly dropped. But our victory was short-lived, because within days Mr Zhao complained that foreigners used too much hot water and should take their showers with the Chinese in 3rd Brigade. From that day on we would make the twice-weekly walk across the prison to the main showers, which were located in the same building as the kitchens.

My first visit to the large concrete box was something of an adventure. It involved walking up a long staircase past the kitchens, which I'd never seen before. The foreigners had nicknamed the austere, industrial-sized concrete room 'Auschwitz'. More than one wing at a time would use the shower so it was an opportunity to meet some of the inmates we'd normally only see from a distance. In the winter the room was icy cold and we'd have to stand naked waiting for the archaic plumbing system to groan and splutter before the water came, which was often cold when it did. The trick was to get lathered up and rinsed as quickly as possible, otherwise you'd be left covered in soap suds and have to wait another three days to wash it off. Once I got the hang of it, I found it a pleasant enough break from the monotony of life on the wing. After all, we got to walk across the jail to a different building twice a week. Some of the other foreigners were less happy with the arrangement, and Gareth got into a fight with a couple of Chinese guys on our first trip to the new wash place. After writing a report to Captain Xu, it was decided that foreigners who wished to wash in the 8th Brigade washroom could do so as long as they only used one bowl of hot water. This was absurd since the bowls were barely large enough to get you wet, let alone rinsed; still, most of the foreigners stopped going to Auschwitz for their showers, while Jürgen and I continued to make the twice-weekly trek with the rest of the wing. Meanwhile, Mr Zhao was happy to have got his own back on our group after losing face over the issue of forced labour.

Another change came about when it was reported that I'd been seen talking to Pakistanis while doing the shitbuckets. It was decided that from that day on, foreigners would no longer get to empty their own buckets. Instead, a small team of Chinese prisoners would take care of the whole wing. Larry, who had a bad knee and hated having to traipse up and down the stairs every day, was happy, but the others were angry.

Emptying shitbuckets was a pretty odious task, but it was an important break from the monotony of life on the wing. It was 15 minutes of exercise and an opportunity to see another part of the jail. The location changed most days, depending on which drains were available, and sometimes we'd get a nice stroll through the courtyards to parts of the jail we'd otherwise never see. Although I wasn't the only foreigner who talked to prisoners from other wings, it was me who had been reported and consequently I was to blame for the loss of the privilege.

I was also under fire for communicating with McLoughlin, whom the other foreigners had not spoken to for months. I'd maintained from the start that while I understood he was prone to violent outbursts and was rather too friendly with some of the guards, I wished to remain neutral. For a while this had been easy enough, and Tommy was happy to ignore the other prisoners while chatting to me from time to time. But inevitably problems began to emerge when it was discovered that Tommy had access to our mail. He had friends in the intellectual wing who were responsible for translating not only our letters but also reports anybody wrote to the guards. We also had friends who were translators, as these people were often brought in to mediate between ourselves and the officers, and we soon learned that McLoughlin was regularly writing reports that were critical of our group. Meanwhile, Larry, who seemed to be permanently at war with the authorities, was at loggerheads with Captain Xu, who was refusing to send a letter he'd written to Shanghai People's Court demanding an appeal of his case. I was caught in the middle of all this hostility and it wasn't long before fists started flying. McLoughlin punched Larry in the face, and reports were written by both parties blaming the other.

I tried to keep a distance from the disputes, but it became an increasingly difficult position to maintain. In spite of the violence, I felt that McLoughlin had a more pragmatic approach to dealing with the situation than Larry, whose attitude did himself, and our group, no favours. It was all very well that he wanted to appeal his sentence, but it was pure fantasy to believe his combative feud with Captain Xu would advance his case. In truth it was a waste of time anyway, since the People's Court could never admit it had made any mistakes. Larry was banging his head against a wall. Tommy, on the other hand, had decided that the way forward was to 'go Chinese'. He began to consider himself a regular prisoner and took part in all the activities that the Chinese did. He volunteered to work and even learned 'patriotic' songs. We all thought he'd lost the plot, though I felt it was his estrangement from the foreigners' group that was exacerbating the problem.

The rise of Mr Zhao to number one prisoner status proved an unlikely bonus for Tommy, who found a kindred spirit in our loutish new leader. An expert at ingratiating himself with slippery authority figures, McLoughlin quickly moved to side with Mr Zhao against the other foreigners, heartily endorsing the Reform Through Labour issue as well as the hot-water dispute. As the only foreigner who worked, McLoughlin felt that he should get special privileges denied other prisoners, specifically an opportunity to obtain merit points, which in theory at least could lead to a sentence reduction. This put me in a very difficult position as I was the only foreigner who was still on speaking terms with the volatile Scotsman, and my loyalty towards the foreign group was put into question. As McLoughlin was actively involved in the anti-foreigner purge, I was forced to take sides with 'my people', the foreigners. Needless to say, from then on I became McLoughlin's enemy, and he threatened to have my girlfriend's parents' house in St John's Wood burned down by his gangster pals. This was cause for concern, because he was the only prisoner who had access to sending mail outside the usual channels – via a prisoner with a connection to a bent guard. Every so often he would remind me of this by singing the Rolling Stones song 'Play With Fire', particularly emphasising the line about the mother who owned a block in St John's Wood, with his own twisted modifications to the lyrics.

He continued to write thinking reports to Captain Xu, emphasising his progress over the rest of the foreigners and reporting misdemeanours we'd committed. What he didn't realise was that the translators were passing on information to both parties and we got to read what he was saying in his reports.

To underline the new order on the wing, Mr Zhao put McLoughlin in charge of the washroom, which required that he monitor the amount of hot water the other foreigners were using. This was ridiculous given the new 'bowl-of-water' rule for foreigners, and nobody had ever taken any interest in how much water was being used before. The latest rule was clearly designed to wind up the foreigners. The increasingly barmy Scotsman relished his new position and began to patrol the room at shower times, filling large vats with scalding water and joking how easy it would be to 'slip' and pour the contents over the naked occupants. Incensed by the new regime, the foreigners banded together to complain about the intimidating living conditions, but instead of writing a report that would be ignored by the guards, it was agreed that everyone would mention the situation at the next consular meeting, which was coming up. When the day arrived, a meeting was held to discuss the issue, and in the presence of the head warden and the consular staff from the British, German and American embassies, McLoughlin and Mr Zhao's racist and intimidating agenda was exposed. The plan worked: McLoughlin lost his job in the washroom and Mr Zhao lost interest in humiliating the foreign unit.

Not to be outdone by our small victory, Captain Xu announced that from now on the foreigners would have to fall in line with the rest of the prisoners and take part in Reform Through Education classes. Captain Xu spoke no English and may well have been illiterate (all his paperwork was done for him by prisoners from the intellectual brigade), so when the big day arrived for the foreigners to begin their education, the task was passed on to the jovially ineffectual Captain Mai. Mai spoke very little English, but brought in Jin Feng, the elderly lifer from the brainy wing, whose English was reasonably coherent even if his translation skills were haphazard and prone to vague meanderings.

Jin Feng was a *liumeng*, or sexual hooligan, and had been in and out of prison since the '60s. We never worked out what his crimes had been, but he'd grown up around foreigners in the foreign concessions before the war. The son of a Christian pastor, he'd been educated at a Christian school, where he'd learned to dance the rumba, tango and waltz. It wasn't hard to see why he'd fallen foul of the Communist system, being both a Christian and prone to 'bourgeois' Western habits. He'd even given himself a Western name: Joseph King. He was tall for a Chinese and had been something of a dandy in his earlier years, given to wearing Western blazers and cravats at a time when most Chinese were wearing blue or green Mao suits. He reminded me of the bellhop I'd met on the morning of my arrest, whose cultured manner had singled him out for persecution.

The text we were to study was the Chinese Law, a sprawling tome that supposedly protected the rights of the people who lived under its edicts. It was peppered with obscure caveats and fuzzy interpretations of buzzwords like 'democratic' and 'human rights', but the classes became an occasionally fascinating insight into the murky legal quagmire that was Chinese law. This provided an opportunity for the foreigners with legal issues to pursue their own agendas, while the hopelessly inept Captain Mai looked like a man drowning under the barrage of angry questions. Typically he would announce through the interpreter, 'Every person has a right to see a lawyer,' at which point everyone would burst out laughing in his face until it turned from red to purple as he pulled out a handkerchief to wipe the sweat from his brow. 'Every person has the right to appeal his sentence!' he muttered sheepishly as we rolled in the aisles giggling. Occasionally he'd drop a bombshell: 'The Chinese people's police have a right to confiscate the property of some criminals!' and we began to speculate how many people had had their homes stolen by bent coppers.

I couldn't help but feel sorry for Mai; he didn't want to take the class any more than we wanted to attend it. It was difficult to work out whether he believed much of the material himself. He'd been in the jail long enough to know that whenever someone came in with a death sentence, their right to appeal was little more than a formality. Miscarriages of justice were unheard of because it was inconceivable that the state could have made a mistake in the first place. The innocent minority were meant to show the same repentance in the eyes of the powers above as the guilty majority. While the Chinese were forced to reconcile themselves to their fate, the foreigners could dispute their treatment and speak out. Mai had never been in a situation where an individual, let alone an entire group of prisoners, could contradict his point of view. For us, it was an important victory. We'd escaped the crucial factor in the Chinese prisoners' enslavement: their own capitulation to the state ideology.

But we were privileged; we lived outside the Maoist bubble that still engulfed much of the nation. Captain Xu knew this well, which is why he was eager to pass the job on to anyone he could find. He knew that the bumbling, well-meaning Mai would be able to take flak from the infidels, and he probably had a few laughs with his mates about it. Perhaps they'd taken bets on how long the classes would last, because Xu had long since realised that the foreigners couldn't begin to understand the notion of repentance as the Chinese were made to know it. He'd told me to my face, 'You don't belong here.' And he was right. We were a disruptive influence on the smooth running of his wing. The language barrier was the tip of the iceberg; beneath it lay a chilling history of fear and terror.

Though originally scheduled as a bi-weekly, four-hour gathering, the increasingly rowdy meetings quickly became a ninety-minute, once-a-week opportunity for the foreigners to vent their spleens about the atrocious legal limbo that the law had left them in. Before long the meetings withered away to nothing, though Captain Xu announced with typical fanfare at a work-unit meeting that the foreigners had made good progress with their education reform. Then Mai delivered the news we'd been dreading: from now on the foreigners would be required to write thinking reports.

The idea that one is required to abase oneself and constantly repent belongs to a pre-modern religious age long abandoned in the West. But to the Chinese it had become quite normal. They didn't do it because they believed in it, and they certainly didn't do it because they liked it. It had been a feature of Chinese life since the formative years of Mao's tyranny in the caves of Yan'an in the 1930s. Everybody willingly subjected themselves to it because they knew that they could be next. Even the top brass in the Communist Party and Red Army were purged successively until the dictator's death in 1976. I'd seen people weep before his waxwork cadaver at the giant mausoleum in Tiananmen Square. Were they weeping for him? Or for the tens of millions of their countrymen who'd died as a result of his monstrous ego? Maybe they wanted to see him in the flesh, having been denied the dubious privilege during his notoriously secretive life, during which he rarely ventured out of his luxurious palaces. But his legacy had lived on in the form of thinking reports, and everybody had to write them. So the Chinese would do what they were told, otherwise the oppressive state apparatus would crush them underfoot like cockroaches on the hard stone floors of the prison block.

But to us it seemed like the first step on a slippery slope towards our loss of independence, not to mention self-respect. Nobody could see any sense in getting involved in it. Nobody except Tommy. It came as little surprise to the rest of us that he would volunteer to do it. It was well known that he'd been doing it for a long time off his own bat. Everybody was furious. 'A chain is only as strong as its weakest link,' said Gareth bitterly. He was right, but I could see Tommy's rationale for doing it. The guy had 15 years, and the warders had told him that if he played the game he'd get his sentence reduced. As far as he was concerned, he was doing the sensible thing. I could see both sides of the argument, but was more sympathetic to the rest of the guys' view that we were best off not getting involved in the system. Also, it was clear that Tommy's separation from the group had taken its toll on his mind. He was becoming too Chinese for his own good. As usual, Larry was at the other end of the spectrum and refused point-blank to be a part of it. But, as I saw it, his 15-year term was destroying his mind, too. His health was poor, but he insisted on doing anything he could to stop the guards from helping him. His strategy for coping with the burden of his sentence had failed miserably, and in spite of his stubbornness he increasingly looked like a broken man. Jürgen and Ludwig were no more enthusiastic about the prospect of writing the self-criticism reports, but felt that if it got the Chinese off our backs it was worth the effort. Ultimately we didn't have much choice, so we all swallowed our pride and began writing the same grovelling letters as the rest of the prisoners.

For me, it was no big deal to write a few hundred words of bullshit once in a while to placate the guards; in fact, I quite enjoyed it. Besides, I wouldn't be getting any time off my sentence anyway, so it made no difference what I wrote about. My first report was about pandas and how I hoped the Chinese law protected their animal rights.

'You don't understand,' said Mai, 'you're supposed to write about your crime.'

'But I haven't done anything wrong, and anyway, pandas are more important than foreigners carrying a bit of dope about.'

For the next report, I wrote how happy I was that the Chinese government were having a crackdown on Pakistani falcon smugglers who were stealing the birds from China to supply the lucrative trade in Saudi Arabia.

Captain Mai eventually stopped caring what I wrote, but I carried on doing the bare minimum because he had a job to do and we all had to play the game. He was also the only officer who seemed to care about our welfare, and once even bought me some medicine from outside the jail in his own time. In the world of *Porridge* he was our very own Mr Barraclough, and I appreciated his voluntary acts of kindness.

The reform meetings brought a bit of levity to the wing as Mr Zhao's reign of oppression dragged on. Personally, I didn't care about the lack of showers or the report-writing; what got to me was the breakdown of communications with my Chinese friends. Officially we were not supposed to mix, but as long as the number one didn't mind, nobody said anything. Under Mr Zhao, all my friends ignored me. In fact, they would not even give me eye contact, even though we all lived on one corridor. I'd been sent to Coventry. I was invisible. An outcast. My friend San Peiwa, who had enough clout to override the number one's orders, had been released, as had Mark, so it was just me and the four foreigners. I missed hanging out with the hunchback and the other characters I'd come to know, and though there were 75 guys in a tiny area, I became isolated for the first time since leaving the detention centre.

There was a violent undercurrent to the new regime, too, and Larry was often at the centre of it. His behaviour had been ignored most of the time before, but now the gloves were off and the guards were getting fed up with his attitude. Where most of us would make some kind of half-hearted effort to be civil with the guards, Larry would find some small point of principle to cause a fuss. He had many issues, both legal and medical, that brought him into contact with Captain Xu, which required a bit of humility and diplomacy on his part. Needless to say he wasn't having any of it, and often ended up shouting and banging his fist on the table. A gang of Chinese prisoners would then drag him off down the corridor and into his cell with a punch in the mouth. It was frustrating to watch because I sympathised with him while realising that he was wasting his time. Prison officers had no powers outside of the day-to-day running of the jail, and it was shooting the messenger to pretend they did. Throwing a tantrum with a screw because you wanted to see a lawyer or doctor was entirely counterproductive, because you were alienating your one link to the outside world. Even if the officer was your best friend it was still pointless, because in China the idea that you would even contest your sentence was unthinkable, as it would be construed as questioning the system, which was always right. Larry's case was hopeless, and the best he could hope for was a sentence reduction, which required a recommendation from the officer in charge. The more he complained, the more time he would serve.

The Chinese prisoners disliked him too, which was ironic because Larry would happily have put himself in the dock to protect their human rights. If he saw some prisoners assault a new arrival at the jail, he would make an official complaint in writing and demand an audience with the captain, who'd laugh at him. Afterwards, the prisoners handing out the beating would find something to report Larry for and so the cycle would continue until Larry was back in the guards' office complaining or being reprimanded. Worse still, punishments were invariably applied to all the foreigners, so our group would be blamed for Larry's tantrums. We didn't mind because everyone respected Larry's principles, even if they were counterproductive, and there was never any doubt that he would stand up for us in any dispute with the authorities.

I had an important advantage over the other foreigners: I'd been to boarding school before I went to prison. In fact I'd been to a number of them, from a young age, and there are many similarities between these two institutions: the single-sex environment, the separation from loved ones, the power structure. My early altercations with the bully Hunan had reminded me of school: how new boys were abused, only to become abusers themselves as they moved up the hierarchy. No doubt I had been both, though I never became a prefect and thus never managed to cause others too much misery. In Ti Lan Qiao, the top flight of prisoners were often bullies; indeed, it was part of their job description, and they would probably have lost their position if they'd failed to toe the line. The humiliation of newcomers was de rigueur – unless, of course, they were the relatives of Communist Party big shots. You were being hardened up for your own good. At boarding school, prefects would send you on long runs before breakfast, followed by a cold shower. In jail, it would be slaps around the head and sitting cross-legged in a cell for hours. The other foreigners didn't have such a background, but it felt fairly normal to me.

Another key feature of both these establishments is that you have to get used to living with a bunch of people whom you might not necessarily like. Day-school children might hate being at school and despise their fellow students, but come four o'clock they can go home to their friends and parents. Living with people 24–7 is a very different situation that requires a good deal of flexibility to navigate the power structure of same-sex environments. I generally loathed my many years at boarding school, but the experience certainly came in handy in jail. And yet regardless of whether the pupils liked it or not, there were always the school holidays to look forward to; meanwhile, prison was relentless, and there was always someone at the end of his tether for whatever reason. And this, presumably, was why guards and inmates celebrated events like Chinese New Year or female-inmate dance troupes. It was the nearest the state could get to emulating a family environment, which was crucial for letting off steam. Without it, Shanghai Municipal Prison would have been a very dangerous place indeed.

Even the lifers' block got to let their hair down once in a while and were given 'cooling' parties where they'd sit in the sun outside for an hour or so every few weeks. I'd got to know some of them when emptying shitbuckets, and while they didn't speak English, a smile and a handshake was enough to form some kind of a bond. They had a much harsher regime than we did and often worked in shifts round the clock to get out the orders of whatever they were making. One of the longest-serving prisoners had been a strongman for the Gang of Four, the counter-revolutionary movement led by Mao's last wife, Jiang Qing. He was a mountain of a man, twice the size of the average Chinese, and had been in Ti Lan Qiao since the group had been put on trial shortly after Mao's death in 1976. Like his boss and her cronies, he'd been given a suspended death sentence, but while she eventually committed suicide, having been released on health grounds in 1991, he'd survived. I estimated he'd probably be released in around 2001, after 25 years, though it's possible he got out not long after Deng Xiaoping's death in

1997. Had Madame Mao's coup against Deng been successful, he could have ended up as mayor of Shanghai, or even warden of Ti Lan Qiao prison. Either way, he must have had some tales to tell.

We also got a cooling party, and unlike our exercise periods as a foreign group, the whole wing was allowed to sit in the courtyard lapping up the sunshine. I was the only foreigner who didn't have any sunglasses, and the rare burst of sunshine made me squint. Years earlier I'd got conjunctivitis from a filthy towel in a Taipei hotel, and my eyes had never been the same. I think the disease had burned my retinas, and from then on I always kept a pair of sunglasses nearby. In prison I forgot all about them, as I'd never needed them until today, and I joined a small group of Chinese sitting in a spot shaded by the shadow of a guard's watchtower.

It wasn't the first time I'd been 'blinded by the light'. Two years earlier, Rosie and I had gone sightseeing, something we rarely did. We'd taken the train from Delhi and I'd slept most the way.

'Agra's a dump!' everyone said. 'See the Taj and get out.'

The train pulled into the station in time for breakfast. A boy of maybe 13 stood on the platform spying on the passers-by. His face lit up with a smile as we approached, before averting his gaze towards an elderly couple who dutifully tossed a coin into the battered baked-bean can around his neck. The taxi driver slouched as he entered the fray of dusty traffic fumes. He never asked us where we were going; he didn't have to. On the side of the road, an old man was selling paperweight concrete domes inlaid with mirrored tiles and multi-coloured agates from Rajasthan. I narrowed my eyes as we got out of the cab, having left my sunglasses back at the hotel. It was still dark when we'd left at 5 a.m. and they'd been the last thing on my mind, but as we approached the glorious marble palace it was invisible to me. My scrawny eyelids wrapped shut like roller blinds before the white-marble colossus, and I had to make a curve out of my hand like a golf cap to see through my scorched eyelashes.

'Oh my God, isn't that just beautiful,' cooed an American woman to her husband, 'and to think he built it just for her!'

There was no disputing that the Mughal treasure – built by a maharajah as testament to his unfailing love for his wife – was one of

India's finest, but the relentless midday sun beating on the vast slabs of white stone began to give me a headache. I crouched next to a fountain with my back to the giant mausoleum of love and read the blurb from the Lonely Planet guide, whose glossy illustrations reminded me of what I was missing. Through the warped prism of my sundried retinas, the Taj Mahal became more convincing in pictures than reality.

We went to eat at a nearby restaurant, intending to return for sunset. Walking back an hour or so later the sun was beginning to wane, and we decided to stop for a smoke after finding a small gateway leading to a garden where a concrete stairway traversed the side of the wall to a roof terrace. The sun collapsed over the garden wall, leaving a peachy hue between the two pillars either side of a doorway leading to the street below. Silver-tailed monkeys swung down from branches to see who the visitors were as the birds broke out in a twilight cacophony that echoed across the courtyard.

There were no other tourists in the garden, as if the famous monument next door had robbed it of its attraction, but this only added to its appeal for us as we sat smoking beneath a tree. If we wanted to see the Taj again before our train left we'd have to leave immediately, but the garden had begun to work its magic on us, and its enchanting spells of natural beauty overshadowed the world-famous shrine barely a stone's throw away. The garden had come alive with its vibrant mix of plants, animals and birds, while the neighbouring building that everyone had come to see stood stone-dead in this dusty town: a colossal and beautiful corpse holding up the sky. By contrast, the garden needed no representation by men; it simply existed, as it had done for thousands of years before the Taj Mahal had been thought of. In a leafy corner stood an ivy-covered statue of the monkey god Hanuman, the weeds strangling its granite torso after years of neglect. We wondered if it had been built by some great monkey king in remembrance of a loved one.

Back at the station, the same boy we'd seen in the morning was hustling tourists on the platform and seemed to be doing good business. His angelic smile greeted us from a couple of carriages away, beaming under the glare of the canopy lights. As we got nearer we began to notice his feet bulged from beneath his baggy trousers, ballooning into hideously cartoonish spectacles with grotesque elephantine toes.

'My friend,' he called out, 'you want photo?'

I pulled a camera out of my bag and snapped a close-up of his waifish smile. He seemed disappointed that I ignored his lucrative malformations, but his smile outshone the gloomy cards that fate had dealt him, and I had no appetite for tourist freak shows.

A whistle blew and the train started to hiss. A hand came down from the stairwell and hoisted me up into the carriage. He was a Sikh businessman from the Midlands on his way back home to England after visiting family and friends in the Punjab.

'Well, what did you think of the Taj then?' he said, stuffing stray hairs into his beard net.

'I think it's beautiful,' I replied, not wanting to bore him with my story about the forgotten sunglasses.

'You should see the Golden Temple in Amritsar,' he said, referring to the holiest Sikh shrine. 'I think you'd be impressed.'

'Yes, I'd love to, but I'm leaving India in a few days,' I said.

'Me too, I can't wait,' he said, perking up. 'This country's too bloody hot, don't you think?'

'Yes, I suppose it is,' I said as the train picked up speed.

Shanghai was hot, too, and the longer the summer went on the hotter it got, as the vast concrete buildings, courtyards and walls heated up. Even if the weather changed outside it took weeks to cool down in the jail, in much the same way as it had taken weeks to warm up after the winter. The prison seemed to be around three weeks behind the temperature outside its walls, and when cooler winds blew as the seasons changed, you could still feel the summer heat oozing through the walls of the cells at night. And it wasn't just the heat. Shanghai is one of the smoggiest cities in the world, and Ti Lan Qiao is slap-bang in the middle of the city: a steel and concrete island surrounded by fetid rivers and smoke-filled skies.

I wondered what Rosie was up to in South East Asia. She'd sent me photos of her travels, which I'd Blu-tacked round the back of my cell, out of general view. She was grinning between the animated trees of Angkor Wat, gazing at the sandstone peaks of Halong Bay and surfacing mischievously from a Vietcong tunnel shaft in Hue. She was seeing the places we'd talked of seeing together, and I was jealous. She'd even taken a PADI diving course now I was out of the way: something I'd always wanted to do, but which she'd never shown any enthusiasm for. Perhaps my dreams were rubbing off on her?

Gareth was missing his wife, too. He got a visit once a month like the Chinese, and he spoke in Mandarin under the beady eyes of Captain Jinn, whom he loathed. Jürgen and Ludwig got a visit from the German consul, Mrs Sievers, a kindly lady who clearly sympathised with them. There was bad news from back home: Jürgen's dad had died. His family had already sent a letter, but he hadn't received it since foreigners' mail tended to get delayed in the bottleneck of the translators' office. Larry had also had a visit and had taken the opportunity to rail against the guards for not posting his appeals for a retrial to the high court. I imagine the US consul thought he was living in cloud cuckoo land.

I wasn't thinking about visits. Time was racing now, and even thoughts of Rosie were less frequent. I was getting into the rhythm of jail life and sort of liked the tempo of the place, which swam round my brain to the music of Howlin' Wolf's 'Wang Dang Doodle'. Boarding school had been my dry run for prison, and I think I coped better with the latter. I'd got used to the monotony of it all, with its 24–7 routines that never changed. Such certainty can put your mind at ease, and lends itself to a Daoist 'in the moment' type of mindset. I was becoming institutionalised, and it felt good.

1|0

Peshwari Mangoes

Before Mr Zhao's reign as number one prisoner had prevented the foreigners from emptying their own shitbuckets, I had got to know my Pakistani friend Khalid better. We only had a couple of minutes to speak at the drains, but he'd often made a point of coming along to say hello. His work unit was involved in the most tedious job in the prison, which involved separating threads of cotton all day long. He also wore a uniform and spoke fluent Mandarin, since he'd done most of his time pretty much on his own on a straight Chinese wing. The Pakistanis had been unfortunate to have fallen between Chinese and foreigner status, and had been put through the system as sort of honorary Chinese, with few of the benefits that either party enjoyed. I felt sorry for them because they had a tougher time of it than we did and didn't have the kinds of connections the locals had to get more interesting work. Like me, Khalid was 'coming down from the mountain', being in the home stretch of an eight-year sentence. He had the kind of chilled-out demeanour that people take on as the light at the end of the tunnel looms brighter, and I had enjoyed our meetings. We'd exchanged magazines and he'd given me a copy of the Koran to read.

One day he'd given me a tiny piece of hash that he'd found in the hem of some clothing, years after his arrest. It was less than half a gram in weight and had the dry, grainy consistency of Xinjiang hash rather than the sticky texture of the stuff from his home country. When I'd got back to the wing, I'd begun to feel nervous having the contraband in my possession and decided to drop it down a hole between the floorboards where no one would find it. I never saw it again.

One of the pleasures of prison life is the amount of time one has to reflect on the past. On the outside, life is far too hectic to spend hours thinking about former adventures, but for prisoners it's a full-time occupation. I thought a great deal about Pakistan, the place that I had bought my hash and, as a result, brought disaster upon myself. I trawled my mind for clues as to how the foolish idea had come to me, and the surrounding circumstances that might have put me off the ill-fated mission. I thought about the days before I'd set off from Peshawar and how my illness had clouded my judgement as I lounged around on the roof gardens of guesthouses, smoking joints and drinking mango juice from old-fashioned dimpled pint glasses.

The evening before I bought my hash, I'd sat in the garden of the guesthouse drinking mango juice with a couple from Madrid. It was their last night in the country and they were flying back home the following morning. Juan and Maria said they'd come to Pakistan to buy stones to make into rings and pendants to sell at the markets in Paris and Berlin. I suspected they were junkies whose dependency on the white poppies of Afghanistan was their real reason for being in the country. Both had geranium-blue eyes with tiny pupils that struggled to peer out beneath their encroaching eyelids. Maria was prone to nodding off mid-sentence, leaving her partner to pick up where she left off before jerking back in her chair to smile in agreement with him. They showed me samples of their work that were made of beautifully crafted silver inlaid with semi-precious stones. She wore a scorpion necklace with green tourmaline eyes that peered out from a carved onyx head, while the body consisted of a row of rectangular slabs of garnet, their smooth surfaces like tiny bottles of red wine. Its tail was fashioned out of Maori jade with a minute faceted diamond on the tip, which caught the last rays of sunlight that crept over the hotel compound.

'Go and see this guy,' said Juan, handing me a name card. 'He'll look after you.'

I took the card as the couple wandered back to their room, holding hands. They'd been together for 18 years and seemed very much in love. Their laid-back existence – drifting between Europe and the Hindu Kush, buying stones and working with their hands – seemed like a charmed life. It was the life Rosie and I had had, though neither of us had succumbed to the melancholic darkness of opiate addiction.

The following day, I went looking for stones. The muezzin's call rang out across the street from a battered megaphone as I stood outside the shop. A handsome young man with fluffy stubble on his chin quickly opened the door, ushering me away from the oppressive heat of the bazaar into a small room with a large, patterned carpet hanging from the wall and a few cushions in the corner.

'Welcome, please, my name is Islam,' he said with a convivial smile, his milky teeth gleaming like moonstones. 'I will make some tea.'

The curtain at the back of the shop fluttered as he came back with my tea. We sat across from each other, he with his long white *jalaba* and me in the baggy new trousers I'd bought in Saddar Bazaar the day before. I'd discarded my jeans within 24 hours of arriving in the city; it was 40 degrees and rising, so the heavy denim fabric had clung to my legs like dead skin. The flowing arabesque calico allowed the warm air to circulate round my legs and groin, and for the first time since arriving in the country I felt comfortable.

I lit a cigarette and leaned back on a cushion, pretending to sip on the sickly-sweet tea that made my lips cringe. Islam unlocked a large safe at the back of the shop and produced a handful of large, white paper wraps, and I sat up inquisitively as he squatted down next to me and began opening them. The first contained maybe a hundred small cabochons of lapis lazuli, their azure, dome-like surfaces speckled with tiny golden nuggets. I took a handful of the small treasures into my palm and began sorting them by size and shape. The round stones reminded me of the blue mosque in Esfahan, a place I'd often wanted to visit and had seen many photos of, while the oval-shaped ones looked like the tiny eggs of some exotic mythological bird.

Looking up, I noticed that Islam had opened the other wraps and laid them out on the carpet next to the brass teapot. In one there were two or three dozen pieces of the blue rock that had been tumbled into lovely smooth shapes. I'd seen this process in the stone-cutting shops in the back streets of Jaipur, where hundreds of pieces of amethyst were rolled around a barrel for days at a time, their purple, crystalline formations grinding incessantly until all their surfaces were immaculately smooth.

'More tea?' asked my host, unaware that I'd barely allowed the sugary fluid to touch my palate.

'Water, please,' I replied.

He returned with a glass in one hand and a metallic filing tray in the other. A piece of black velvet covered its contents, and he peeled it back to reveal an exquisite array of lapis trinkets. There were carvings of elephants and monkeys, tiny plates and bowls like doll's-house accessories, and a selection of bead necklaces. I sifted through the pile of beads with my fingers; their cool pastel surfaces had a prickly, jade-like sensation, and I was reminded of running my hand through vats of olives I'd picked in Andalucia some years before.

As we talked I found myself absentmindedly fumbling with a string of the blue droplets, which I wound round my fingers as Arabs caress their worry beads. The custom has no equivalence I can think of in Western societies but is a feature of most Islamic states, and as I ran the cobalt spheres through my palms a peaceful sensation emanated from the stones, a fitting antidote to the stifling heat of the midday sun.

Back at the guesthouse I showed the stones to the landlord, but he had other business on his mind. The police had been round with a warrant to search the Spanish couple's room after they'd been arrested at Karachi Airport with a kilo of smack.

All the prisoners I talked to had encountered ominous happenings prior to their arrest. Tommy had gone out of his way to get busted by insisting on smoking hash openly on the train to Shanghai. A policeman on the train had asked him to put it out, and Tommy had got paranoid and got off the train in the middle of nowhere. Then he decided to take out the dope and leave it in the waiting room of the train station, but was seen doing it by a cleaning lady, who reported him. My own journey had been littered with bad omens, from the fact that I'd got hepatitis to the string of obstacles that had almost prevented me from getting to customs in the first place. It seemed silly to think about it now, but like my colleagues I'd gone to great lengths to make my own misfortune. The only rational conclusion to come to was that we'd subconsciously engineered our downfalls for obscure reasons that would eventually become apparent.

In the meantime, I had to make sense of my fate by accepting that it was of my own doing and therefore the right thing to have happened. That the monasticism of prison life was something that I needed, even if I didn't want it, and I realised that somewhere along the line I might as well get happy and enjoy it. This was helped no end by the news that Mr Zhao, our number one prisoner and arch-enemy of the foreigners, was on his way out after serving his sentence. Better still, he was to be replaced by my favourite Chinese friend, Chen Yong Ho.

Chen was a proper Shanghai guy, from the right side of the river if not the tracks. He'd been in jail before, knew how to play the system and had risen swiftly through the ranks. He and his mates had been selling monosodium glutamate, the taste enhancer much moaned about by Westerners who think Chinese medicine is useful for serious illnesses. They'd been selling it by the ton and had been making a good profit until one of their gang had grassed them up. MSG was a government business, so the bootlegging scam had brought the full weight of the law down upon Chen and his pals, who got the rooster treatment. Chen ended up with 13 years, while his partner, who had grassed him up, hoping to receive leniency, got a suspended death sentence. The news that he was to be the new number one lifted our spirits no end as the wing returned to normal. Suddenly Chinese were allowed to talk to us again, and old friends began to apologise for the frosty relations that had characterised the months under Zhao's xenophobic leadership. Tommy's spell on easy street came to an end, too, as Chen quickly decided he was an idiot who couldn't be trusted and removed the powers the former number one had bestowed upon him. My relations with the Scotsman improved, too, as he began to accept that I couldn't take sides with him against the other members of our small group. We started to enjoy having a laugh with the Chinese again, taking the piss out of them and making fun of the guards, who also began to relax under the new regime, and by the time my last Christmas came about I was happy and contented.

The New Year brought out the best in the Chinese. A carnivalesque atmosphere came over the wing as huge celebratory posters, wall hangings and fairy lights lit up the grey walls of the prison. The top brass from the warden's office made rare appearances to check on the welfare of the staff and inmates, while the guards cracked a few smiles once in a while. Reform Through Labour speeches were suspended and replaced with Western movies and Chinese pop music. For a month the people united in an orgy of benign nationalism, drawing on their Daoist past to rise above their misfortunes and encouraging foreigners to do the same. The rat-a-tat-tat of firecrackers ricocheted down the streets beyond the prison walls to remind us all of our close proximity to the world outside. Prisoners in punishment cells were allowed out to mix with everyone else, and trustee prisoners visited their counterparts from other blocks. And then there was the food. Quotas from the jail's shop were doubled, as were the family-visit allowances. Cabbage and rice was suddenly transformed into stir-fried prawns and sweet-and-sour pork. The daily rice rations went from small, brownish-grey husks to fat white grains with no stones in them. Dried mango, tangerines, and sunflower and melon seeds arrived on trucks in industrial quantities, wheeled around the prison by inmates with sack barrows. Families brought in Christmas hampers, which prisoners shared and swapped. The corridor became a festive food hall, with salamis hanging from the bars while the grey Formica tabletops were littered with seasonal fruits and jars of pickles as the aroma of steaming vats of pork bellies and chicken wings wafted through the air.

The opulence of the festivities was a trade-off between the prisoners and their captors. After 11 months of the drudgery of everyday life, the New Year acted as a valve to let off steam. The state – notoriously cruel and unyielding – was rewarding its subjects with a rare show of benevolence. Of course, the same could be said of Christmas in the West, but the sheer scale and duration of the festivities in China seemed closer to some kind of sumptuous inversion of the Muslim holy month of Ramadan.

Kang, a petty thief doing five years for stealing bicycles, gave me a fresh mango, my first since Pakistan. Mangoes held a hallowed – if comical – role in the Cultural Revolution. In 1968, Mao had been given seven of them as a gift from the Pakistani government, though it's believed that he didn't like to eat them himself. This was at the peak of the 'Bombard the Headquarters' campaign designed to weed out the 'bad elements' who were gaining too much power and thus needed to 'learn from the masses'. Mao gave the mangoes to different worker-peasant cooperatives, an act widely viewed as a criticism of the Red Guards. The pieces of fruit quickly took on sacred significance and were paraded around the country. One of the mangoes was put into a glass cabinet in its own carriage and carried for weeks on a slow train around the countryside to be viewed by the people. Hundreds of thousands lined railway tracks for a glimpse of the sacred fruit. Another was kept in formaldehyde, while one of the communes kept theirs in a massive tank of water and allowed the workers to drink its Mao-infused contents. Before long even the embalmed mango began to go rotten, so waxwork replicas were produced in glass cases with a picture of Mao on the front. You can still buy 'original' replicas of these on the Internet today for $800.

As well as being Shanghai's main prison, Ti Lan Qiao served as a kind of sorting house where prisoners were brought to be processed before going off to other jails and labour camps. Because the Eastern cities were so overcrowded, some prisoners with very long sentences could exchange their Shanghai citizenship for a short sentence with privileges in far-off regions of the country. Some of the labour camps were in such remote areas that there were no walls or bars needed to keep the prisoners in, and they might end up getting a paid job, too. However, they could never come back to Shanghai and would have to spend the rest of their lives away from the city of their birth. This was an established system outside prison, too, and poor families living in Shanghai could get a resettlement package to go and live in places like Tibet and Xinjiang. For most Shanghainese it was a fate worse than death, but for many there was no other choice. If the government wanted to knock down a residential area to build a fancy hotel or a golf course, the inhabitants had little choice other than to relinquish their residency permits and take the government's offer of a new home and work unit thousands of miles away. There were incentives, too. Colour TVs might be thrown into the bargain, or a larger living space than the resident had had in Shanghai. This is why today there are more Han Chinese in Tibet than there are Tibetans.

In the summer, about a hundred transit prisoners turned up on our wing. Most of them had come from a labour camp and seemed to miss it. They said the work was hard in the labour camp, but their free time was much more relaxed. They could buy cigarettes, food, even beer, and there was plenty of fresh air; crucially, there was also almost no ideological reform. The relentless brainwashing that was considered the key to salvation in Ti Lan Qiao had not been part of the programme in their previous jail, and they loathed it now. Because the cells were already taken, the new arrivals slept on the wooden boards in the middle of the corridor or on makeshift mats. I enjoyed having new Chinese to chat to, but some of our senior prisoners felt their discipline was being undermined and fights broke out. After a couple of weeks, the inmates were split into groups and packed off in a huge police convoy of buses and trucks to a prison train headed for the camps in the west of the country.

After they left it was decided that it was too hot to stay in the cells any more, and some of the Chinese got to sleep on the landing where the inmates passing through had slept. Just as the wing was freezing in winter, it became unbearably hot in the summer. It took a while to warm up, but by August the concrete-and-steel structures turned into an inferno. Most Chinese slept three to a five-feet-by-seven-feet cell, so when it started to get really hot it made sense to open up the wing at night. There were large electric fans, too, translated into Mandarin as 'electric wind'. Because there were not enough fans to go round, I shared one with Grumpy next door. Grumpy had been convicted of having sex with his ten-year-old daughter and kept a low profile on the wing. The fan was placed between our two cells, blowing fresh air all night. Chinese would shift our fan so I got his cool air, but I moved it back when I discovered what they were doing. I felt uncomfortable assuming the man was an evil paedophile; he could well have been innocent of the allegation, as I suspected were a number of other people I'd met. In a country where prisoners meet their lawyers ten minutes before they go to court, the actual hearings are little more than a formality. Add to that the widespread use of torture, which is always good for getting innocent people to admit to crimes, regardless of whether they committed them, and the mind boggles as to the number of innocent people there must be in the Chinese legal system. But even if he had been guilty, there's something distasteful about the treatment of child-abusers in jail. I have noticed that the most unpleasant prisoners are usually at the forefront of this type of bullying. It's as if they hope that tormenting such people will somehow make them feel better about their own crimes and failings. This is a feature of all prisons around the world, I guess, and I wanted no part of it. It came as little surprise to learn later that at least one of the fan-shifters was a convicted rapist.

The heat brought many prisoners out in a rash, and the jail sold bottles of alcohol-based aftershave to splash on their skin. It smelled like a mixture of menthol, tiger balm and Brut 33, and it worked well. It was a pinkish liquid in a glass bottle that left a cool, dry sensation, as well as drowning out the inevitable body odour of so many perspiring men. Most of the foreigners wet-shaved their heads in the summer, which seemed to perplex the Chinese, who thought it uncouth, I think. The guys on death row and the lifers' block had shaved heads, so I suppose the practice had unsettling connotations for them. Instead, a group of prisoners would get out the clippers and give everyone a crew cut once every three months. Elderly men were allowed to grow beards if they wanted, and there was an aged Korean guy in the lifers' block who'd been in the jail at least 20 years who reminded me of paintings of the great Daoist sage Laozi.

Summer was the watermelon season, and they arrived by the truckload. They were ridiculously cheap, and the foreigners always bought at least six each. The Chinese taught us how to make watermelon salad out of the rind. This involved scraping the hard, dark-green layer off first before thinly shredding the yellowish pulp, which is then soaked in salt. It was a laborious job with a blunt knife, and after ten minutes in the salt there wasn't much left. We then washed the salt off and added light soy sauce, sesame oil and sugar; it produced a tasty crunchy salad that I'd happily buy in a restaurant.

Our new number one, Chen, made the most of my shiatsu skills. I was happy to oblige. He was a good bloke and had always been a friend to me. As head prisoner he had a lot of admin to do, consisting mainly of doing the guards' paperwork for them. Reports had to be written about the prisoners' progress towards their reform and the hierarchy of trustees who ran the place. Mr Sun, the convicted rapist, was still the 'eyes and ears' of the guards as head of the shadow surveillance team. His job was to organise the monitoring of all the prisoners, regardless of rank, so it was important for him and the number one to synchronise their reports before handing them over to the guards. Some of Chen's flunkies were leftovers from Mr Zhao's time as number one, but they couldn't have been nicer under the new leadership. Even one particular prisoner I'd never got along with, and with whom I'd had a showdown after I'd found him in my cell, was civil towards me. Zhu Go Hua, the hunchback, was allowed to be my mate again, and I massaged his head when he had migraines.

A young new prisoner called Qian turned up. He was 21 but he looked 14, with a weedy physique and thick glasses. He looked like a school kid who'd wandered into the jail by mistake. His English was excellent since he'd worked as a clerk in a foreigners' hotel, and was a good deal brighter than most of the guys on our wing. He'd been caught with his hand in the hotel till and got an eight-year stretch. In the first week, he cried a lot and the top prisoners took him under their wing. Being more intelligent than most, he learned the rules quickly and was moved up to group leader of the latest batch of new arrivals. As the best English speaker on the wing, he was sometimes drafted in to translate for the foreigners. Before long, he was eating on the number one's table and became a trustee.

My Mandarin was very basic – though I managed to make myself understood most of the time – but it was good to have someone around whom I could speak to in normal English. I asked Qian for Chinese lessons, but as usual it was against the rules. It was easy to forget that officially there was supposed to be no communication between the Chinese and us. We all lived in the same corridor, but were supposed to ignore each other. Under Mr Zhao this rule had been strictly enforced, but even though things had improved drastically, being seen by a guard talking to a foreigner was risky and a punishable offence.

Every few months, there was a bed-airing day when we'd take our futons and pillows up to the roof. The view from the top of the building was a treat, as was the fresh air. We had a bird's-eye view of the iconic Shanghai tower we'd nicknamed the 'spaceship building'. The roof was surrounded by a small concrete wall and a large mesh fence. Our building was higher than some of the other brigades', and we could see the roofs of other buildings. One of the brigade roofs was covered in plants and vegetables and looked like a giant rectangular oasis, while the kitchen brigade had huge drums of cooking oil and steaming chimneys. The terrace was the size of a football pitch, with heavy-duty ropes hung across upon which we draped our futons and pillows. The Chinese had a uniform way of folding their bedding and hanging it, while the foreigners did their own thing. If the weather was nice we were allowed to relax and catch a few sunrays, and when we went back to the cell block the bedding had halved in weight. The dust these days generated would cause an allergic reaction in me, and my nose would run constantly for an hour or so afterwards. Captain Mai noticed the discomfort it caused me and bought me some 'joint-venture' antihistamine pills. Joint venture meant a combination of Chinese and Western medicine, manufactured by Western businesses joining forces with their Chinese counterparts. Mai said he always bought joint-venture goods because the Chinese stuff was useless, which I entirely agreed with.

He also took me to the dentist when I had toothache, generally caused by chipping my teeth while biting on stony rice. A news story turned up in the *China Daily* about a gang who'd just been sent down for putting a ton of small stones in their rice to bring up the weight. They got long sentences, which I was not sorry to hear about.

The trip to the dentist with Mai was an eye-opener. There must have been a hundred guys waiting to go in, but Mai queue-barged and got me in the chair in ten minutes. There were two dentists working side by side with a chair each, so you could hear the guy next door groaning as the dentists chatted. The dentists wore guard uniforms with white coats over the top and left the door wide open so the people waiting could watch. There was no anaesthetic, and the place ran on an 'if in doubt, pull it out' basis. I'd been terrified about the impending visit, but the toothache got worse and Mai said he'd make sure they did a good job. Jürgen had been not long before me to have a wisdom tooth out. He came back looking like the Elephant Man, with a bulge in his jaw the size of a tennis ball, but he'd lived to tell the tale. Now I was in the chair with a hundred convicts ogling me, so I had to put on a brave face. Fortunately, it wasn't as bad as I was expecting. The tooth was dead, and the dentist yanked it out without too much pain.

Being in a dentist's chair reminded me of my first ever encounter with a Far Eastern white-coat years earlier in Japan. I had a lingering dose of non-specific urethritis from my escapades in Thailand and booked myself into a clinic as soon as I got my first pay-cheque from the karaoke bar where I worked. The surgery was pristine, with pretty girls fussing over me and lulling me into a state of security before the doctor pulled a curtain around the area and asked me to lie down on a bed. He then put on a pair of surgical gloves – which I'd come to associate with airport customs officials – and rammed two fingers inside me before squeezing the prostate gland. I'd never felt such agony in my life and remember letting out a high-pitched squeal as the doctor continued with a smile on his face. The pretty girls' faces dropped as the curtain was opened and they looked at me writhing on the bed. I was in a state of shock when I handed the doctor a 10,000-yen note for his services and walked back to my guesthouse, but the more I thought of it, the more convinced I was that I'd been sexually abused by this man. I considered going back and confronting the pervert, who I imagined had wanked himself off afterwards, but I knew I would never be able to back up my claim. As an Amnesty International member, I often get grisly reports of tortures involving such practices – often involving sharp, heated or electrical implements of one kind or another – and they always upset me more than any other equally hideous reports.

On the way back from the dentist, we walked past a group of convicts awaiting execution. They were hog-tied and chained to each other as an open-sided truck stood by. They were to be paraded through the city as an example to the others, roosters for the chop, and a police film crew were on hand to record the occasion for the evening news. I asked Captain Mai what he thought about it, and he looked uneasy and told me to move along. The condemned men stood in line as guards and soldiers began prodding them onto the truck for their last drive around the city. I lingered in the doorway of 8th Brigade, watching the doomed men as Mai checked me in, and my dreaded trip to the dentist found a new perspective.

Rosie had mentioned in a recent letter she might have a chance to come and visit. She was working as a tour guide in Vietnam and had a few days spare. Mai announced out of the blue that the big day had come, so I threw on the best T-shirt I could find and we left for the reception area. Captain Jinn was a senior officer in charge of foreigners' visits and was waiting for us at the bottom of the staircase. Jinn was loathed by the foreigners, though I never had much to do with him. Larry wrote him endless letters about legal issues, which I imagine Jinn threw in the bin, while Gareth understandably detested his racist attitude towards his half-Uighur wife.

We walked into one of the more civilised prison reception rooms, and there sat Rosie with the British vice consul. She looked lovely in her pastel-coloured hemp dungarees from the Golden Triangle, with a big grin on her face. We hugged and had a quick kiss before Jinn told me to sit on the opposite side of the table. Prison visits can have a surreal quality to them. With so much to say in such a short space of time, it becomes hard to think of anything to say at all. Instead there were long silences, interspersed with a few giggles and resigned smiles. I had a large bushy beard, which I'd been planning to shave off before her visit, but for some reason I hadn't bothered. Perhaps I wanted her to see the new me: unattached, independent and oblivious to the notion of looking good for someone else. We talked about mutual friends and goodwill messages passed on from family members as I made my way through her packet of Camel Lights. She looked happy and said I looked well under the circumstances, and we both knew the worst of our ordeal was over. I was 'coming down from the mountain', and felt confident enough not to bother asking what was going on in her private life. It didn't seem to make much difference any more; our life together had been torn in half, and there was no saying whether we had a future together when I was released. Either way, we were the best of friends and no amount of time apart would ever change that.

Jinn looked at his watch and it was all over. In some ways, it was a relief. Rosie said my sister was thinking of visiting if I wanted, but I said I'd rather she didn't. I'd be out in a while and visits slowed down the passing of time. We kissed goodbye, and I nodded to Mai that I wanted to get going. I turned in the door to see Rosie's beautiful face looking back at mine, then turned back and walked quickly back to 8th Brigade.

Later that day, our number one prisoner and my good friend Chen asked how my visit had gone, and did I think we'd marry when I was released. For the first time since my arrest I said I had no idea what the future held. Our love had become like the decayed tooth in Yukio Mishima's *The Temple of the Golden Pavilion*. Just as the student of Zen Buddhism destroys the temple that, to him, has become like a decayed tooth, a throbbing pain that always wants to make itself known, ceaselessly nudging and cajoling him into recognising its existence, I realised I was better off without my past. So I let it go, and it let me go. The following day I shaved off my beard.

11

One-Way Ticket

Captain Xu announced that a major event was to take place in the prison, and the foreigners were asked to take part. These occasions were more for the benefit of the guards and local dignitaries than they were for the prisoners, and some high-ranking Communist Party cadres would be invited. Our jail band, the Reformers, had played at other events and we always got a great response from the audience, singing our favourite songs and larking around for the other prisoners, but this time it was just Jürgen and me doing Johnny Cash's 'Folsom Prison Blues'. It was also one of the few occasions to see the girls from the song-and-dance troupe, the small crew of women from 9th Brigade. The members of the dance group were amongst the prettiest in the jail and put on entertaining shows that they were rigorously trained for. I was reminded of the lengths to which the state in Communist countries like North Korea goes in putting on public exhibitions as propaganda exercises, with their immaculately choreographed, dazzling displays of colour, so at odds with the real-life conditions of most of the population.

The show took place in the Great Hall of the Prisoner, a huge concrete block the size of a large cinema, with around a thousand seats. I'd played guitars in pubs and bars before, but this was Hammersmith Odeon. Waiting to go on stage we could see the audience consisted of convicts at the back and sides, with a large contingent of uniforms and civilians in the choice seats in the middle. Warden Lai was there, schmoozing the guests with his immaculately Brylcreemed Elvis quiff and full police uniform. We ran through Johnny's famous jailhouse tune from the live *At Folsom Prison* album, and it occurred to me how well behaved the inmates were. In the film of Cash's 1968 shows there were no civilians, whereas here were Shanghai's hardest criminals mixing with the local Communist Party cadres and citizens. There was a feeling that in spite of their crimes, the prisoners were still part of a community.

Captain Mai waited in the wings while Jürgen and I strummed our songs, and he congratulated us warmly afterwards. We were growing to like Mai more and more. He wasn't the sharpest knife in the drawer, but he was a good soul and he took genuine pleasure in seeing us play. He even let us hang around for a while after our performance, and we found ourselves backstage with the dance troupe from the women's brigade. One of the girls reminded me of a girl I'd known when I'd first arrived in Asia ten years earlier, and her memory stayed with me as I lay on my cell floor that night.

I'd flown to Bangkok on a one-way ticket in 1985. An old school friend, Philip, was doing a gap-year tour of Thailand, Burma and India, so I joined him for the first leg with no particular plans beyond that. We'd met at a Thames riverboat party a few weeks earlier, on the day I'd been fired from my job as a runner for a Soho TV-commercial production company, and when he told me of his plans I knew it was my cue to get out of the UK. I had enough money to pay for the flight and survive for a few weeks until I could get a job. I had no idea what I might do there, but it seemed like a good idea at the time, and I had no desire to get another job in England, where I'd become increasingly bored and restless. My earliest childhood memories were of a wooden globe I had in my bedroom. I would spin the ball around, close my eyes and prod my finger onto a random spot. Wherever my finger landed would be a place I would one day visit. Usually I'd end up in the middle of the Pacific Ocean, but sometimes I hit land and I'd look the place up in a picture atlas to find out more about it. I didn't really care where I went, but I knew from a young age I wanted to leave England. Now I was 20 years old and the dream was becoming a reality.

I went through my father's old copies of *National Geographic* magazine looking for anything I could find about Thailand, or, as my grandfather pronounced it, 'Thighland'. Glossy photos of Buddhas, pagodas and elephants adorned every page. There were pictures of the country's much-loved king in his various guises, from ice-cool sax player in a zoot suit to wizened statesman. According to the text, Thailand had capitalised on its close relations with the Western world and brought great prosperity to its people at the same time as neighbouring countries had floundered under the impoverishing influence of 'Red' China. Wealth distribution had been slowed down by corruption and economic mismanagement, while democracy and human rights were more of a luxury than a birthright, but the nation was flourishing under a 'benign' military junta presided over by its compassionate monarch. I went to Norwich library and found more books about the country, including the seminal Lonely Planet traveller's guide, *Southeast Asia on a Shoestring*. I was happy to see how cheap Thailand was compared to the UK and that there was the possibility of getting work teaching English. If all else failed I could get an onward flight to Australia, where school friends were living and working, so I pieced together a plan to get out of England for good and make a new life somewhere else. I couldn't wait to get on the plane.

I assumed my first night in Bangkok would be spent in a hotel or guesthouse, but on arrival Philip informed me we'd be staying with friends. The motorised rickshaw rattled through the streets of the capital as we sat sweating in the back with my rucksack at our feet. The driver lit a cigarette at some traffic lights and took a slug of cough medicine-like liquid from a bottle of Lipovitan vitamin drink, allegedly a pick-me-up as well as a health drink. I thought the driver was wasting his time taking vitamins. It was dark, but the air was hot and clammy, while the carbon monoxide fumes from the thousands of unrestricted vehicles were almost tangible. Some tuk tuk drivers had scarves or surgical masks wrapped round their mouths to keep the worst of the toxic vapours at bay, but they were fighting a losing battle against their noxious surroundings.

The tuk tuk pulled up outside an apartment block adjacent to the Nana Hotel in one of the city's more affluent suburbs. I handed the driver a note and Philip led the way up a flight of steps to a green door with a peephole that resembled a cell door. Seconds later the door sprang open, revealing a one-room apartment with a sleepy Thai girl standing in the entrance.

'This is Miaow. This is her place.'

We shook hands as she yawned and apologised for the mess, but she had no reason to: the place was clean and tidy, if a little cluttered with clothes and bedding. On the windowsill sat the biggest bottle of Johnnie Walker Black Label I'd ever seen, with a sunken handle so you could carry it like a suitcase. Around the walls were pictures of Caucasian men with beautiful Thai girls on their arms. Philip thrust an ice-cold bottle of Kloster beer in my hand and winked. I noticed there was only one bed in the room, which took up most of the space.

'So, this is where I've been staying for the last few days.' He grinned, looking rather pleased with himself.

'Lucky man, she's fucking gorgeous!'

'No fucking, actually; we're just friends.'

'Yeah, right!'

'No, it's true. She and Nok and I kip down together, but that's about it.'

'Nok?'

'Yes, that's her friend, she sleeps here as well, and yes, she's even more beautiful than Miaow.'

'So where am I going to sleep?'

'I'll sleep on the balcony with Miaow and you can hop into the bed with Nok.'

I'd yet to meet Nok, but I immediately approved of the sleeping arrangements. Philip wound up the bamboo roller blinds and opened a door that led out onto a balcony with a thin mattress on the marble floor. I took out a duty-free Marlboro, but then Miaow asked if I'd prefer some Thai stick. She handed me a four-inch bud of sticky green grass wound around a thin stick. I held it to my nose and inhaled its sweet, pungent aroma.

'You like?' she enquired, knowing full well what my answer would be.

'I like very much, thank you, Miaow.'

I sat on the balcony bed and rolled a thin joint of straight grass, while Philip replenished our beer bottles and poured us a shot of Jack Daniel's each. Above our heads a fan whirled silently as the sound of the Doors' 'L.A. Woman' wafted up from a street-level bar below.

'That'll be Woodstock,' said Philip. 'It's the local rock-and-roll bar, run by an Aussie bloke. It's a go-go bar where the girls dance to '60s music. We'll check it out later, if you like?'

'Sounds fun. Maybe tomorrow.'

'Fine. Why don't you make yourself at home and we'll be back in a bit. Miaow and I are invited to the opening of a friend of hers' bar in Patpong.'

I had no intention of going anywhere; I'd barely slept a wink on the plane and had got quite pissed in the transit-lounge bar at Moscow airport. What's more, the weed was starting to kick in, and though I was a seasoned hash smoker, I was not prepared for the buzz this stuff was giving me. I poured another shot of bourbon, took a swig of beer and lay back on the bed, looking at the fan on the ceiling. I imagined I was on the set of *Apocalypse Now*, recalling the scene in which Martin Sheen, wearing only a sarong, cuts himself while punching a mirror after doing some kind of convoluted t'ai chi exercise. Jefferson Airplane's 'White Rabbit' was playing at the Woodstock Bar below, and I wondered what Nok was going to be like.

Twenty-four hours earlier, I'd been sitting in Heathrow airport with my one-way ticket in my hand, wondering what I was getting myself into. I often got butterflies in my stomach before I left home, but this time I had no plans, or even a ticket, to go back. I had enough money for a few weeks and then I'd have to get a job, whatever work I could find. It had been days since I'd spoken to Philip about my flight-arrival details. Would he be there to meet me? What would I do if he wasn't? Now these worries were a million miles away. The booze and weed were taking effect, and I slid effortlessly into a deep sleep.

A soft nudge woke me, and I rolled over to find a sleek body next to mine. I scanned my brain for a few seconds, but the computer in my head crashed under the weight of information overload. My eyelids flopped shut, then opened again to see the chopper blades overhead. I blinked and sat up. Outside it was light, but a sheet had been hung over the bamboo blinds, bringing a pinkish hue to the room. At the edge of the window a shaft of light shone into my eyes, its misty particles suspended like fairy dust at the head of the bed. Wiping a fine layer of moisture from my brow, I spied a sink in the corner of the room and remembered how dehydrated and thirsty I was. While pouring a glass from the tap, it occurred to me that it might not be a good idea to drink the water. Just then a hand touched me on the shoulder, and I turned to see my sleeping partner, with her long dark hair and ivory-white teeth, standing beside me wrapped in a pastel-blue sarong. She leaned over to a small fridge in the corner of the room and pulled out a plastic bottle of mineral water, which she held up to my lips with a smile.

'You are Philip's friend?'

'Yes, and you must be Nok?'

It felt strange shaking hands with someone I'd just woken up next to, but it seemed like the right thing to do, so we both giggled awkwardly as we officially touched for the first time. Nok pulled a cord next to the window and reeled in the bamboo blinds, revealing my first daylight glimpse of Bangkok down below.

'You take shower?'

'Yes, thank you.'

The toilet I'd used the night before doubled up as a shower, and as the water washed over my body I could hear my new friend singing along to the radio next door. My first day in the Thai metropolis was getting off to a start I could not have imagined in my wildest dreams, and I scrubbed myself as if I were washing away my old life to make way for the better days that lay ahead.

We sat in an American burger bar having breakfast. Nok assumed that, like many of her Western friends, I would not enjoy the local cuisine, so we sat eating a horrible chicken sandwich wrapped in a Stars and Stripes napkin.

'Let's eat Thai food for dinner, Nok; I can eat this kind of food where I'm from.'

'OK, but first I'd like to take you to my apartment.'

'I thought you lived with Miaow?'

'No, I've been staying with her, but I have my own place. Would you like to come and stay?'

We took an air-conditioned taxi for 15 minutes and pulled up outside a high-rise apartment block. She insisted on paying the fare, which was just as well since air-con taxis were not really in my backpacker's budget. I stood next to her in the lift, with my rucksack at my feet, admiring her lithe body. She had a stunning figure and large obsidian eyes that peered up at me as she smiled. The apartment had little in common with Miaow's place. The main room was three times the size of the other place, with glass sliding doors showing a panoramic view of Bangkok. I headed straight for the cassette player while she disappeared into the shower next door. On top of the machine was Neil Young's *Decade* album, which I slipped in and then pressed play. 'Cortez the Killer', one of my favourite songs, was playing. I was in heaven. To this day I'm unable to listen to songs like 'Old Man' or 'Ohio' without being transported back to that apartment all those years ago, such is the associative power of music.

Nok appeared again, with a brief sarong barely covering her body, and took a cold beer out of the fridge for me before returning to the bathroom. Wandering around the room, I noticed a number of photographs of her with a red-headed guy I guessed to be around 35. There were pictures of him with his parents taken at some Midwest barbecue, and one of him wearing a yellow hard hat, standing shoulder to shoulder with an Arab wearing a red kaffiyeh. Nok had mentioned her boyfriend over breakfast. He was an American working for an oil company in Saudi Arabia who kept a place in Bangkok for R & R. She was a kept woman in his absence but clearly had no trouble making cash on the side. After a couple of beers, we decided to go out and find a suitable place for me to have my first Thai meal. I wanted to go to one of the colourful street stalls I'd noticed across the road from the apartment block, but Nok insisted on taking another air-con taxi to a market area a couple of miles away. We came to a bustling street with an open-air restaurant every five yards. Outside each stall was a large sloping table covered in ice with an immaculately arranged selection of colourful seafood. Behind the chilled marine offerings, a man stood next to two large gas rings, tossing the food in a wok. Next to him, a woman with a huge, razor-sharp meat cleaver sliced vegetables and chopped up squid, whose inky entrails she rinsed in a large vat of water. Nok spoke to her in Thai, and she looked up to smile at me while continuing to slice the food on the wooden block in front of her. Her face was friendly and welcoming, and she waved her head towards a couple of free seats available a few feet away. I was convinced she was about to cut open her fingers with the dangerous-looking knife in her hands, but no doubt she could have done her job with her eyes closed. I ordered a bottle of Kloster beer and Nok bought a small bottle of Thai whisky and a big bottle of Coke. I tried a sip of her drink without a mixer, and it tasted more like cheap rum than anything you might find in Scotland.

'Is this a good spot to eat?' enquired an ashen-faced couple from the north of England.

'Dunno, just got here myself.'

They sat down on a bench across the way, she with her back to us while he glanced at us from over her shoulder. He looked mildly envious as he admired Nok's sleek stature. His missus looked older than him, and when she began to read an English translation of the menu he took the opportunity to grin and wink at me. I tried to crack a smile when I felt a hand on my thigh. Turning, I saw two bowls of rice and a massive plate of mixed seafood before us. Prawns the size of small lobsters lay next to tiny pink crabs and jade-coloured clams, while the squid glistened like purple coral. Within seconds, another plate arrived with steaming stir-fried vegetables over dried noodles.

'There's nowt wrong with that then,' said the Englishman across the way, though I was unsure whether he was referring to the meal or the girl.

'Ooh! Look at the size of those shrimps,' said his wife, turning to look.

The meal tasted as good as it looked and cost less than the third-rate KFC-style dive we'd eaten in earlier. Afterwards Nok wanted to take me back to Nana Plaza, where her friend had a bar. I suggested we take a tuk tuk that was a quarter of the price of an air-con taxi, but she wouldn't have it, saying tuk tuks were dirty. The bar in the plaza was run by a German guy and his Thai wife, who looked like junkies and probably were. He wore a pink Balinese shirt and slacks, and had long blond hair and pale-blue faraway eyes with pinhead pupils. She looked like Siouxsie Sioux in 1979, with thick make-up obscuring her cratered complexion. They were friendly and warm and gave me a drink on the house on account of my being Nok's friend. I propped up the bar while Nok did her rounds, sidling up to chubby Americans perched awkwardly on bar stools. I got chatting to a friendly guy from Texas who worked in the oil business in Qatar. A pretty girl called Phong joined us and the

Texan bought her a Coke. She had a friend in tow, who sat next to me before Nok hissed and waved her away. The bar stereo was playing the Beatles' *Rubber Soul*, which was fine with me. I'd been into punk music in my early teens, but later I'd fallen in love with the sounds of the '60s and rarely listened to any current music. In Bangkok it was as if the '60s had never ended, and there was still a large community of Vietnam veterans who'd stayed on after the war and married Thai women.

Philip turned up after a while with a new pair of girls I didn't recognise that he'd met in a bar on Patpong road. The manager of their club had offered him a job as a doorman, which involved handing out leaflets and hustling foreigners into choosing his place over the myriad bars on the strip. He said he'd probably give it a miss and take his flight to Rangoon sooner than expected. Bangkok was doing his head in, and he wanted to go down south to Koh Samui when he got back. He gave me a card for the go-go bar that had offered him a job and told me to contact a guy called Barry. We made vague arrangements to meet at a bungalow on the island, and he disappeared with the two girls.

Nok was busy with her American friends, so I flagged down a tuk tuk and showed him the business card Philip had given me. He nodded and off we went through the traffic towards Patpong. We pulled up outside a bar called Suzie Wong's and I paid the fare. Young Thai girls lingered in the doorway and grabbed my arm as I walked past. Inside another two girls took over, sitting me next to a stage and bringing me a cold beer. A fat Western-looking man was on the stage with two girls. They were taking turns to suck him off, but his penis was flaccid and he couldn't get it up. Our eyes met, and I noticed his were pinned. Another junkie trying to pay for his next fix, I thought as I glugged on my bottle of Singha. A girl to my left tugged on my shirt and pointed across the room to a guy in a black Jack Daniel's vest with a handlebar moustache. It was Barry. I left without saying hello and took a tuk tuk back to Nok's bar.

She was waiting with an air-con taxi. I climbed into the back as an American at the bar winked at me. Nok had her hand on my lap all the way back to the apartment. When we got there, she walked straight into the bathroom and turned on the shower. After a couple of minutes she came out and handed me a towel with the shower still running. I cleaned my teeth as the cool water splashed over my grimy skin, then I wrapped myself in a sarong and walked into the main room. The room was almost dark, but I could see her silhouette in the shadows by the bed. The bamboo blinds allowed horizontal bands of light to shine on the wall, giving the room a film-noirish feel. I lay beside her and she rolled over for a cuddle, then raised her right leg up to my waist until I could feel her moist, warm parts rubbing up against my thigh. Running my hands through her hair, we tried to kiss, but I felt awkward and told her I just wanted to hold her for a bit.

'You don't like me?'

'I think you're the most beautiful woman I've ever met,' I said.

I wasn't lying, but something was holding me back. I lay there frozen, wondering why I was unable to make the most of the greatest opportunity that had ever come my way. But the missed opportunity would be replayed, again and again, with a very different outcome, as I lay in my cell in Shanghai prison many years later.

I got up and lit a cigarette, which I smoked out of the window as Nok slept. A cool breeze blew across the Bangkok skyline, and I felt a chill for the first time since arriving in the country. Then we fell asleep in each other's arms.

A sticky pool of warm clammy juice trickled between the follicles of my chest hairs into my belly button, where it quickly crystallised in the freezing air of 8th Brigade. The nightwatchman paused momentarily outside my cell door before continuing on his ten-minute rounds of the wing. After a minute, I reached over to my shitbucket and tore a few pieces of toilet roll off to wipe myself down. I wondered what kind of life Nok had ended up with. Had she married one of her American boyfriends who worked in Saudi and returned to some sleepy town in Idaho or Texas to bring up his kids? Or had she, like me, fallen through the cracks, condemned to while away her days pondering what might have been?

Thinking of what had become of the beautiful Thai girl and my unforgettable introduction to the country, my mind drifted back to my second visit to Thailand, which had been a very different experience and changed the course of my life for ever. Hard drugs demolished much of the sense of morality I'd previously possessed. High-quality heroin was easy to come by, usually bought in small glass phials for a few dollars. Unlike the 'brown sugar' from Afghanistan and elsewhere in the Hindu Kush, 'Chiang Mai White' was a highly refined and insidious form of the drug. It had a soft, fluffy texture and was extremely powerful when snorted in even the tiniest lines. An English friend, Jonathon, and I had got into it after we found ourselves hanging out in a guesthouse near the Khao San Road in Bangkok's backpacker area. We were both heading for Japan, where we planned to teach English, but we had several weeks in Thailand before our respective flights left.

These were fun times, but the drug drastically altered my personality. Perhaps it would be truer to say it unleashed dormant character traits that would have surfaced anyway, but there was no question that heroin was a catalyst that had a profound effect on my behaviour. I'd always been afflicted by a sense of guilt, though it was never clear why, and heroin is the friend of those who wish to lay down such burdens. This is why junkies find it very easy to lie, cheat and steal from even their closest family and friends. Heroin will take your conscience and kick it for six every time. No questions asked; its powder dissolves the soul.

My music taste changed, too, and after years of listening to my singer-songwriter heroes I fell in love with the drug-addled Rolling Stones. I'd always thought there was something a bit naff about the Stones and had never really appreciated their music. My teenage punk heroes had dismissed them as overblown rock poseurs who'd 'sold out'. I was familiar with their big hits and there had been a few greatest-hits albums around the house when I was a kid, but now I discovered the brilliant sequence of albums between *Let it Bleed* and *Black and Blue*, a period in which the once squeaky-clean pop group degenerated into a down-and-dirty rhythm-and-blues outfit, turning out a succession of superb albums best appreciated at four o'clock in the morning with Class A drugs running through my veins. *Exile on Main St.* was my favourite, closely followed by *Sticky Fingers* and *Beggars Banquet*, and we stocked up on bootleg cassettes from the multitude of street vendors on Khao San Road. The only 'current' album that came close was The Cure's *The Head on the Door*, whose lyrics we interpreted as containing endless references to heroin, real or otherwise. I'd met Robert Smith and Simon Gallup at Norfolk's premier punk venue, West Runton Pavilion, years earlier, and the singer had given me a guitar plectrum as a gift, while both scribbled their names on my arm with a biro. Now I was lying on the tiny guesthouse bed listening to 'Kyoto Song', convinced every word was written for me.

My lovely Thai girlfriend Lek was not impressed with my new habit and flushed the powder down the loo when she found it. I was twenty-one, while she was at least five years older and had seen the stuff destroy many of her friends who'd fallen prey to its sinister charms. Jonathon and I bought another phial and hid it on a ledge under the guesthouse stairs.

'We shouldn't do this stuff every day,' said Jonathon, 'or else we'll get hooked.'

I agreed, so we settled on every other day, which quickly reverted to every day. No other drug is quite so good at deluding its users into thinking a day has passed when it hasn't.

I got a bit of work teaching English, which I thought would be good practice before the move to Japan. Jonathon was dabbling in petty crime, kiting credit cards 'borrowed' from other travellers, so I went along for the buzz. The card-owners would go to one of the islands in the south and after 24 hours report their credit cards missing. In the meantime, we'd go on elaborate shopping sprees determined by the spending limit on the credit card. We ate in five-star hotels, and in the gold shops of Chinatown we bought two-thousand-dollar gold chains. I was terrified of the armed guards in the gold shops, who sat in the corner with shotguns on their laps, staring at us while we waited for confirmation from the credit-card company. The spoils were divided between the card-owners and Jonathon, while I'd get to enjoy the freebies along the way. Some of the shops we went to were in on the scam and allowed us to buy what we wanted, even checking the card limits for us. We stocked up on clothes for English-teaching in Japan, as we only had jeans and T-shirts, and soon we had several outfits to make us look like 'real' teachers.

Though I was happy to benefit from these shopping trips, I didn't have the nerve to do them myself. It seemed suspiciously close to stealing, and even the smack did not lead me down that road. Had it done, I imagine

I'd have been an even worse thief than I later became drug smuggler. I'd always had jobs and crime never really suited me; I was too honest for my own good and my conscience would have plagued me.

Sex was something my conscience found rather easier to approve, and the heroin opened a Pandora's box of debauchery. On my first visit to Thailand the previous year I'd had a beautiful girlfriend called Lek, a bar girl who'd come to Bangkok from a small village near the Cambodian border. When we'd met, I was down to my last few hundred dollars and was planning on going to Australia to work. She had her 'paying' boyfriends, who were usually older men, while I was what she called her 'love' boyfriend. There were strict rules in the guesthouses about 'working' girls coming into the rooms at night, but the family who owned the place befriended Lek and allowed her to stay when she liked. She continued to see her customers, but always came to me at the end of the night and kept her other dalliances to what she called 'short time'. In spite of the slightly unorthodox arrangement they were happy times, and when I left to find work in Australia we kept in touch and rekindled our relationship upon my return.

Australia had been hard work, but I'd saved every penny I could in the six months I was there. I wanted to see Asia, and the land down under held little interest for me. I'd got a string of lousy jobs and kept my head down, starting with the dismal fruit-picking season in Victoria state. I'd heard you could make decent money in the orchards, and perhaps if you arrived at the right farm at the right time and knew the right people, you could. But for me it was a disaster, and I barely earned enough to feed myself while living in a grubby shack in the outback. I'd hitch-hiked from Melbourne, a pleasant enough town, and on the first day I was fired for picking unripe fruit: the only fruit available at the time. I was thrown off the farm there and then, and nearly got arrested for vagrancy by some hick coppers in a four-by-four. They reminded me of the rednecks in American films about the Deep South, while I was the black drifter one step away from a chain gang.

Things improved when I got to the next farm and by chance ran into some old school friends from Norfolk taking a year out before university. They were on their way to Sydney and said I could join them later on. With a new plan of action, I needed to come up with a couple of hundred quid to make it to the big city and applied myself to the loathsome task of picking pears for ten hours a day. I hated the work and spent the evenings getting drunk on cheap, nasty booze with Aboriginal lads. With barely enough saved to buy the bus ticket, I decided to hitch to Sydney instead and got a ride with a psychotic truck driver who scared the hell out of me. He drove one-handed and used the other to rant to his mates on his CB radio, using his knees to keep the steering wheel steady while he changed gears. Presumably his mates were up ahead, telling him what the traffic was like, because he was uninterested in which side of the road he was driving on and went round blind bends on the wrong side. I was exhausted and needed to sleep, but he wanted company and said I could get out and sleep on the side of the road. I stayed awake all night.

We pulled into an industrial estate on the outskirts of Sydney at six in the morning, and I found a pie shop opening for the early morning bake. My friends Bobby and Simon had got a place near Bondi Beach and were sharing with two Kiwi girls and their cousin Stu, a guitarist and recovering heroin addict. I took an immediate liking to Stu, a very chilled-out guy and good company. It was cramped, but they said I could stay for a couple of days until I found my own place. I stayed five months and slept on the sofa for a peppercorn rent. We all signed up for an agency called Dukes and were rarely out of work. Some of the jobs were OK and some of them weren't. They kept sending me to a powdered-milk factory for ten-hour shifts, and I'd have to spend an hour washing the disgusting, sticky grime off my body afterwards. The foreman was a sleazebag who liked to brag about getting the 'cherry' of 13-year-old Filipino kids on his visits to Manila. I wanted to punch his fucking lights out.

It was shitty work, but I was earning and saving around a hundred dollars a week. If I kept it up I'd fly back to Bangkok with a couple of grand in my pocket, enough to hang out for a while and fly on to Japan. At the end of the week we'd go to a bar called the Bourbon and Beefsteak, an all-night drinking den in King's Cross. This was the start of my penchant for bourbon, which climaxed the following year in the karaoke bars in Kyoto.

Bob Dylan came to town with Tom Petty and the Heartbreakers, and

I saw them twice: my one extravagance while in Australia. The first time I got so drunk I have no recollection of the show whatsoever. I can only remember being woken up by the prod of a policeman's truncheon on the side of the road a good mile from the stadium. Later I talked Bobby and Simon into coming to a second show, which they reluctantly agreed to in spite of the expensive tickets. The gig was in one of those awful aircraft hangar-style venues, better suited to corporate events, but I did remember the show. Unfortunately I got thrown out for lighting up a cigarette in the squeaky-clean dive and stood out on the street while Bob played 'Like a Rolling Stone'.

I was still thinking about Lek, but I started to meet new girls and before long had a new girlfriend of sorts. Belinda was cute, but we weren't well suited. She had a junkie boyfriend called Lance whom she was still seeing, while her sister, Judy – whose flat she lived in – had a boyfriend who was on the run for armed robbery. Judy was cute too, but I felt they were both damaged. They'd had a difficult upbringing and had been removed from the family home by social services. Judy's boyfriend, Bill, was a bad lot. I took an immediate dislike to him and was not surprised to learn he was violent and abusive towards her. Fortunately he only arrived intermittently, usually late at night, as the police were looking for him. They caught up with him in the end and he went to prison for many years.

After six months my visa was running out, and I had my two grand saved, as well as the second half of my return flight to Bangkok. Bobby and I took a few days out to see more of the country and caught a bus up the coast to a place called Surfers Paradise, a hideous Torremolinos-like resort that I hated. It was off-season, and we holed up in a cheap motel, drinking and watching TV. The beach was deserted, as was the town, and the sea was choppy, with danger signs every hundred yards. Perhaps it's unfair to judge a holiday resort off-season, but I got the impression it would be even worse full of people. Soon I'd be in Thailand and the last thing I wanted to do was spend the money I'd saved in this dump.

Within a week, I was back at the airport waiting for my flight. Belinda and I had parted company on good terms, and I'd given her a silver St Christopher pendant my mother had given to me. Some years later I got mail from her with a San Francisco phone number included so I could call her. We spoke for a while, and I was pleased to discover she was happy and settled with an American guy. She'd had a shitty start in life, but things had turned out for the better. She asked if I wanted her to return the St Christopher, but I told her to keep it, saying that maybe if we ever ran into each other again I'd have it back. Unsurprisingly, I never saw her or the necklace again.

Back in Thailand I wanted to party before going on to Japan, and I had the cash to do it, for a while at least. Jonathon and I moved away from the backpacker district to a guesthouse near the Malaysia Hotel, an old Vietnam War R & R hangout. It was an agreeably seedy neighbourhood, with a small cafe bar frequented by Vietnam veterans and over-the-hill bar girls. The Americans tended to be bearded, with Jack Daniel's vests and Harley Davidson tattoos. Many had tried to settle back home, only to find they missed the 'edginess' of the war zone and the girls they'd met in Saigon. With fond memories of the region, they'd used their army pensions to come back, start businesses and settle down with willing Thai girls. The Malaysia Hotel was a dump that had seen better days and looked more like a nasty block of flats than a hotel. It was a notoriously 'smacky' neighbourhood, and the hotel was at the very centre of the sleaze. It was common to see ambulances parked outside and another dead junkie being taken away. In the basement there was a 23-hour bar, but you could take your drink and sit in the garden for the hour that they were cleaning the place up. It became our end-of-the-night local, where we could have a nightcap and stumble home to our crummy guesthouse down the street.

We met a couple of Londoners called Tony and Ronnie, who'd just come from Australia with thousands of pounds' worth of traveller's cheques, which they'd 'lost' on arrival. They successfully claimed them back from American Express, even though Ronnie had cashed in the originals on a quick jaunt to Singapore. Now they had money to spend and they wanted to have fun. We started going out to bars and clubs, buying Captagon 'slimming' pills from the pharmacy and drinking all night. We went on a blitz of one-night stands and before long had acquired a variety of STDs.

It wasn't my first visit to a clap clinic; I'd been to one with Lek after picking up a 'dose', as Ronnie called it, on my previous visit to

Thailand. Lek had taken me to a central Bangkok hospital, where we stood in a huge line for over an hour before being seen by the doctor. The patients were mainly women, but there were men, too, and even Buddhist monks in saffron robes. Eventually we got to the front of the queue, which opened into a large room containing curtained-off cubicles with a bed in each, and a man sitting at a small table with a Bunsen burner. In his hand he held a small tool that resembled a tiny model of the immersion heaters we'd had at boarding school to boil water for Pot Noodles. It had a wooden handle with a long wire sticking in it that coiled up at the end and back on itself. The Bunsen burner was there to clean it between patients. Nobody spoke English, but Lek asked the doctor to see me and explained the problem. He asked me to drop my trousers as he stuck the grim instrument into the blue flames to kill off my predecessor's germs. Then he stuck the end in a bucket of water to cool it down.

'Are you sure you don't mind coming to the Thai hospital?' Lek had asked me earlier. 'There is a *falang* [foreigners'] clinic, but it's very expensive.'

'If the Thai hospital is OK for you, it's OK for me,' I said.

Now I was regretting the decision, but it was too late. The doctor plunged his knobbly wire into my urethra and wiggled it around to get a sample of the discharge. The sensation was both agonising and ticklish, and I let out a yelp as he dragged the wire back out before wiping it on a piece of glass with my name attached. I pulled up my jeans and underwear, and he handed me the sample back and called for the next person, as he waved his tool over the Bunsen burner again.

We managed to find a seat in a huge waiting room that looked more like a train station than a hospital. I figured the worst was over, until I saw the size of the injection heading my way. Our numbers had come up on the wheel above the entrance to the waiting hall, and we'd been called up to take our samples into a doctor's office. The door was slightly ajar, and I was standing outside rolling up my shirt-sleeves when I saw a man lying on a bed. The syringe looked like a veterinary hypodermic for delivering horse tranquillisers, and I'm the kind who is scared of tetanus jabs. The doctor held the dreadful contraption up to the sunlight and squirted out the air pocket before plunging it into the man's stomach. I turned to look to Lek for reassurance, but she'd already gone in to have her check-up and was nowhere to be found. Finally it was my turn, and I lay down as the doctor thrust the stainless-steel spike into my gut, where he left it for what felt like an eternity.

Now a year had passed, and we were waving down a tuk tuk on the side of the road on the way to sort out our respective 'doses'.

'Bangkok Hospital, please,' said Ronnie, as we set off through the city smog.

'Let me tell you a story,' I said, and began to recall my tales from the previous year.

'Make that Nana Plaza on Sukhumvit Road instead, please,' said Tony.

So off we went to an English-speaking clinic in the posh part of town, which charged us five times as much, but it was worth every penny.

Tony and Ronnie were not impressed with our use of skag. They were a few years older than us, with a lot more common sense, and when I turned up at their rented flat with an American Vietnam vet called Steve it was the last straw. Steve was a junkie living in Kathmandu who had been hired by a distraught Canadian family to find their son, who'd gone travelling the year before and had not been heard of since. He'd been trekking in Nepal, but had flown to Bangkok at some point and had subsequently gone off the radar. Steve seemed a strange person to entrust with finding anyone, let alone dealing with the police and embassy staff. He looked like Dennis Hopper in *Apocalypse Now* and had a full-blown heroin habit. We'd met in the cafe opposite the Malaysia Hotel, where he was staying, and he'd taken one look at my pupils and decided I was a good person to help him find some gear. We scored a phial and stopped by at Tony and Ronnie's place, where Steve fell asleep on Tony's bed and had to be lifted out of the room.

'You gotta knock that shit on the head, Dom,' said Tony, 'or it'll be too late before you know it.'

He was right. My brief flirtation with smack was getting out of hand, and it was time to get a grip. It was getting me in trouble, too, and I found myself in a fight with a ladyboy at six in the morning in the bar of the Malaysia Hotel. He'd kissed me with thick red lipstick on my brand-new white shirt, and I'd called him a stupid fucking faggot.

Three people had to drag him off me, and we both got barred from the sleaziest bar in town. My body couldn't take the powder, either, and I was prone to projectile vomiting out of the windows of taxis. The force of the jet from my stomach was such that it didn't even touch the sides of my mouth. Thai girls I was sleeping with started telling me to get out of the country. 'Thailand no good for you,' they said. 'This one no good,' they said, rubbing their noses.

It was time to take their advice and go. My second visit to the country had seen me go from being a squeaky-clean kid who liked to smoke the odd spliff while listening to Van Morrison's *Moondance* to a strung-out loon lying dazed in dingy hotel rooms listening to the Stones' 'Sister Morphine'. My personality had changed and would likely never be the same again. Lek had been replaced by a long line of girls whose names I couldn't recall, although we remained friends. I hadn't visited one temple in three months, but I'd got drunk in half the bars in town. I'd swapped museum visits for clap clinics, malaria pills for tetracycline. I was gaunt and skinny, with sunken eyes and pallid skin, and rather than wait for Lek to do it for me, I emptied my last phial of heroin down the loo.

Tony and Ronnie were also leaving, heading back to London to get jobs, having blown the proceeds from their traveller's cheques scam, while Jonathon flew to Japan to meet his English girlfriend. I was on my own and the fun had gone. I had enough money to buy a ticket to Osaka, with a short stopover in Hong Kong, but I had to clean up my act before going to Japan, where drugs were frowned upon. I moved back to the Chuanpis Guesthouse behind Khao San Road and spent my last days with normal backpackers, eating good food and steering clear of any chemicals. I felt like I'd been through a maelstrom and now I'd been spat out the other side, wondering what the hell had happened.

'You crazy boy!' said Lek, sliding her hands through my hair.

We were making up for lost time, lounging around the guesthouse drinking juices and counting down the hours till I'd go away again. I promised to send her some cash when I got up and running in Japan, and that I'd be back soon to see her. She was the only thing that had been constant about my first year away from England, and I'd missed her terribly when I'd gone to work in Australia. Now I was on my way again, and our time together was coming to an end. She had a new 'money' boyfriend, an older man from England whom I had a beer with at a street bar. He seemed a nice enough bloke and looked after her well. She was hoping to get married to give her family the life she wanted for them, and had saved all her money to build a house in her home village in the countryside. Her family were everything to her, and her own happiness was secondary. I was the opposite and was only really interested in myself. Perhaps the heroin had made that easier to deal with.

Lek wanted to come to the airport with me, so we took an air-con taxi across the city. We were still good friends, and she was concerned about the state I'd got into. I felt I ought to give her a little cash before I left, so I asked the taxi driver to pull over outside the Nana Plaza bureau de change. As I pushed open the taxi door there was a crash, and a guy somersaulted over the bonnet of the car and into the road in front of the cab. He got up shaking his wrist, which was clearly bruised, and started having a slanging match with the cab driver. The driver helped him pick up his motorcycle taxi, which was lying on its side, and then they both began to assess the damage. The taxi door was slightly dented, but the bike's petrol tank had a large bump in it and would need to be banged out by a mechanic. Obviously they both decided I'd be footing the bill. Lek was outraged, sensing that they would be getting the spare cash I'd planned to give to her, and she was right. I ran into the money-changer and cashed in a hundred and fifty dollars, and gave the hundred to the bike guy, which I told him was all I had. Then I slipped Lek the fifty and told her to go home so she didn't have to pay to get back from the airport. We kissed goodbye on the side of the road before I got in the cab and drove to the airport. She was still standing there in her pretty pink dress, smiling at me as I turned to look out of the back window. I never saw her again.

12

Sex and Drugs and Mao Zedong

I became a barfly as soon as I hit Asia. I guess I'd never been able to afford it in England, and most British pubs were dreary places in the early '80s. Also, there didn't appear to be any licensing laws and you could drink 24–7, which I did my best to make the most of. It didn't matter whether you were in Bangkok, Seoul, Taipei or Tokyo: when one bar closed another opened, and if you were skint you could always buy a hip flask-sized bottle of whisky or vodka from a vending machine. I was addicted to Coca Cola, too, and drank endless cans of it to keep the never-ending hangover at bay. There were various speedy drugs available over the counter, like the Thai slimming pills Captagon, which kept you up all night and made you feel like committing suicide when they wore off. The thought of taking them today makes my mind reel, but I had some great nights on the town with them and loved the confidence-enhancing rush they gave me.

If you got bored with the legal drugs available, there were always dealers around to find something else. Japan, with its harsh legal system and outrageous prices, was the hardest place to buy drugs, but if you knew a yakuza you could get hold of *shabu*, a frighteningly powerful type of amphetamine. This came in pure crystal form and cost a hundred dollars for a mini packet. It seemed like a rip-off until you realised how little you could get away with taking. A single tiny crystal gave you a massive rush if smoked on tinfoil, while a medium-sized line would make you feel like Superman for 36 hours. An American musician friend taught me how to get the most out of the stuff by putting it in a mini spice bottle with a lollipop stick spiked through the cork top. We'd then get a mini blowtorch lighter and heat up the glass while spinning the stick between our fingers. If it got too hot the crystals would start to turn brown, so the trick was to wave the lighter around the base of the bottle at just the right distance while inhaling the fumes. Once the lighter was turned off, the hot liquid would recrystallise immediately and be usable later. The comedowns were devastating and left you feeling like your life was, to all intents and purposes, over. The depressions got so bad I had to give the stuff up while I was still sane.

Work was a mixture of market-trading, English-teaching and busking, and the yen was at its peak. A good run of work in Japan would bankroll a year in cheaper Asian countries. Busking in Japan reached its zenith around this time, and various duos and troubadours would vie for the key spots in the bar districts of the big cities. My favourite was outside the public toilets on Kiyamachi Street in downtown Kyoto, which had a stage of sorts, with male and female entrances either side. Large gangs of students and office workers would congregate while their mates had a pee, and it was not uncommon to make twenty dollars off one song. A gangster once gave me a hundred dollars for singing 'Wild Horses' to him and his girlfriend, but usually it was couples that wanted to hear Beatles ballads like 'Yesterday'. Salarymen, the name given to the blue-suited white-collar workforce, tended to favour cheesy country songs like 'Take Me Home, Country Roads', which I hated singing. I'd plead with them to let me play Merle Haggard's 'Sing Me Back Home' instead, but after I'd sung it they'd demand to hear 'Country Roads' all the same. 'Let it Be' and 'Stand by Me' were probably the most requested songs of all, but I built up a deep dislike for both and would sing 'You've Got to Hide Your Love Away' or 'Help!' instead, which would usually keep them happy.

It was hard to argue with the punters, because if they requested a song they invariably paid for it. Unlike many countries, where busking seems closely related to begging, street singers (as we were known) were effectively human jukeboxes. The choice of songs mirrored those found on the karaoke machines in the local bars, and most people knew all the words and sang along. Musicians would come along and have a strum while I popped off round the corner to the beer machine. I'd learned this trick from stories I'd heard about the legendary blues harp player

Little Walter, who liked to invite wannabe harmonica players up on stage while he went off drinking or chasing women, only to leave the hapless victims on stage for the majority of 'his' set. Some people would give you beer instead of money, and occasionally I'd be invited to go to one of the local restaurants, where I'd be plied with drinks and delicious food. Weekends were naturally the busiest, and it was possible to play from six in the evening to two or three in the morning. On the really good nights, the atmosphere became carnivalesque as great swathes of human traffic descended upon the street, bombarding my guitar case with hundred-yen coins. Every so often the local police would move me on and I'd go for a few drinks at friends' bars and come back an hour or so later, but as a rule they'd smile and wander past uninterested.

While I was busking, Rosie would be hostessing in one of the many expensive clubs in Gion, Kyoto's main bar district. This entailed sitting talking to Japanese businessmen and pouring their drinks. I'd worked in such places myself on earlier visits to the country and knew the routine well. Each customer had his own 'keep bottle', which sat on the shelf behind the bar. Each time he visited the bar, he'd drink from the same bottle and only be charged for the ice and water, which could cost him a hundred dollars alone. When the bottle was finished he'd be obliged to buy another one, and this was how I earned my money. The *mama-san* (landlady) would invite me from my place behind the bar to have a drink with the customers. Generally speaking, Japanese people couldn't drink much, and when they did it tended to be *misouari* (whisky and water) with very little whisky in it. As soon as I sat at the table I'd be given a half-pint glass with almost no water in it, and by the end of the evening the customer would be obliged, at great expense, to buy another keep bottle, while I'd be totally legless. If the punter was a bourbon drinker, which I had an unhealthy tolerance for at the time, I'd happily drink until the new bottle arrived, but I quickly developed an aversion to the local whisky and would pour it down the sink while the customer was out of sight. It made no difference to the *mama-san*, who made a good profit out of my drinking habits, and all the customers had company accounts, which they were happy to invoice for their expensive habits.

There was one particular customer that we dreaded. He was a senior executive at a major Japanese corporation. He always came to the bar late, in a state of advanced inebriation, and would flail around to traditional Japanese music, groping the hostesses, who treated him like a naughty schoolboy. The hostesses would ply him with salty snacks, which would get caught in between his protruding yellow teeth. He spoke no English whatsoever, but would insist on talking to me in slurred Japanese, pinging vile globules of slimy squid snacks in all directions. One night I missed the train back to Kyoto, and he asked me if I wanted a lift in his taxi. Reluctantly, I agreed. Throughout the journey his hand slid across the seat into my crotch, until I put an elbow in his ribcage and he roared at the taxi driver to kick me out. We were in the middle of nowhere at three in the morning, so I refused and the cab continued to his house. On arrival I discovered we were still a good 15 miles from Kyoto, so I demanded he pay the driver for the remainder of the journey. He was outraged and tried to leave me to sort it out with the driver. Finally, his wife came out of the house in her dressing gown, reached into his jacket pocket for his wallet and gave 10,000 yen to the driver. As the taxi pulled away, I saw him collapse in the driveway of his home.

Although reluctant to take a hostessing job when we first got to Japan, Rosie took to her new line of work and was soon earning good money. After a while, her customers started to ply her with expensive gifts and day trips to local cultural events and sushi restaurants. I started to feel jealous and resentful that I couldn't afford to do the same for her, but she put my mind at rest and we started to make plans to take the money we were earning back to India to invest in jewellery and crystals to sell in Europe. The success rate of Western couples in Japan was not good, with the men invariably being tempted away from their partners by the pliant, exotic Japanese women they came into contact with as English teachers or bar workers. Having lived in the country several years earlier, including 18 months with a local girl called Miya, I was less enamoured of their coquettish charms and was more in love with Rosie than ever. My Japanese girlfriend Miya had been a *maiko-san* from the age of 15 but had given it up instead of graduating to be a geisha like many of her friends. Whereas geishas were all over Japan, *maikos* – meaning dancing girls – were only found in Kyoto and were comparable to apprentice geishas. They studied for two years under the most conservative *mama-sans* in the old part of Gion and were hired to dance at exclusive banquets all over Japan. As well as dancing, they were expected to be expert in tea ceremony and playing the shamisen, the three-stringed cat-skin instrument that looks a bit like a banjo. But Miya was more interested in rock and roll than traditional arts, and had opted out of the intensive training necessary to make the transition to geisha that her mother had enrolled her in. My feeling was that she had not wanted to continue in a profession that would likely lead to her having to compromise her integrity, but she never admitted it to me.

Even though Miya had given it up, she still had an apartment paid for by her benefactor, a wealthy and very aged local businessman. Her former colleagues Satomi and Mimi lived with her, along with several cats, and within weeks of our meeting I moved in too. The household was entirely nocturnal, and we rarely got out of bed until after dark in the winter. Miya had a hostessing job in an upmarket Gion club, while her friends worked as geishas around the country. She'd spend at least two hours getting ready for work, but her friends took around four hours to put on their faces and kimonos. The transition was extraordinary as these rather plain-looking girls morphed into exotic dolls.

Miya's work had led her to meet many celebrities and she knew the composer and occasional actor Ryuichi Sakamoto, a major star at the time who'd collaborated with David Bowie on Nagisa Oshima's *Merry Christmas, Mr. Lawrence*. Although she was trained to mix with the great and the good, she liked a bit of rough with the smooth, which is probably where I came in. I was more interested in gang culture than tea ceremony, and I'll never forget seeing hundreds of Japanese lads on motorbikes having showdowns with the police in Kyoto. I'd often hang around on the streets late at night, watching the bike-gang subculture known as *bōsozōku*. I could hear them long before I saw them, as their modified exhausts turned Kyoto's main drag into Brands Hatch. Police sirens screamed from all directions as the police set up roadblocks, creating a wall of uniforms across the road. It was a game, but a dangerous one, as the bikers never wore helmets and the police took swipes at them with batons before leaping out of the way to avoid being run down. Sometimes the police would simply throw their truncheons at the bikers, and a few people were hurt, particularly if the bikes crashed. An ambulance was usually on hand to pick up the pieces afterwards. The police often resorted to dragging a spiked chain across the road, at which point the bikers would move locations, but often the bikes would mingle with other traffic, preventing such drastic measures from the cops. It was a great sight, and in typical Japanese style it involved an elaborate, ritualised dress code including kamikaze bandanas, Imperial flags and yakuza-style punch-perm haircuts. Some of the hard core *bōsozōku* went on to become gangsters, but more often they grew out of it in the same way as mods and rockers did in England in the '60s. Like the cherry blossoms of Kyoto their youthful exuberance soon faded, but at their peak they reminded me of the kinds of kids seen in movies like *Rebel Without a Cause* and *Rumble Fish*.

Miya knew some high-class yakuza, too: rich Koreans with legitimate businesses in the construction industry. In fact, we lived on the cheap in a flat owned by one of them, which made Miya nervous, as it was not a good idea to be indebted to such people.

Kyoto often hosted major gatherings of high-level yakuza, and it was common to see lengthy convoys of white Mercedes-Benz cars with blacked-out windows arrive in the Gion bar district. Immaculately dressed hoods with perm hairdos and sunglasses would stand beside their cars, waiting for the bosses to arrive in their black cars. The police kept well out of their way and seemed to look upon them more as military top brass than gangsters.

Once we'd met a yakuza on the riverbank in Arashiyama, one of the most beautiful places in Japan, famous for its cherry blossoms, cormorant fishermen and expensive fish restaurants. He was sitting alone drinking beer, throwing stones into the river near where we went swimming, and invited us to drink with him. He had a full-body tattoo suit, as well as one and a half small fingers missing: a sign he'd upset his boss on several occasions. We got chatting, and I discovered he'd spent 15 years in prison for a murder his boss had committed. The police knew he was innocent, but bosses rarely went to jail, sending their underlings instead. In return for his sacrifice, he'd been rewarded by being made the boss of one of the most exquisite parts of Kyoto Prefecture. He drove a huge, top-of-the-range, jet-black Mercedes and carried the first ever mobile phone I recall seeing.

He wore a navy kimono with a black T-shirt underneath and, like many Japanese gangsters, had tattooed eyebrows that looked odd with his shaved head. The more he drank, the more he insisted on trying to fondle me, much to Miya's amusement, who laughed as I pushed his hand from my crotch again and again. I guess the 15-year stretch had taken its toll.

Like many yakuza he was of Korean descent, a discriminated-against minority. To this day many Koreans still have to queue up at Japanese immigration centres to renew their papers, despite having lived in the country for many generations. The largest single group of yakuza members in the western Kansai region – at least in the lower echelons – are *buraku* people, the descendants of outcasts from the feudal period. Traditionally these people worked in occupations associated with death, such as tanning, slaughtering animals and undertaking. They lived in ghettos separated from the main communities and are still discriminated against today, though many thrive as market traders and, of course, gangsters.

Years later, Rosie and I were invited to a *buraku* party in a suburb of Kyoto. We'd been selling crystals and jewellery at Kyoto's various flea markets and had got to know some of the other stallholders and the *buraku* organisers that we paid for the space. When we arrived, we discovered we were among the few guests without full-body tattoo suits. Even the women had them; something I'd never seen before. The first thing they did was give Rosie an envelope with a 10,000-yen note in it as a gift, while I walked around admiring the fabulous designs on their skins.

While my relationship with Rosie went from strength to strength, my friends went from Yuki to Kyoko to Suki to Midori and back again to Yuki. Sometimes it seemed like a handful of girls was being passed around from foreigner to foreigner, which was pretty much the case. Western girls living in Japan tired of the endless philandering of their male counterparts, who seemed, at times, to be living like Roman emperors with a retinue of nubile young women at their beck and call. Some went out with Japanese guys, who were generally shy and often intimidated by Western women, but sometimes these relationships lasted longer than the men's, which rarely went beyond the casual fling.

Unlike the Japanese, the Chinese were far more prudish about sex.

In Communist China, shows of passion were reserved for expressing revolutionary zeal rather than personal fulfilment. Almost all forms of entertainment were banned unless they were seen as furthering the Party agenda. Love between individuals was a bourgeois distraction from the more important collective passion for nation and leader. Mao had encouraged the people to have as many children as possible, causing a population explosion that has still not been successfully contained. His rural background had led him to believe that the more children a family had, the more hands there would be to work the fields, but China was changing fast, with a huge migration of people from the countryside to the cities. In 1979, three years after Mao's death, Deng Xiaoping attempted to reverse the trend by implementing the one-child policy. While the policy was undoubtedly a practical response to a dire population problem, it nevertheless imposed further the state's interference in the private lives of the Chinese. In the early '90s, things were changing – in the large cities at least – and yet that most primal of human urges was still dominated by the state.

Still, even in the darkest days of the Cultural Revolution there had been at least one Chinese man enjoying himself. Mao had a voracious sexual appetite that seemed to grow with age. His underlings organised 'Cultural Work Troupes' when he made his rounds of the provinces. These gatherings usually involved dance troupes from which the ageing lothario had a wide choice of young 'volunteers' to regenerate his ailing *yang* (male essence) with the *yin shui* (female water) from their nubile young bodies. Like the emperors of old, Mao believed the Daoist tradition that a regular dose of youthful vaginal juices would prolong his life. He was particularly fond of orgies with several girls at once and did not confine himself to the pleasures of women alone. Handsome, muscular young men were required to perform his nightly massage, which often involved more than a rub-down of his back.

As in many countries, homosexuality is taboo in China and was only recently removed from the list of mental-health disorders. Yet same-sex relationships are well represented in ancient Chinese texts like *Water Margin* and *Dream of the Red Chamber*, which Mao held in high esteem. In some respects the Chinese belief system is less hostile to homosexuality than its Western counterpart, and none of their religions consider it sinful. While the *yang* is primarily a masculine energy, it is also acknowledged that every *yang* contains an element of *yin* and that some men have a great deal of *yin* in their *yang*. One of the ancient Chinese terms for homosexuality, 'the passion of the cut sleeve', refers to a Han emperor who cut off his sleeve in order not to wake the much-treasured male concubine who lay in his embrace.

The top prisoners in Ti Lan Qiao had only two people in their cells, and I suspected from my first week in the prison that some inmates had close relationships. For example, Gao Zhengguo, the number one prisoner upon my arrival, had shared a cell with T'an Ji, the prettiest cellmate on the whole wing. T'an clearly had rather more *yin* than most other prisoners on the wing and had not been in the jail long enough to have a two-man cell, so I'd assumed from the start that they did more than share the same shitbucket.

At the height of summer some of the Chinese prisoners slept outside their cells, as it was considered unsanitary to have three people lying in a five-feet-by-seven-feet space. One evening, it was not yet lights-out when I walked down the corridor to get some water, and Chinese lay around on mats in their boxer shorts. Many lay against each other or slouched in their friends' laps. It was not a sight you would be likely to see in a British prison, where privacy could be easily achieved with the click of a cell door, but neither was there necessarily a sexual dimension to it. However, on this occasion I saw one of the more senior prisoners, Wu, being fondled by a younger inmate. He had his shorts down to his knees and his legs apart, and he watched me walk by without any show of interest. I was not even convinced this was a sexual act since Wu – a tough-guy gangster from Guangzhou – did not appear particularly aroused.

I'd also experienced what Mishima called 'forbidden colours' in Ti Lan Qiao. A young lad from the punishment unit downstairs had a job cleaning the shower area. At the end of the room stood a large steel gate that divided the room into two and enabled trustees from downstairs to get hot water. I'd say *ni hao* to him from time to time, and I often noticed him looking across through the bars when I was having a wash. He spoke no English, but my Mandarin had improved and I was able to throw together a few rough sentences to make small talk. He always had a pleasant smile for me, and I could see him peering up from his mop as I threw warm water over my naked body. After finishing my shower one day, I decided to introduce myself and called him over to the bars. He peered down the stairs to check nobody was around and moved his mop and bucket closer, before holding out his hand to meet mine. His hand was clammy and limp, the closest thing to *yin shui* I would likely experience in prison. I held it for some moments as we gazed at each other, and a pulsating energy flooded through my veins into my dick and I was hard. His groin was pushed up against the bars as his grey flannel trousers bulged and our handgrip tightened. Then a door creaked open on his side of the gate and his hand shot to the head of his broomstick as he lurched back, plunging his mop back into the bucket of milky, chlorinated water. A bell rang out and a flood of Chinese began to pour back into the wing from the work area. We never touched again.

13

Going Home

Captain Xu announced the foreigners would be having their photos taken, so we were marched off to a large greenhouse-style building on the other side of the jail. There were hundreds of plants in pots along a wall and a solitary chair had been placed in front of them, with an officer standing by with a camera on a tripod. Although I was told to come along, the purpose of the photo was designed more for the other foreigners, who had been away from home a lot longer than I had. With the exception of Gareth, whose wife visited regularly, family visits were few and far between, and the prison had decided it was time to give us an up-to-date picture to send home to our families.

Captain Mai presided over the photo session, which Larry did his best to get out of on the grounds that it was little more than a propaganda exercise. He was probably right, but the rest of us were always up for an opportunity to get out of 8th Brigade and see a new part of the jail. We were a motley crew, and the years in jail had not been kind to any of us. I'd gone bald and Jürgen had gone grey, while Larry and Tommy looked older than their years. We all had a grey pallor from the lack of natural sunlight, and Gareth had put on weight. Larry's health had deteriorated, and a knee injury had stopped him taking part in the few exercise periods available. With Mark gone he was the only vegetarian in the entire prison, and little effort was made to accommodate his dietary habits. While the rest of us got a meat dish once a week, Larry would be given a hard-boiled egg and cabbage. Mark had made a point of making friends with inmates from 3rd Brigade, where the food was prepared, and had seen to it that he and Larry got healthy meat substitutes like tofu and fruit. Now there was nobody to help him, and he looked increasingly haggard. He wrote reports to complain, but any report had to go through Captain Xu, his nemesis and the target of many rants. The people he needed on his side all hated him and so his condition deteriorated until the US consul stepped in to ask for help with his food requirements. The consul pointed out that his life would be better if he was less antagonistic towards the prison staff, who had no control over his attempts to appeal. If he wanted better treatment, he had to be more diplomatic and play the game. Of course the first step of reform was acknowledging one's crime, and Larry was still trying to appeal his sentence on the grounds that he'd been blackmailed by gangsters. Given that the consular staff were aware of his record of drug busts in other Asian countries, it's highly unlikely they believed his story any more than the Chinese did.

The other foreigners were beginning to question their position within the jail's educational hierarchy. Chinese inmates who played the game appeared to be getting sentence reductions – albeit minuscule ones – while they were not. McLoughlin had long since bought into the Chinese way of doing things, but due to his violent outbursts he found he was going one step forwards and two steps back. Gareth and the Germans began to wonder whether it was time to succumb to at least part of the Reform Through Labour programme to see if it actually made any difference. I was far from convinced, but I understood their predicament. They had nothing to lose and could conceivably have something to gain. Had this initiative been proposed by Captain Xu I would have treated it with contempt, but I'd come to believe that Captain Mai could be trusted to help the foreign group if they helped themselves. The question was whether Larry would do his part or whether he'd undermine the efforts of the others or, indeed, be undermined by them. It was a huge step, because the foreigners had been exempt from working for years, but now we were being brought into the Reform Through Education system, which in itself was related to work. The Chinese had been clever to introduce the educational part of the system first, but it later emerged as something of a Trojan Horse as labour was ultimately an important part of reform.

My own time in Ti Lan Qiao was drawing to a close, but there was little cause for celebration. My colleagues were years away from release, so I kept a low profile and tried not to look too happy. There was little chance of me getting any reduction in my sentence but neither was it out of the question, so when we were called to a Reduction Meeting, friends joked that I might be leaving that day. The whole wing was herded into a large room where several judges sat in uniform on a podium. Names were read out and prisoners stepped forward to be congratulated. By the end, it turned out that all the foreigners except myself and Larry would be given some kind of reduction of between six and eight months. Nobody was exactly ecstatic with this outcome, but it was better than nothing. It meant that the guys who were almost four years into an eight-year stretch were coming up to their halfway point and they, too, would be 'coming down from the mountain' soon. Some Chinese friends also got a few months off, but with sentences well into double figures it was hardly noticeable. With little to look forward to but years of drudgery ahead, they plodded on, like Sisyphus rolling his ball upwards.

'Within a few weeks, you'll forget you were ever here,' said Larry, who'd been through a similar routine several times and seemed to know what he was talking about.

The foreigners wanted me to send some more books, and Larry was eager to point out that if I didn't do it soon, I'd probably forget to do it altogether.

'If you get half a chance, don't forget to stick a trip under a postage stamp for me, will you?'

'I'll see what I can do.'

The final weeks of a prison sentence can be unnerving. A huge weight is being lifted off your shoulders, while other burdens are only just making themselves known. Time, which has hitherto spun like a calendar in a Hollywood film, begins to grind to a halt, and the days linger where before they'd flashed by. The outside world – which in my mind had been perfection itself – starts to look less appealing. The light at the end of the tunnel comes into focus, revealing a humdrum world with all the pitfalls and pressures that were there before. It is no longer the Xanadu it appeared to be when you first got arrested. The illusion dissolves before you like a mirage in the desert as the release date approaches.

An illuminating prison book had been circulating our wing, written by a guy called Bo Lozoff, entitled *We're All Doing Time: A Guide for Getting Free*. Bo is an extraordinary man who has spent many years working in prisons with some of the most dangerous individuals on the planet. His message is that freedom – or lack of it – has little to do with walls and is, rather, a personal journey of enlightenment. It may sound like a banal observation, like money doesn't buy happiness, but he backs it up with many examples, not least the number of people who return to prison after their release. Now the walls around me were coming down, and I began to question the nature of freedom and happiness. I realised that I'd had many happy times in prison and that at some of the saddest times in my life I'd been free. The worst part of my prison journey had been the early days in the detention centre. And yet I'd been blissfully happy to see the full moon appear through the slim band of the steel shutters on the window as I hung from the bars at night. I'd spent eight months lying on a dirty mattress, but my dreams had been splendid. The mornings were crushing, but the nights had filled me with hope. The move to the prison had vastly improved my physical life, but something had been lost in the process. In the detention centre my mind had been almost kaleidoscopic, overflowing with an energetic and boundless optimism. I'd found it very easy to convince myself that the future would be bright, even though there was little evidence to support this rose-tinted view. Now I was facing another hurdle. Freedom.

My incarceration was the physical manifestation of another factor.

I'd run out of road.

Days before my arrest, I'd met a young couple on the bus between Kashgar and Urumchi in Xinjiang. It was a long journey through the desert, and we shared a room one night in a small village along the way. They were young and new to travelling, and every moment was savoured as they recalled their adventures to me. When it was my turn to speak I sounded jaded, even to myself. I must have sounded like the ageing hippies I'd met in Goa in the late 1980s, moaning about how it wasn't as good as it had been in the '70s. But if travelling had lost its allure, what the hell was I going to do with the rest of my life? I'd done much of my travelling on my own, and enjoyed it, most of the time. Years earlier I'd written in a notebook, 'Aloneness is a precious gift, and loneliness its bastard offspring.' Now the aloneness had given way to the loneliness.

In Urumchi, I got food poisoning from a street stall. After the bland monotony of the food on the bus ride, the big city was a foodie's mecca. Muslim men sat beside small charcoal fires cooking mutton threaded onto bicycle spokes, and I must've eaten ten of them. Years earlier, I'd got serious food poisoning in Bangladesh and had spent Christmas Day stranded in a guesthouse in Chittagong. Food poisoning can seriously zap your energy at the best of times; on top of hepatitis, it laid me up for a week. I took an excursion for a couple of days to the oasis town of Turfan. Its boulevards were festooned with grapevines that dangled in my face as I strolled around aimlessly. I fancied a drink, but my hepatitis had put an end to that. I was in the wine capital of China, drinking sodas and yogurt drinks. There were sand dunes on the edge of the town, but I didn't have the energy to walk up them. I wanted to smoke, but my lungs leapt out of my ribcage after every puff. My greatest traveller's asset – being able to get on with the locals wherever I was in the world – had deserted me, too. I was invited to take part in a pool game and nearly got beaten up for refusing to pay a gambling debt I'd never agreed to.

I took a train from Urumchi in the far west of China to Lanzhou in the centre. The trains were all sold out for days to come, and I had no ticket but got on the train anyway: a 48-hour journey with no seat. I didn't have the energy to stand up, so I squatted between the third-class carriages. Chinese in Mao suits looked disapprovingly at me on their way to the loos, while train officials charged me for the seat I never got. Kids hawked cigarettes and packet noodles through the bars of the windows and ran off with my change. The toilets went from unsanitary to unspeakable – even the cockroaches scrambled under the door to get out of the way. At one point I thought my guitar bag, which contained my hash, had been stolen, and I ran through the train looking for it. Alas, the one time in my life I *needed* to be robbed, I was 'saved' by a guard who'd put it on a rack above one of the bunk beds in the sleeper carriage.

The train stopped in the middle of the night for what seemed like hours. A group of soldiers got off for a walkabout, so I joined them.

It was freezing, but the air was fresh for the first time since I'd got on the godforsaken train. I walked along the embankment close by the carriages, beyond which was a steep ravine that fell into total darkness. I heard a passenger inside spit and then felt it on the back of my neck. I don't think it was aimed at me; I was just in the wrong place at the wrong time. Everything was wrong. After eight years living in Asia, I'd never felt so bad. I'd reached the end of the line.

So where do you go when you've run out of road? When the train line simply runs out of track? Well, each to his own, I guess, but prison was my solution to the crisis. Let's face it: you don't travel thousands of miles across three international borders with half a kilo of hash in your bag if you wish to stay out of jail. I was sick in mind and body, and I wanted out. I could have joined the Foreign Legion, but I'm not the army type. Uniforms don't suit me, anyway. I could have got religion, but I've never really *done* religion. I've dabbled, sure. In fact, just before I left my hotel room to cross the border into China, I could hear the sniffer dogs barking at the Pakistan customs stop in Sost. I briefly made an Islamic prayer, prostrating myself three times, but it was fear that was driving me, not worship. No, I'd long since reconciled myself to the fact that somewhere deep inside I wanted to go down, and I was lucky enough to have been able to climb up again.

And there was something epic about the trip I'd made that seemed to suggest the adventure was some kind of grand finale. After entering China from Sost and driving over the Khunjerab Pass, there was a wonderful drive back down the mountain along a dead-straight road into the desert. After the barren rock faces of the Indus Valley the road went flat, and as we approached the Chinese border a rosy-cheeked kid in a green uniform had stood to attention. Our driver gave him a carton of Marlboros, and the long descent began through hundreds of square miles of melon fields. Running parallel with the road was a sleek turquoise stream, no wider than a small car, which formed an electric-blue border between the tarmac road and the green melon fields. It had an artificial, neon-like quality to it, as if it had been transported from a kitschy Las Vegas hotel. And the mountains along the way reminded me of the Pinewood Studios set of the Himalayas in Michael Powell's great *Black Narcissus*. And there were women everywhere, hunched over melon plants in colourful clothes with babies on their backs: a welcome sight after the dismal masculinity of northern Pakistan. My journey was reckless but often beautiful, with a cinematic backdrop of stunning scenery and striking landscapes. If you're going to screw your life up, there are many worse places in the world to do it.

Chinese friends were eager to spend time with me, as if my impending release imbued me with a sense of freedom that might rub off on them. I thought of the American prison song 'Midnight Special', which refers to the light from the interstate train that passed the jail at the same time every night. Folklore had it that prisoners who managed to clamber up the bars and allow the train to 'shine a light' on them would be going home soon. Now I'd been bathed in this light, and even prisoners I'd never had much to do with wanted to come up and say hello. My small hunchback friend was particularly sad to see me go and would miss the head massages I'd been giving him. He still had double figures of his sentence to go and did not mix well with the other prisoners. It would be harder for him than most others, and after several years inside he still hadn't really settled down. Another friend named Li had become the wing's star artist and was given commissions to paint propaganda paintings, which he was very good at. Gareth was also painting a lot, and we were all invited by Captain Mai to visit the prison art exhibition in the main building.

As well as paintings, there were huge wooden carvings and stone sculptures that any Western art gallery would have been grateful to add to their collections. Local dignitaries visited the displays and many of the art works were for sale, though I doubted the artists would get much of a share of the takings. Many of the artefacts were reminiscent of the Maoist propaganda posters of heroic peasants and happy workers toiling for the motherland. The colours were garish and the characters always had rosy cheeks and proud smiles. I wondered how long the Communist Party could keep its grip on a society that was changing so fast. Next door in North Korea, the Kim dynasty had complete control of outside influences and had turned its nation into a kind of slave state. Meanwhile, China was developing so quickly it was hard to see how the rigid dogmatism of the Mao years could be perpetuated into the twenty-first century. People had food in their bellies for the first time in decades and contact with the outside world had never been greater, but the devastating crackdown of the Tiananmen protests had sent a clear message to those hoping for political freedom.

There were a number of political prisoners in the intellectual wing upstairs from us, and many had life sentences. Even so, some were being fast-tracked for early release as their crimes no longer carried such severe punishments. Everybody knew that 45 years after Mao declared that his people had 'stood up', China was finally getting up off its knees. Without Mao it might have happened much more quickly, but either way there was no going back now. For many of my friends, the city they returned to would be barely recognisable as the one they'd left. From the shower-room window we could see the Shanghai skyline was in a constant state of flux, with hundreds of giant cranes giving birth to huge new buildings. I'd lived in the city for two and a half years and yet had spent less than two and half hours walking its streets. When my time came to leave I would be escorted to the airport and sent on my way, but I'd be back some day. I'd asked the judge Mr Shen if I would be permitted to return to China, and he'd assured me I'd be welcome. I was already looking forward to my next visit and sensed that I was going to miss the country once I'd left. China had changed my life; there was no doubt about that. Whether it was for the better remained to be seen, but it would never be the same.

I wondered what had become of Liu. Was he still in that dire room in the detention centre, waiting to go to court? Had he even been charged yet? We'd gone from best mates to arch-enemies, but now the resentment had faded and I felt more sorrow than anger. What were his wife and son going through? Never knowing when he would be home. All I knew was that he hadn't come to Ti Lan Qiao, because otherwise I'd probably have run into him at some point. Our old cellmate Yen would be released within a couple of years and go back to his wife and kid. By then his executed brother would be a distant memory, rarely mentioned outside close family. The bitterness I'd felt towards him and Liu seemed silly now. A friend in Kyoto had written to me to say how lucky I had been to have cellmates at all. He'd spent 13 months in solitary confinement in Japan for a minor dope bust. It had driven him crazy and he'd never really recovered. I'd shut myself off from my cellmates, but they were still there and they kept me sane. Many of China's most famous dissidents had endured years on end in solitary confinement for 'crimes' we encourage in the West, such as exercising freedom of speech. Ti Lan Qiao was like a holiday camp compared with what they'd had to cope with. I was acutely aware of how fortunate I'd been. Many of my Chinese friends had been tortured with electric batons and grisly beatings, while I'd always been treated with respect. I'd been lucky that my case did not involve anybody else, though even my friends could still not truly believe me when I told them that. They didn't understand my crime, and in two and a half years in prison I never met – or even heard about – a single Chinese convicted of a marijuana offence. There were loads of heroin dealers, and many of them were executed, but we never saw a Chinese dope dealer, and the foreigners often speculated whether the weed, which grew on the side of the road throughout the country, was even illegal.

Our number one, Chen Yong Ho, made my last weeks a pleasure, and we spent many hours together. I wondered how his wife and kid would cope without him for so many years, since his time to serve also ran into double figures. He had a calmly Daoist attitude to the situation, while acknowledging his marriage might not survive the years ahead. Like most Chinese I met, he was not one to indulge in self-pity but rather accepted whatever life had to offer. Another prisoner told me this was Chen's second time in prison, and he was furious that this had come to my notice. He never mentioned it again, and I never enquired further.

My studies declined as the countdown drew nearer, and I played less guitar and stopped writing letters altogether: I would be out before they reached their destinations anyway. I spent hours staring out of the window at the lifers' brigade opposite – a punishable offence, but now my minor transgressions were ignored, as they had been on my arrival. Lifers I'd got to know would smile and hold their fingers up, one fewer each day. They were as happy for me as I was sad for them. Most would be released one day, as even life sentences in China are usually completed in less than twenty-five years, but a huge chunk of their lives was being taken from them. They worked longer hours than our brigade did, too, often late into the night if orders from Japan and America were pending.

I wondered what the golfers in California would say if they knew their hats were being made by slave labour.

There was a major clearout of the death-row landing downstairs, and a human chain of condemned men handcuffed together were boarding a bus in the courtyard below. Along with us foreigners, they were the only people in the jail that were not issued with uniforms. Most would be staying a maximum of three months, so the prison saved itself the expense. Their heads had been shaved for the occasion, and a line of prison officers were herding them onto the bus. Some of the more loutish officers snarled at them and prodded them with sticks, but most were respectful, even sad. I asked Chen Yong Ho what he thought about it, and he said he did not agree with the death penalty. I asked Captain Mai the same question and he was non-committal, suggesting to me that he, too, did not agree.

'But this is China,' he said. Boy, if I had a dollar for every time I'd heard that phrase.

It was March 1996, and my release date was the tenth of the month. I'd been arrested on 11 September 1993, a day of the month that would become enshrined in the collective memory of the world. Back then, 9/11 was a day like any other, but not for me. As Solzhenitsyn said in *The Gulag Archipelago*, 'Arrest is an instantaneous, shattering thrust, expulsion, somersault from one state into another. The gate to our past life is slammed shut once and for all.'

Now I was walking the corridors, sighing heavily; I was winding down, as if a spring inside me was slowly uncoiling. The door to my past life was reopening, but would the outside world be different? Would I be different? I'd found it necessary to wean myself off Rosie and move on. It had pained me, but it was for the best. From our letters, I got the impression she, too, had moved on. She had a new life, and perhaps a new man. We were destined to be the greatest of friends, but our idyllic love affair was probably over. I would leave prison a single man, and in this respect, at least, the gate to my past life was well and truly shut. In other words, the life ahead of me bore little resemblance to the dream world I'd filled every waking hour with throughout the early days of my incarceration. Since my arrest I'd cushioned myself from reality on every step of the journey. First I told myself the customs men who arrested me would give me a slap on the wrist and send me on my way. When this turned to dust I managed to convince myself I'd be released when I got to court, and finally I believed I'd only do half my sentence. At no point did I believe I'd lose the love of my life. Now I had to face the fact that I'd been wrong on every count, and freedom had a bitter taste.

The other foreigners were similarly delusional; in fact, they were worse than me as the burden of their long sentences encouraged them to cling to a number of possible release dates that were largely fantasy. They, too, had hoped to get out at the court stage, only to discover their crimes carried sentences in excess of murder tariffs in their own countries. Then there was the appeal process: a wonderful daydream to entertain oneself with when you're looking at 15 years behind bars, but basically worthless.

'They'll probably kick us out with Mark' was the favourite when I first arrived. But Mark went after completing his sentence. And the rest of us stayed. The next hope was 1997, as the Hong Kong handover loomed. This event would be a momentous occasion in Chinese history, but I was sceptical of the idea that it would be considered an opportunity to release a handful of dope smugglers. Still, I kept my own views to myself – the last thing they needed was to have their wishful balloons burst by me. My Chinese friends had no such illusions – they knew they'd have to do at least 90 per cent of their sentences, and in some ways they were happier with this knowledge. Misplaced hope can crush you time and time again, but for the Chinese there was only reality, which they accepted without complaint.

A new batch of prisoners turned up. They sat on the tiny blue plastic stools that I'd seen so many times before, as senior prisoners clouted them round the head and shouted at them. They were being introduced to writing thinking reports, the ongoing sagas of how they'd come to 'let down' the People. One looked too young to be in prison and was terrified, but he'd get used to it after a while. I didn't bother to ask what they were in for, and they probably wouldn't have told me the truth anyway. They'd stepped into the tunnel just as I was coming out the other end, and we were worlds apart. They were looking through the 'wrong' end of the telescope, while my own view was out of focus.

Captain Mai called a meeting to remind the foreigners about their obligations to the Reform Through Labour programme. He wanted them to work alongside the Chinese cutting bits of loose thread off cooking aprons. The garments were destined for Japan and had labels of the French designer Pierre Balmain sewn into them. Larry refused to touch them on the grounds that it was slave labour and illegal according to international law, but the other foreigners agreed to take part. It was a bitter pill to swallow and there was little evidence that work was related to sentence reductions, but if it got the officers off their backs it was worth it. I was spared the task because I was about to be released anyway, so I sat with Larry chatting about his intransigency to the authorities and how it might affect his health and hope of parole. I told him I thought he was crazy and that things would likely get worse if he split from the foreign work group. He had little to gain and much to lose, but he was a stubborn bastard with too much pride, which is rarely good.

'The Chinese are going to fuck you over sooner or later, Larry. You could die in this place and nobody will ever know.'

I wasn't joking. His health was very poor, and he was well into his 50s, with haggard skin and a constant stream of minor ailments. He looked ten years older at least and could barely walk the five yards to his cell. He'd been hospitalised and had spent a lengthy spell in the young offenders' punishment unit for going on hunger strike. He was almost old enough to be a grandfather to his fellow inmates. Now he was taking on the Chinese again, and it could only end in disaster. I pointed out that had he been Chinese, he'd have been beaten so badly he'd have shaped up long ago. He'd have been hog-tied, doused in water and given electric shocks until he begged for forgiveness. Or else he'd have died of 'natural' causes. Regardless of whether his stance was morally correct, he looked like an arrogant American waving his passport in the hope of preferential treatment. His was the petulance of the privileged, and the Chinese were having none of it.

While the other foreigners were being reformed through labour, I was starting to pack up my possessions. There wasn't much, but even in prison it's possible to acquire all sorts of junk, from soy-sauce bottles to a selection of notebooks. One of the first things I'd done on my arrival in Ti Lan Qiao was to write out the classic Daoist text the *Dao De Jing*. The book was very short, but I'd spent so many hours consulting the

Sage in the I Ching that when I eventually found a copy of the original text I decided the best way to acquaint myself with it was to write it out by hand. It's not the sort of thing that I'd ever have considered doing before or since, but in jail it seemed like a therapeutic pastime. I also had two large diaries, one of which had a record of my favourite quotes from the dozens of books I'd read. In the detention centre I'd started out making pencil marks in the margins of my books, but after sentencing I had access to a great selection of other people's books so I made a point of writing down my favourite lines. I also had a record of every I Ching session since my arrest and was struck by the frequency with which the hexagrams pointed towards Chapter 36, 'The Darkening of the Light'.

I had a postman's sack-sized pile of letters received from friends and family, which I decided to edit down. It was tough deciding which ones to keep, but I couldn't be too sentimental about it. Some friends had written multiple letters, for which I was hugely grateful, and I had many from kind strangers associated with the charity Prisoners Abroad. Another letter was from a friend in Spain who was living in a small town in the mountains near Granada. She'd suggested I come and stay if I fancied getting out of England after my release. I kept the letter.

One of my prized possessions was a postcard of a temple in Nara, the ancient capital of Japan. It was no ordinary postcard; it had been sent to me in a letter from my friend Freddy in Kyoto. He'd been to see Bob Dylan at a Buddhist festival in Nara, and being a good hustler had managed to get backstage and meet the great man. He told Bob I was in jail in China and asked could he send me a message, so Bob scribbled 'Hi Don, Best Wishes Bob Dylan' on the back. Apart from misspelling the last letter of my name, I was elated at the thought that for a few seconds, at least, I'd been in the thoughts of one of my great heroes.

Jürgen and I would miss playing guitar together. We'd spent hundreds of hours sitting at the end of the landing, with me strumming the rhythm and him playing the lead. When you play so much with someone, you get a rapport going and are able to second-guess each other's next move. After a while, the two styles fuse into something else entirely and the music begins to take on a life of its own. Now he'd have to go back to playing on his own and tapping his foot to keep the rhythm. Music was his life, and he did little else but sit in his cell playing the blues. I think he'd found a kind of happiness that insulated him from his surroundings and harsh predicament.

Ludwig would pass his time banging away on his noisy typewriter, which drove Gareth crazy. He never talked about what he was writing and was an intensely private person. He was younger than Jürgen and had gone off travelling for a few months only to find his brief adventure turn into a protracted nightmare. He wasn't a hustler, and I couldn't imagine buying dope from him. I got the impression his smuggling trip was out of character, a brief diversion for which he'd paid a heavy price. I felt sorry for him, but it wouldn't be long before he, too, would be 'coming down from the mountain'. For him the worst was over, and he'd leave prison a wiser, and still young, man.

Gareth had become something of a linguist: he spoke passable Chinese and was in the process of learning Spanish from a Teach Yourself book and cassette course. He spent a lot of time painting, too, and had a talent for it. While my relationship with Rosie had withered over the years, his with his wife had blossomed, and she was living in Shanghai and visiting every month. His journey from rural Wales to Xinjiang had ended in disaster, but the future looked bright for him and his wife. He was a man who knew what he wanted from life and would find happiness soon enough. Prison isn't the worst thing that can befall a person; if you're wise enough to use the time well, it might even be a blessing.

For Tommy, it was a long, hard road ahead. His stretch was still in double figures, and he'd regressed into an infantile hoodlum with too much time on his hands. Unable to concentrate for more than five minutes, study was of little use to him, while his estrangement from the foreign group had cut him off from any grounding influences. His response had been to become a sort of honorary Chinese: volunteering for menial work assignments, learning patriotic songs and kissing the backsides of the guards. Had he been a real Chinese, his antics would have been met with so much violence that his temper would have been quashed long ago. Instead he was lost between two worlds and was respected by neither. And yet he was often good company and was expert at making the Chinese laugh with amusing impersonations of prisoners and staff alike. He had a childish enthusiasm for new ideas, only to toss them aside as his attention span faded. He bought a guitar but never played it, took an Open University writing course but never followed it through. Finally he decided to become a model prisoner, before punching someone in the face. There was a nice guy in there somewhere, but the petulant thug trumped his best intentions every time.

Captain Mai held a meeting on 9 March in which he praised the foreigners – minus Larry – for their contribution to the Reform Through Labour programme. By showing their willingness to work, they were one step closer to a sentence reduction that would speed up their release dates. He also said that I'd be going home the following morning and had to be packed and ready to leave at short notice. Now it was official, my Chinese friends stopped by to congratulate me on the happy news, and I tried not to look too pleased with myself in front of those with very long sentences ahead of them. The consul had booked me a flight back to London with a stopover in Bangkok, as it cost the same as a direct flight and I felt Thailand would be a good place to unwind before seeing my family again. I'd spent a lot of time in Bangkok over the years, and it felt as much like home as anywhere else in Asia. England, on the other hand, felt like a distant place that I had no great desire to live in ever again. I'd left on a one-way ticket eleven years earlier, with no plans to go back. Now I was returning with a one-way ticket, but at least a stopover in one of my old haunts would break the back of the culture shock ahead.

Winter was still lingering, and a chilly breeze blew through 8th Brigade as my cell door clicked shut for the last time. It was a sound I'd come to quite like, signifying the end of another day and the start of the dream world in which there were no walls, bars or concrete. The night-watch team patrolled at ten-minute intervals, slouching down the corridor and writing up their reports on prisoners' bowel movements. I'd boxed up a selection of my favourite books and dedicated the rest to the Shanghai Municipal Prison library, so for once I had nothing to read. In 24 hours, I'd be sipping a cool beer on the Khao San Road and eating fried snappers in my favourite street market. Rosie was in Vietnam but would meet me in Thailand in a week or so, and we'd fly back to England together. What the future held for us was anyone's guess, but it didn't seem to matter much any more. The spell had been broken.

I thought of my first night in jail, after 13 hours of police and customs interrogations, pacing the wooden floors of the detention-centre cell beneath the glare of strip lights. I'd lain on my bed with mosquitoes circling like famished vultures and cried myself to sleep. I thought back to the kindness of Yen and Liu in those early days and the captain who'd assured me I'd get 'short time'. And he'd been right – even though he'd known nothing and was simply trying to cheer me up – the time had gone quickly in retrospect, though it didn't always seem like it while it was happening. I'd got lucky in the end and my sentence had been 'a holiday', as my Chinese friends liked to point out. I'd passed through the dragon's belly and out the other side.

Captain Mai turned up at around 8.30 and asked me to come to the office. I had to sign some papers, and he gave me a bag with the gold ring my mother had given me on my seventeenth birthday. On our travels, Rosie and I had bought a cabochon of lapis lazuli, which we had laid into the ring by a jeweller friend. Now it sat on my finger after two and a half years in a dusty envelope, with its azure blaze set off by the sunlight streaming through the bars. I wanted to keep my Ti Lan Qiao 'necklace' as a souvenir and had hidden the plastic card with my photo and prison number in the lining of my jacket. The photo had been taken on my first day in the jail, with me wearing a red, green and gold spliff-smoking Rasta T-shirt. Along with my number was a stamp of the red star of the Chinese Communist Party and the words 'drug peddler'. While patting me down, Mai found the jail ID and confiscated it, which was a shame. Surely I'd earned this one token of my time served?

The Chinese were all at work next door and we'd already said our goodbyes, but Chen Yong Ho had come to see me off and we shook hands. His day would come, but not for many years. I felt bad for him, but he was happy for me: a true test of friendship. The foreigners were happy for me, too, I think, or at least they were happy to be reminded that sooner or later they, too, would be leaving the clutches of the Chinese penal system. And then I was gone. Mai marched me down the stairs, and I glanced along the death-row landing. These prisoners would soon be leaving, too, and their families would never see them again, unless their last drive was captured on state TV. All the cells were locked, with a few trustees milling about and guards sipping green tea. Lawyers would be arriving shortly with unsuccessful appeal papers and wills to sign. I thought of the old man I'd met in the cells beneath the courthouse, how I'd given him a tissue to wipe the snot and tears from his face as he waited for death. He'd probably been too old to have been much value as an organ donor and died without benefit to the state: a small triumph, I suppose.

We were on the ground floor, where Mai stopped to fill in a short form to notify the brigade they were losing one of their members. A guard I recognised smiled kindly at me. He was bald, like me; my follicles had not taken well to imprisonment, even though I'd kept my hair shortly cropped anyway. We walked across the yard towards the main prison building, and once I got a few metres from 8th Brigade I turned to see my comrades vying for a view through the bars. I had my bags in my arms and my guitar over my shoulder and gave them a final salute, and they waved back as we turned round a corner for the last time.

A police minibus was waiting and Captain Mai handed me over. We shook hands and he looked quite overwhelmed with emotion, and for a moment I thought I could see a tear in his eye. It was moving for me, too: partly because it was a momentous occasion in my life, but also because I'd grown quite fond of Mai, who, along with the captain in the detention centre, had always shown kindness towards me. Both men had been considerate and had always been prepared to step outside the robotic limitations of their jobs to show a little humanity to those in their care. The Party they represented was cold and officious, but they embodied the warmth of many individuals within it, and I shall remain eternally grateful.

There were no handcuffs involved as the police van drove through the streets of Shanghai, but neither was I free. I asked a guard to stop and buy me some cigarettes with the cash I'd had on me at the time of my arrest, and he agreed, though I was to stay in the van. I opened a fresh pack of Marlboros and passed them to the officers, who accepted, and lit one up myself, flicking the ash onto the road through the barred window of the minibus. I thought back to my first drive across the city in a police car and how I'd desperately tried to convince myself it would all be OK, that they'd probably just deport me from the country. The spotty driver with his siren blazing and the English-speaking policewoman I'd tried to be nice to in the hope they'd let me go. They'd run every red light on the journey, barging their way through the traffic as if they'd caught an international terrorist. Now my driver was slumped in his seat, arm out of the window, eyeing the pretty girls on Nanjing Street and taking his time.

The vice consul, Jackie Barlow, was waiting outside the airport in a chauffeur-driven consular car, and the officer passed over my two boxes of books, cassettes and various other bits and bobs I'd acquired. They were to be handed over to the embassy and shipped back to England at a later date. The airport looked more Japanese than the kind of building I'd come to associate with China. Everything was new, and the bulk of the passengers were men in Western suits. There were no ramshackle shanty towns of hungry-looking peasants like I'd seen all over the country at train stations; this was the new China, a country ready for the twenty-first century.

I was lighting up a cigarette when one of my guards stopped me; I was not yet free and I was already breaking the law. Just two and a half years earlier, it would have been strange to see people *not* smoking; now they were trying to turn Shanghai into Singapore. A smiling girl from China Airlines came over with my ticket, which she handed to Jackie Barlow.

'This is as far as I go,' Jackie said. 'These men are going to see you to the plane.'

I thanked her for her help over the last couple of years, and for bringing cigarettes along to our prison visits, which she wasn't obliged to do. We'd got a few old newspapers from the embassy, too, and it was always good to get a copy of the *Sunday Times* once every three months. She'd been a valuable link for my family and had kept them up to date on any legal developments in the early days, when nobody knew what the hell was going on. The Shanghai consulate was at the forefront of trade between Britain and China, so a couple of jailbirds must have been pretty low on their to-do list.

She walked off towards the car park. I felt a hand on my shoulder, and we made our way to the departure area. There was no hanging about in airport lounges: the plane was waiting for me.

'Good afternoon, sir, welcome to China Airways. I hope you enjoy your flight.'

The air hostess didn't seem to have noticed that I was accompanied by two police officers, but when I turned they'd already gone. I got a window seat at the back of the plane and sat watching the pretty hostesses go about their work.

'Did you enjoy your visit to China?' asked a businessman, looking up from his stocks-and-shares newspaper.

'Oh, yes. It's a very interesting and beautiful country.'

'How long was your visit?'

'Not very long; I was just here on holiday.'

'Very good.' He smiled.

He put his head back into his newspaper, and I gazed out of the window as the plane gained momentum before slipping into the crystal-blue sky.

Epilogue: The Road to Madrid

The Triumph spluttered and snorted along the motorway, carburettors gargling under the weight of its steel frame, my life bungeed to the back rack in a tower of fabrics and CDs. A pair of panniers drooped over the seat like basset-hound ears, flapping noisily against the scorching exhausts in time to the engine's mechanical rhythms. Birds of prey hovered over the highway as orange trees blurred into formless tunnels of amber-green over the sticky asphalt. The road was empty, as if it had been laid out before me and would disappear behind me, while my two wheels screamed along its temporary surface, oblivious to the world that lay beyond it. As if from nowhere, a Mercedes-Benz slid past as I maintained my ninety-miles-an-hour cruising speed, and I looked up to see two small kids pointing and laughing out of the back window as the silver bullet shrank into the distance, and then I was alone again.

The silhouette of a bull grew from a black speck on the horizon into a giant tarmacadam beast scuffing its hooves at the foot of a mountain, wedged between a bank of olive trees clinging precariously to the rocky hillside and a dried-up ravine that snaked down the granite facade into the valley below. I glanced back to check on my load, as had been my habit for the last few hours, but something was missing. My right hand, numb with the vibrations of four hours in the saddle, unclenched the throttle as the engine chugged down the gears to a stop on the side of the road. Again I looked round in amazement at the luggage on the back of my bike, its zip bursting with the few items of clothing it seemed worth taking back to England. Everything was where I'd tied it before leaving Andalusia the night before, except the spare crash helmet that had sat on the top of my bag, fastened down by a spider-web bungee strap. I leaned over the saddle of the bike to see if the helmet had slid down the side and was somehow lodged between the mudguard and the pillion handrail, but there was nothing. I took off my own crash helmet, stepped back from the kerb and then walked along the road. I slid down to my knees in a squat among the roadside scrub.

And then I laughed. I wanted to cry, but I couldn't help myself; it was too absurd to take seriously. I knew in that instant that my life had changed – that there was no going back, that I'd have to get a job, that I'd never play cat and mouse with customs officials again. It was the end of an adventure that had lasted the best part of a decade, turning my life into a lottery whose successes only underlined their futility.

The helmet had weighed little more than a kilo, and 800 grams of that was dope: the result of a laborious hollowing-out-and-packing job taught to me by a friend in the mountains near Granada. Now I stood on the side of the motorway, gazing back up the road behind me, as the slipstream of a passing truck blew dust in my eyes. A pair of Hoopoe birds flashed by in a chequered orange flutter and rested on the base of an olive tree. They were spying on me, chuckling to each other as if they were in on the joke that had brought about my abrupt change of lifestyle. In the middle of the road an ochre-coloured lizard crouched on the relative safety of a white line, looking left, then right, before scuttling across to the island between the two roads. I knew which way I was going now.

I briefly toyed with the idea of retracing my journey to look for the £4,000 Riff mountain crash helmet that was presumably lying beside or in the road somewhere between here and Almería. But to have done so would have been to admit failure in understanding the strangeness of fate and the unconscious dreams and desires that make us do such idiotic things.

In spite of this philosophical interlude, my stubbornness was unable to let go of the thought of my livelihood lying further back down the road. What if it had only just fallen off and was only a couple of hundred yards behind me? Four grand's worth of Sticky Moroccan waiting to be picked up by a stranger who'd probably never know why the crash helmet was so unusually heavy and unbalanced. Or picked up by highway police and thrown in a ditch to keep it away from the traffic, where flies would drone and buzz curiously around it as the vegetable matter inside began to rot. Then I thought of the prospect of turning up at Plymouth from the Santander ferry with fifty quid in my pocket and no job, my plans to move down to Brighton with the proceeds of the scam blown out of the water. I'd have to sign on the dole and do some menial job that paid peanuts. There'd be no more whimsical flights to Goa or drop-of-the-hat jaunts to Pakistan or Thailand. I'd be stranded in the place of my birth with no quick and easy exit strategy. My wings would be clipped and I'd be forced to endure an avalanche of 'I told you so's' from jealous acquaintances who'd never know the life I knew. And it was a good life: it was the last great folk adventure, pitting your wits against the banal, sticking two fingers up at the cardboard cut-out facades of convention, the dreary rat race in which there were no free lunches but everyone was conditioned to believe they had a vested interest in making someone else rich.

And to give up now would be a betrayal of beliefs I'd begun to hold dear. I would be vindicating the authorities: all the customs men from Heathrow to Osaka who'd stuck their fingers up my arse, the police officers who'd stripped me naked and subjected me to endless hours of interrogations, the judge who'd sent me down, the screws who'd refused me my mail when it was 18 inches from their noses.

But this rage against power and authority had its flip side, too. There were the customs men who were only doing their jobs, the judge who'd come down to my holding cell at the courthouse in Shanghai with a handful of cigarettes and the first decent meal I'd seen for six months. The captain of the detention centre who'd shown me genuine kindness and reassurance when I had no idea whether I was going to get 15 years or a slap on the wrist. The prosecutor who looked like Stan Laurel, who gave me a carton of Marlboros to smuggle back to my cell. The prison guards who'd always had a sympathetic smile.

Even so, I wasn't ready to give up yet, so I climbed onto the Triumph and burned along the motorway to the nearest slip road in order to backtrack on myself in search of the crash helmet that contained my livelihood. It was a long shot, but fuck it: I'd do my best to keep the adventure going.

233

The first road off the motorway snaked around the hillside and over a flyover to a small roundabout with an offshoot back onto the Andalusia route south. I hunched the machine over onto its side to manoeuvre around the 240-degree bend and opened her up as the back wheel slipped from under me and sent the bike sliding down the gritty roadside to a stop beneath a buzzing pylon. A passing Spanish man pulled over to the kerb and asked me if I needed any help, but I wasn't hurt and the bike seemed OK in spite of losing an indicator. Above, a huge signpost split into two soared up like my own twin towers, pointing south to Andalusia and north to Madrid. I was momentarily dazzled by the choice of the two destinations, knowing full well what each signified for my future. My life has been peppered with such choices, and I have to say I've frequently made the wrong ones, ignoring my intuition and following my ego, throwing caution to the wind and doing foolish things to test my luck or simply to make my life more interesting.

I'd grown tired of running away, and there was nowhere else I really wanted to go. The travel bug that had driven me since my teens had lost its allure. I'd got busted in China because I no longer cared what happened to me; in fact, subconsciously I wanted to get caught, I wanted out. I knew as I looked up at that sign and the fork in the road in front of me that I had a choice, and that in our often murky lives options rarely appear with such clarity but instead are shrouded in contradictions and mixed feelings. And in that simple sign, a multitude of other signs burst into my consciousness, as if I were two different people vying for control over my destiny. I questioned whether my life had been a fraud, whether my picaresque lifestyle belied a deep selfishness in which I was the only person that mattered. I thought of my mother flying across the world to see me in court, standing in her red dress, so beautiful and dignified, and what it would do to her to hear of me stuck in some dungeon for years. Again. I began to question whether I really wanted to spend the rest of my life hanging out with people whose lives were one long holiday, itinerant expats who'd fly into an airport with a couple of suitcases once a year and then take another year off to 'recover'.

In truth it was a boring life, and the consequences of failure were catastrophic. But worst of all, I wasn't very good at it. Sure, I'd made some money along the way and spent many long months living off the proceeds in various exotic locations, but my modus operandi was haphazard and my days of freedom were numbered. It was only a matter of time before I'd hear the monotonous clang of cell doors, see the 24–7 strip lighting and smell the rancid stench of slop buckets. I'd grown accustomed to the reassuring prompts of bells ringing: the wake-up bell, the breakfast bell, the work bell, the break bell, the lunch bell, the shower bell, the dinner bell, the meeting bell, the bedtime bell, and on and on . . . Nobody told me what to do any more; therefore, I didn't know what to do with myself. I wasn't so much a rudderless ship as a pinball careering around from one thing to the next in the knowledge that sooner or later I'd slip between the paddles and be sucked back into the machine, only to be churned out at some later date and have to start all over again. It was a cruelly dispiriting game that I was destined to lose time and again.

I sat on the bike, pondering these thoughts as the sun hid behind the road signs in front of me. A light wind blew between the canyons, leaving a chill in the air, while a fine layer of pink dust from the Sahara lodged itself between the scratches on my petrol tank. I lit a cigarette, which I smoked clumsily through leather motorcycle gloves as a pair of Guardia Civil police officers pulled up beside me in a jeep. They asked me if I was OK, and I said I was fine as I turned over the engine to leave, but the carburettors were flooded from the bike lying on its side and the machine wheezed and coughed wearily. The cops pulled over to the side of the road and came to take a closer look as the starter motor went flat again. Then one of them walked round to the back of the bike and motioned the other to help, and the two men pushed me along the road in neutral before I slipped into second gear and opened up the throttle, which spat out the excess petrol and roared triumphantly. I waved to my helpers, who stood by their car looking pleased with themselves, and for a split second considered asking them if they'd found any crash helmets on the roadside today.

The gritty desert wind stung my eyes and made them stream as I hit a hundred miles an hour, creating rainbow prisms on the tips of my lashes. I pushed down the tinted visor on my helmet and the hills around me glowed with a cool green hue as the sun bounced off them into the valley below. I felt the rush of air between my legs and up the sleeves of my leather jacket, circulating round my body as the bike leaned in and out of the bends all the way north to Madrid.

Postscript

Many years have passed since I boarded the plane at Shanghai airport for the last time. I sent a parcel of books back from London, which was warmly received by the foreigners' unit. I also sent Larry an LSD trip under a postage stamp as promised. When he was eventually released, he wrote to say how much he'd enjoyed it. The foreign unit at Ti Lan Qiao prison was closed shortly after I left, and all the prisoners were moved to a new jail called Qing Pu, about 45 minutes' drive from Shanghai. By all accounts it was an improvement for the foreigners, with much better facilities and exercise opportunities. Ti Lan Qiao was horrendously overcrowded, with some wings sleeping more than three to a cell, and the only exercise areas were concrete courtyards. At Qing Pu, there were large open areas with a football pitch, green lawns and flowerbeds. It was a twenty-first-century prison designed for future expansion to house the ever-proliferating number of criminals and political prisoners. It must have been a relief for Captain Xu, who'd always considered the foreigners a disruptive influence on his wing.

After three years the Germans, Ludwig and Jürgen, were released, while Gareth left some months later after serving seven and a half years of his eight-and-a-half-year stretch. Tommy and Larry ended up doing twelve and a half of their fifteen years, and I heard from Larry on his release. He'd been out for little more a year before getting arrested yet again, flying into Japan, and landed another six-year term. Having done two years in Korea, two in Hong Kong and twelve and a half in China, I would have thought he'd have decided he wasn't really cut out for dope smuggling. With his poor health, I wonder if he'll survive this latest stretch. If he does, this will surely be his final scam (though I wouldn't bet on it).

Mark and I have remained friends, and we have a drink from time to time in London. Jürgen wrote to me on his release and, the last I heard, was playing in blues bands in Germany. I haven't heard from the others, and my contact address has long since been out of date.

Not long after I got out, I got a letter from a Chinese friend who'd been released shortly after me. He was a tailor and was interested in starting an import–export business together. I tried calling him but was unable to get through, and I've had no contact with any other old friends. Only one of the boxes of books and diaries I gave to the consul made it back to the UK, and unfortunately the missing box contained many of my most valuable diaries, including one that had a number of contact addresses hidden in its cover.

Rosie and I split up. It was inevitable, I suppose, and in truth we'd split up the day I got arrested, though it wasn't something I could accept at the time. We'd made a half-hearted attempt to rekindle the relationship in Bangkok a week after I got out, but my old world had moved on without me. I drifted for a long time and briefly returned to scamming to make a buck before giving it up for good. I was probably better at doing the time than the crime and, had I continued, I'd have probably ended up like Larry, on his world tour of foreign jails.

Drugs proved to be the downfall of a number of good friends of mine from Kyoto. One committed suicide after a lengthy spell in solitary confinement in a Japanese prison, while another died in a Kyoto detention centre under what can only be called 'suspicious' circumstances. An old drinking buddy, Jerry, died of a heroin overdose in a Bangkok guesthouse, while others served time in American prisons and a psychiatric hospital. It's no exaggeration to say that our druggy lives – which seemed so innocent back then – proved disastrous for all of us, though in retrospect I was one of the lucky ones.

My love affair with Asia remains to this day, and I sometimes think I'd like to live there again. The jaded cynicism that accompanied my fall has gone, and the thrill of travel has returned for good, I hope. On a recent trip to Iran, I was struck by the parallels between the cult of Khomeini and Mao's Communist version. To be fair to the late ayatollah, his ascetic life was a far cry from Mao's debauched one, but the rigid separation of public and private domains is very noticeable in both countries. Both countries are post-revolutionary societies. An Iranian friend took me to her old high school in Tehran, named the School of Revolutionary Flowers. I imagine there are a thousand schools in China with the same name. In spite of the propaganda, Iran is a noticeably freer country than China, and Iranians are very eager to criticise their government and are not overly concerned about who hears them. Yet Chinese are still cagey about speaking their mind in public, and the vast gulag of prisons and work farms are home to many who have fallen foul of this 'unspoken' law.

A recent visit to Vietnam reminded me of what the Chinese Communists robbed from their people. If Esfahan is the jewel of the Middle East, cities like Hoi-an are the pearls of the Orient. The wonders of Chinese Daoism are alive and well in Vietnam, whose Communist rulers were not afflicted with the deranged philistinism of Mao and his followers. Nevertheless, China remains high on my list of countries to revisit, and hopefully the words of my case judge Mr Shen that I 'would be welcome' will prove to be true when I eventually make my way back to the Middle Kingdom. It's unlikely that when I return to Shanghai I'll run into any old friends, but I'd dearly love it to be so. To share a cold beer with old friends on the Bund would be the icing on the cake and the perfect end to my China odyssey. I also look forward to walking the streets of Shanghai, a city I lived in for two and a half years but only saw from inside a concrete box. Now I see it on TV and it looks like a science-fiction town.

My views on crime and punishment have hardened. The Chinese system is far too harsh, but in Britain it's gone too far the other way. The law no longer protects the innocent, and 'career' criminals are free to make other people's lives a misery. Every week I see dangerous people leave UK courts with shorter sentences than I served for half a kilo of dope. Much of the country has become a no-go area for the weak and the elderly. The UK penal system has also broken down, and many leave with worse drug habits than they had on arrival. I'm grateful to the Chinese prison system to have provided a respite from all drugs, even tobacco, and believe British jails could learn something from the Chinese.

China continues to grow at a staggering rate, though democratic reform has been suppressed and the country is still a totalitarian state in which dissent is met with brutality and oppression. While the elites have engaged in an orgy of hypercapitalism, the old Communist system has been the lot for 'the masses'. The country continues to execute far more people than any other country in the world, and in 2008 introduced execution vans: mobile killing machines manned by 'surgeons' who remove essential organs, which are put on sale by the government.

In 1999, three years after I left China, the Communists outlawed the practice of Falun Gong, the *qigong*-based religion teaching 'truthfulness, compassion and forbearance' whose growing membership unnerved the Party. This has resulted in a monstrous rise in the use of torture, violence and unimaginable cruelty not seen since the darkest days of the Cultural Revolution, and the imprisonment of millions of Chinese in work farms, labour camps and 're-education' centres of various kinds. Reports by all the main human-rights organisations make grim reading, suggesting that the country has gone backwards since my time there. Two years later, the events of September 2001 provided a convenient cover for even more oppression of dissenting minorities, particularly Muslim Uighurs and Tibetans, now labelled 'terrorists'. For many living in the Middle Kingdom, the darkest days of the twentieth century have continued into the twenty-first and, if anything, have intensified.

These oppressive campaigns have proved a boon to the prison industry, as huge swathes of people are put to work in factories across China for no pay, contrary to international law. Neighbouring countries within China's sphere of influence, like Burma and North Korea, have also become little more than slave states and continue to be legitimised and supported by the Chinese Communist Party. Meanwhile, Chinese leaders are feted by Western governments, which can no longer afford to stand up to the country as it takes centre stage in the new economic world order.

It's very much my hope that readers of this book will not allow my own comparatively frivolous experiences in China's prison system to blind them to the desperate and ongoing tragedy befalling millions of innocent people in this part of the world. And this book is dedicated to their struggle.